ANSELM

GREAT MEDIEVAL THINKERS

Series Editor
Brian Davies
Fordham University

DUNS SCOTUS
Richard Cross

BERNARD OF CLAIRVAUX
Gillian R. Evans

JOHN SCOTTUS ERIUGENA
Deirdre Carabine

ROBERT GROSSETESTE
James McEvoy

BOETHIUS
John Marenbon

PETER LOMBARD
Philipp W. Rosemann

ABELARD AND HELOISE
Constant J. Mews

BONAVENTURE
Christopher M. Cullen

AL-KINDĪ
Peter Adamson

JOHN BURIDAN
Gyula Klima

ANSELM
Sandra Visser and Thomas Williams

JOHN WYCLIFF
Stephen Lahey

ANSELM

Sandra Visser and Thomas Williams

OXFORD
UNIVERSITY PRESS

2009

OXFORD

UNIVERSITY PRESS

Oxford University Press, Inc., publishes works that further
Oxford University's objective of excellence
in research, scholarship, and education.

Oxford   New York

Auckland   Cape Town   Dar es Salaam   Hong Kong   Karachi
Kuala Lumpur   Madrid   Melbourne   Mexico City   Nairobi
New Delhi   Shanghai   Taipei   Toronto

With offices in

Argentina   Austria   Brazil   Chile   Czech Republic   France   Greece
Guatemala   Hungary   Italy   Japan   Poland   Portugal   Singapore
South Korea   Switzerland   Thailand   Turkey   Ukraine   Vietnam

Published by Oxford University Press, Inc.
198 Madison Avenue, New York, New York 10016

www.oup.com

Oxford is a registered trademark of Oxford University Press

Library of Congress Cataloging-in-Publication Data

Visser, Sandra, 1965–
Anselm / by Sandra Visser and Thomas Williams.
p. cm. — (Great medieval thinkers)
Includes bibliographical references and index.
ISBN 978-0-19-530938-6; 978-0-19-530939-3 (pbk.)
1. Anselm, Saint, Archbishop of Canterbury, 1033–1109.   I. Williams, Thomas, 1967–
II. Title.
B765.A84V57 2008
189'.4—dc22   2008010209

1 3 5 7 9 8 6 4 2

Printed in the United States of America
on acid-free paper

PREFACE

We have sought as far as possible to make this work a fresh reassessment of Anselm's thought as presented in his own writings. To that end we have been sparing in our references to secondary literature, both in the body of the text and in the notes. We have engaged explicitly with other commentators only when our own way of presenting an issue is dependent on theirs; we have tried to avoid the obliquity of carrying out exegesis by way of positioning ourselves against other interpretations. Nonetheless, we have profited from reading many scholars whose work we do not address directly in these pages. We list those works in the bibliography. We hope it will be evident that the few authors whom we have discussed critically at some length are so treated, not because their views are most deserving of criticism, but because they have taught us the most about Anselm.

We have in general confined ourselves to exposition rather than evaluation, except insofar as philosophical evaluation helps us bring out more clearly what Anselm's arguments and views actually come to. Part of the reason for this is severely practical: the book is quite long enough even as it stands. But more important is the fact that it is impossible to comment intelligently on Anselm's views without first getting clear on what they are, and some of the areas of Anselm's thought that most invite evaluation are the very areas that have been most obscured by bad exegesis. To take just one example: as much as we would like to engage with critics of

Anselm's soteriology in chapter 13, we have our hands full just laying out an adequate presentation of what his soteriology *is*. (As a side benefit, readers who are familiar with the objections that are often brought against Anselm's soteriology will be able to see that if our exposition is correct, those objections are not well taken anyway.) In other cases, any satisfying philosophical engagement with Anselm's views would require a technical apparatus that Anselm simply did not have. For example, he does not have a sufficiently developed metaphysics to wrestle with the problems many contemporary philosophers have raised for the doctrine of divine simplicity that he accepts—problems that Anselm himself clearly does not see. Any defense of the doctrine that we could offer on Anselm's behalf might be Anselmian, but it would not be Anselm's.

After an introduction to Anselm's life and works,[1] this book is divided into three parts. In part I we set out the framework of Anselm's thought. In chapter 1 we explore his approach to what he calls "the reason of faith." Anselm regards the doctrines of the Christian faith as intrinsically rational because they concern the nature and activity of God, who is supreme reason and exemplifies supreme wisdom in everything he does. Because human beings are rational by nature, we can grasp the reason of faith. In chapter 2 we examine Anselm's account of thought and language. Thinking, for Anselm, is a matter of getting objects before one's mind; it is analogous to vision, except that there can be mental vision of nonexistent objects (though, crucially for the argument of *Proslogion* 2, not of impossible objects). One way in which we bring objects before our minds is the use of language. Anselm's philosophy of language is especially concerned with accounting for cases in which this bringing-before-the-mind, called "signification," is unusually oblique or problematic. In chapter 3 we consider Anselm's account of truth, which not only completes his theory of signification but also introduces the notion of rectitude that is the cornerstone of Anselm's understanding of freedom, morality, sin, and redemption.

Because Anselm ultimately identifies truth with God, our discussion of truth leads naturally to part II, in which we consider Anselm's account

---

1. For a discussion of Anselm's influence, see G. R. Evans, "Anselm's Life, Works, and Immediate Influence," in Davies and Leftow, 5–31, at 24–28; G. R. Evans, *Anselm and a New Generation* (Oxford: Oxford University Press, 1980).

of God. In chapter 4 we examine Anselm's arguments in the *Monologion* for the existence of God, showing how those arguments fail because Anselm illicitly takes for granted the metaphysically peculiar nature of the being whose existence he is trying to prove. The failure of these arguments points to Anselm's need for a proof that explicitly and legitimately argues from the nature of God to the existence of God. Anselm supplies such a proof in the "ontological argument" of the *Proslogion,* which we consider in chapter 5. This argument, we claim, was almost immediately misunderstood by Gaunilo, whose incomprehension has been a baneful influence on subsequent interpretations as well. By reading Anselm's reply to Gaunilo as an extension and clarification of the original *Proslogion* argument, we develop an interpretation that shows how both Gaunilo's objection and many subsequent objections to Anselm's argument seriously misconstrue its character. In chapter 6 we explore Anselm's account of the divine attributes in the *Monologion* and *Proslogion.* Anselm's arguments in those works reveal a being that is far removed from the objects of our ordinary experience: a being without parts, without accidents, without location in space or time. In chapter 7 we consider the problems that arise in conceiving and describing this being, and we show how Anselm applies the theory of thought and language laid out in chapter 2 to develop an account of thought and language about God that respects God's transcendence and uniqueness but does not preclude our coming to know truths about God on the basis of rational argument.

In chapter 8 we examine Anselm's development of a claim first broached in chapter 6: that God created all things other than himself from nothing. Anselm speaks of this act of creation as involving an "utterance" or Word by which God made all things. Though Anselm first introduces the Word in the *Monologion* to account for God's understanding of creatures, he develops his doctrine of the Word in such a way that it becomes the first element of his theory of the Trinity. We look in more detail at the Trinity in chapter 9. After examining the metaphysics of the Trinity as Anselm understands it, we turn to his constructive arguments for the doctrine: first for the divinity of the Word, then for the distinctness of the Word from the Father, and finally for the procession of the Holy Spirit from both Father and Word.

In part III we turn from God to creatures, and in particular to the economy of redemption. In chapter 10 we offer a systematic account of the theory of modality that Anselm employs in his discussion of the problem of foreknowledge and freedom. This account of modality is also the essential background for understanding Anselm's theory of free choice, which we discuss in chapter 11. Free choice, understood as "the power to preserve rectitude of will for its own sake," requires the absence of causal necessity (in the precise sense of "necessity" explained in chapter 10). But what is more important to Anselm's account of free choice is the teleological element. Because "rectitude of will preserved for its own sake" is Anselm's definition of justice, free choice is simply the power to be just. In chapter 12 we look in more detail at the nature of justice, examining Anselm's theoretical understanding of morality as well as the practical moral advice we find in his letters.

Anselm notes more than once that he is interested in freedom and morality because he is interested in *salvation*. The free choice that he analyzes is the freedom that is relevant to salvation, and the justice that he commends is the justice without which no one is admitted into heaven. So our discussion of freedom and morality would be incomplete without a discussion of the divine action without which, Anselm argues, salvation would be impossible for all human beings after the sin of Adam: the Incarnation and Atonement. In chapter 13 we examine Anselm's argument for the claim that the death of a God-man was the only possible remedy for human injustice and that God had to offer such a remedy. Finally, in chapter 14 we consider original sin—the injustice that, according to Anselm, is justly transmitted to all human beings who come to exist naturally from Adam—and the grace that eliminates injustice and fits human beings for salvation.

ACKNOWLEDGMENTS

An earlier version of chapters 3 and 11 appeared in *The Cambridge Companion to Anselm,* edited by Brian Davies and Brian Leftow, 179–221, © Cambridge University Press, 2004. This material is reprinted with the permission of Cambridge University Press.

We owe a debt of gratitude to the many people and institutions who have made it possible for the two of us to work together on this project. By awarding Thomas Williams the Alvin Plantinga Fellowship for 2005–2006, the Center for Philosophy of Religion at the University of Notre Dame made it possible for us to work together face to face. Thomas Williams's colleagues in the Department of Religious Studies and the Department of Philosophy at the University of South Florida graciously permitted him to accept the Fellowship in what should have been his first year on campus, and the generous support of a Creative Scholarship Grant from USF's Division of Sponsored Research enabled him to return to Indiana for several weeks to complete the final work on this book. We have benefited greatly from the opportunity to present our work in the Center for Philosophy of Religion discussion group, at the Alvin Plantinga Lecture at Notre Dame, at two meetings of the Midwestern Medieval Philosophy Conference, and to the Philosophy Department at Wayne State University. Brian Davies, as editor of the Great Medieval Thinkers series, offered many helpful comments on the penultimate draft of the book. Leslie Curry's assistance in compiling the index was invaluable. And we are especially grateful to Peter van Inwagen, not only for being a teacher and mentor and a philosophical example to emulate, but for leading the Pew Seminar at Calvin College on the problem of evil, at which our collaboration began.

Sandra Visser would like to thank her husband, Mike Owens, for all his love and encouragement, and for taking vicarious pleasure in our productive days; her stepson, Logan, for staying out of trouble so she could finish; and her sons: Sander, whose initial enthusiasm encouraged her to work hard and make him proud, and whose final desire for her to be done spurred her to timely completion; and Joel, for being so darn cute that she wanted to work hard so she could get home as quickly as possible.

Thomas Williams is grateful to Tom Flint, Mike Rea, and Lucie Marsden for doing so much to make the Center for Philosophy of Religion an exceptional place to study and work, and to all his colleagues at the Center for their role in renewing his delight in philosophical argument and debate. He wishes to thank the clergy and people of Saint Paul's, Mishawaka, for providing a church home in his year away from home. And he is grateful above all for the love, support, and patience of his partner, Marty Gould, to whom his debt is incalculable.

CONTENTS

ANSELM

INTRODUCTION

Anselm's Life and Works

We are fortunate to know a good deal about Anselm's life. Anselm's friend Eadmer was not only an admiring biographer but also a discriminating historian, and his *Vita Anselmi* (*Anselm's Life*) remains an important source. More recently, Sir Richard Southern's excellent—one is tempted to say "unsurpassable"—biography, *Anselm: A Portrait in Landscape,* offers a comprehensive account of Anselm's life and works in their historical, institutional, and political context.[1] Our aim in this introductory chapter can accordingly be quite modest. We present only an outline of Anselm's life and career, emphasizing those aspects of the history that are helpful for interpreting Anselm's works.

Anselm was born in 1033 in Aosta, in those days a Burgundian town on the frontier with Lombardy. Anselm was a bright and likeable boy. There is some evidence that he was particularly close to his mother, Ermenberga, and had a strained relationship with his father, Gundulf. Certainly when his mother died in his early twenties, his father became very hostile and impossible to please, and Anselm left home in 1056. He wandered around Burgundy and France, probably trying out the teaching available from the entrepreneurial scholar-teachers who were so much a feature of that place and time.

In 1059 he arrived at the Abbey of Bec in Normandy. The attraction was almost certainly not the monastic life, since apart from a short-lived bout of religious fervor in his teens Anselm had shown no particular yearning for the cloister, but the celebrated school and its even more celebrated master. The school was not just for monks; it accepted well-born students whose parents wanted them to have a grounding in the liberal arts. The school was under the direction of the prior, Lanfranc, who had a huge reputation as a scholar and teacher. He was also famous as a defender of orthodox Eucharistic doctrine against Berengar of Tours. (The controversy was already in full swing by the time Anselm arrived at Bec, although Lanfranc did not write up his part in it until somewhat later.) Lanfranc taught the standard works of rhetoric and logic and instructed students in the study of the Bible. Before long Anselm was taking part in the teaching himself. It is probably during this period that he wrote *De grammatico,* which is a sort of textbook on logic in dialogue form; it would fit with the kind of education on offer at Bec.[2]

In 1060 Anselm decided to become a monk at Bec himself, after some struggle over whether this was a good thing for his career (and a further struggle over how sinful he was being in thinking about his career). Once he made his decision, he threw himself into monastic life with his whole heart. He was, as Gillian Evans says, "remorseless in his spiritual exercises,"[3] fasting to the point of unhealthiness and depriving himself of sleep to counsel others late into the night.

In 1063 Lanfranc was called away to be prior of the monastery at Caen, and Anselm became prior at Bec. He hated the job. It is perhaps easiest to get a feel for this aspect of Anselm's life by considering a contemporary analogy. Imagine a philosopher whose great passions are for doing philosophy and for training graduate students. Reluctantly, because there is no one else who can do the job and his colleagues are importunate, he agrees to be department chair. He is not naturally a good administrator, and besides, he resents every moment of his administrative duties as a distraction from his "real work" of thinking about philosophy and shaping budding philosophers. But he carries out his duties as well as he knows how, and the unfortunate reward for his conscientiousness is further promotion. He becomes a dean and finally a provost, by which time he is completely at sea, lacking the support of his own deans in his constant battles with the president and trustees. The best he can do is to sneak some time for writing and philosophical conversation whenever he can, and make occasional fruitless efforts to be relieved of his disagreeable duties. Such is the story of Anselm's career from 1063 on. Even as prior he was in over his head. He was bad at handling money, easily flustered when things did not go his way, and inept at getting others to do what he wanted. He asked the Archbishop of Rouen for permission to return to the simplicity of his former life, but to no avail. It would not be the last time that Anselm would seek permission from a superior to lay aside the burdens of office.

Except for some prayers and meditations, Anselm did not write again until about 1075, twelve years after he took over as prior. There are probably two reasons for the long delay. One is simply that he was busy: in addition to his duties as prior, he had taken over the teaching when Lanfranc left. The second, and probably more significant, reason is that Anselm was not the kind of philosopher who writes to get his thoughts in order. Anselm tended to work everything out in his head first and only then write it down. So during that period he was working out his thoughts, no doubt trying them out in his teaching, until he had everything figured out to his own satisfaction. This fact about Anselm's approach to writing helps explain why the dating of Anselm's works, the progression of his career, is of very little relevance to interpreters. Anselm's thoughts do not really develop in any noticeable way; there is no early, middle, and late period, or anything like that. He had his fundamental ideas, and quite a lot of the detail, worked out in his head before he wrote his first book. So in general it is perfectly legitimate to use works from any period of his life to figure out what Anselm thought on a given issue.

Anselm's next work, the *Monologion* (1075–76), was written in answer to a request. This fact suggests another point about his approach to writing that bears on interpreting Anselm. Anselm is highly reactive. Evans talks about his "firefighting" approach to administration,[4] which is exactly right, but something similar is also noticeable in his philosophical and theological writing. Quite a large proportion of his writing is in response to a request or is a reaction to newly minted theological error. As a consequence, Anselm did not always deal systematically with issues even when he had a well-worked-out view. He stuck to the topics people asked him about, presenting only as much of the larger theoretical apparatus as was necessary to deal with the particular question being posed. Yet behind the sometimes widely scattered remarks we can often discern a fully elaborated systematic view on topics that Anselm never explicitly treated in a sustained way. Anselm's ethical theory is one such topic; his theory of modality is another, although he had planned a systematic treatment of modality that he was unable to complete.

In the case of the *Monologion,* Anselm tells us that the request came from the monks at Bec, who "have often eagerly entreated me to write down some of the things I have told them in our frequent discussions about how to meditate on the divine essence." (Note the reference to "our frequent discussions": Anselm had already worked out the arguments of the *Monologion* in his teaching.) The monks not only asked for the book, they dictated the form it was to take:

> Having more regard to their own wishes than to the ease of the task or my ability to perform it, they prescribed the following form for me in writing this meditation: absolutely nothing in it would be established by the authority of Scripture; rather, whatever the conclusion of each individual investigation might assert, the necessity of reason would concisely prove, and the clarity of truth would manifestly show, that it is the case, by means of a plain style, unsophisticated arguments, and straightforward disputation.[5]

Anselm's task was to prove a wide range of conclusions about God "by reason alone."[6]

Anselm's next book, the *Proslogion* (1077–78), was a direct outgrowth of the *Monologion.* Anselm never retracted anything from the *Monologion;* he was never dissatisfied with it in the sense that he came to regard one of the arguments as weak or one of the conclusions as mistaken. But he noticed that it involved, as he put it, "a chaining together of many arguments."[7] He wondered whether he could get the same conclusions—or at least most of them—more straightforwardly, using a "single argument" that proved everything we want proved in one fell swoop. The search for this single argument became an obsession with him. Anselm couldn't sleep, he lost his appetite, and he couldn't pay attention in church—which made him think the whole idea was a temptation from the devil. He tried in vain to stop himself from thinking about it.

Finally the idea came to him. In the *Proslogion* he wrote up the argument and showed how it could be used to generate a wide range of conclusions about the divine nature. The style of the work is just like that of his prayers and meditations, but the method is actually the same as that of the *Monologion:* reason alone, with no reliance on authority. This combination of prayerful style and philosophical content has bewildered interpreters who cannot believe that what is obviously a work of devotion does not rely surreptitiously on premises drawn from faith. Their incredulity, however, simply shows that they do not accept Anselm's version of "faith seeking understanding" (the original title of the *Proslogion,* as it happens). Anyone who thinks faith seeking understanding makes sense will not find anything odd about a purely rational investigation that takes the literary form of a prayer. That's what Anselmian believers do: they prayerfully exercise their rational powers in order to understand what they already believe. If anything, what is odd is that the *Proslogion* is Anselm's only work of that sort.

In 1078 the abbot of Bec died, and the inevitable happened. Anselm begged the monks not to insist on his becoming abbot, and they begged him to accept the job. He gave in. Though he found his new duties even more burdensome than the old ones, he did at least manage to keep writing. In 1080–86 he composed three dialogues: *On Truth, On Freedom of Choice,* and *On the Fall of the Devil.*[8] Anselm described them as "treatises pertaining to the study of Holy Scripture," but they were not Scriptural commentaries in any normal sense. Rather, they exhibited Anselm's techniques of argument and linguistic analysis as applied to a handful of Scriptural texts.[9]

In the meantime, developments elsewhere in the world were threatening to complicate Anselm's life even more. In 1089, Anselm's old teacher Lanfranc, who had been made Archbishop of Canterbury in 1070, died. King William II (William Rufus, so called either because of his red hair or because of his hot temper) left the see vacant so that he could make use of the archiepiscopal revenues—a favorite technique of his for funding his various military adventures. In the middle of all this, Anselm showed up in England in 1092 at the invitation of Hugh, Earl of Chester, who wanted to consult with him about some lands that were to be given to the abbey of Bec. Anselm was afraid that people would think he was angling for the archbishopric, but he went anyway. The monks at Canterbury loved him, and he enjoyed a flattering reception from many people of wealth and influence. There were cynics then, and there are cynics now, who doubt whether Anselm was really as hostile to the idea of being Archbishop of Canterbury as he claimed to be.[10] Our view is that he sincerely and fervently did not want the job. We have already seen how Anselm detested administrative work, and the archbishopric was a huge and demanding administrative position. Worst of all, as archbishop he would not merely have to supervise monks; he would have to deal with William Rufus. And though Anselm could be pretty clueless about the world around him, he was not so innocent that he didn't realize that William would be a world of trouble.

For a while the king ignored the pleas for Anselm's appointment that were coming from various quarters. But when the king fell dangerously ill and began to fear the eternal consequences of his plunder of the Church, he sent for Anselm. At the urging of barons and bishops alike, the king declared that Anselm was the most suitable man for the office of Archbishop. Not a single voice was raised in objection, except for that of Anselm himself, "who wore himself almost to death in his objections."[11] In the end, however, Anselm yielded to the general will and to the unanimous advice of those whom he consulted on the matter. He was enthroned as Archbishop of Canterbury in 1093.

Around this time Anselm was also involved in theological controversy of a sort he found particularly distasteful. A monk named John wrote to Anselm that Roscelin of Compiègne had posed a dilemma for Trinitarian theology: either the three persons of the Trinity are three distinct things, like three angels or three souls, or else the Father and Holy Spirit were incarnate along with the Son. It appears that Roscelin wanted to maintain the standard view that the Son alone was incarnate, so he concluded that the three persons of the Trinity are three distinct things. Anselm immediately began to compose a rejoinder. For two reasons, however, he set it aside without completing it: first, he had heard that Roscelin had recanted;[12] and second, he figured that Roscelin's error was too obvious to require refutation. Neither reason for abandoning the work would hold good indefinitely, however. Some years later, after Anselm had become archbishop, news reached him that Roscelin had recanted his recantation; and "certain brothers," who apparently did not find Roscelin's error as obvious as Anselm did, "compelled" him to explain how they were to escape Roscelin's dilemma.[13] Anselm accommodated his brethren by completing a letter *On the Incarnation of the Word* addressed to Pope Urban II. To the revised version of his solution of Roscelin's dilemma Anselm added arguments about why it was most fitting for the Son to be incarnate, rather than the Father or the Holy Spirit.

Not long after becoming archbishop, Anselm began work on *Cur Deus Homo* (1095–98), an attempt to defend the rationality of the Christian doctrines of Incarnation and Atonement. At the same time, however, his conflicts with the king were growing more and more acrimonious. There were several issues, and it is worth pointing out that Anselm did not always have the support of his own bishops, who were mostly recruited from the younger sons of Norman nobility and were not surprisingly as much the king's men as they were churchmen. At his wit's end, Anselm decided to go to Rome to seek the pope's advice. Three times the king refused permission for Anselm to leave for Rome, but Anselm finally decided to go anyway. The king would not allow him to return to England.

Thus Anselm was in exile from 1097 until William died in 1100. In 1098 Anselm completed *Cur Deus Homo,* though he complains that "if I had been allowed freedom from distractions and enough time to work on it, I would have included and added quite a few things that I have left unsaid."[14] Anselm's great editor, F. S. Schmitt, believed that Anselm would have "included" (or interpolated) the discussions "of power, of necessity, of will, and of certain other things" to which he refers in *Cur Deus Homo* 1.1 and "added" (or appended) a treatment of original sin. Anselm never put his thoughts on power, necessity, and will in final form, but sketches of a discussion of those topics are preserved in an unfinished work that we know as the "Lambeth Fragments." He did, however, supply the missing appendix, a work *On the Virginal Conception, and On Original Sin,* probably completed 1099–1100.

This period of exile kept Anselm busy in other ways as well. In 1098 Urban convened the Council of Bari to discuss reunion of the Eastern and Western churches, and he asked Anselm to defend the Western view that the Holy Spirit proceeds from the Father and the Son, as opposed to the Eastern view that the Holy Spirit proceeds only from the Father. Anselm later turned his speech to the council into *On the Procession of the Holy Spirit,* which he finished in 1102. It was also during this period that Anselm learned about the investiture controversy. "Investiture" refers to the delivery of various insignia of office. The investiture controversy was over the role of laypeople—kings and emperors—in the investiture of bishops and archbishops. It had long been customary for kings to invest bishops with their crozier and ring, symbols of their pastoral authority and sacramental role. Though lay investiture had been prohibited under Pope Gregory VII in 1077, it seems clear that Anselm was happily ignorant of the whole controversy; he had accepted the pastoral ring and staff from William Rufus when he was made Archbishop of Canterbury. Anselm was therefore deeply distressed at the Vatican Council of 1099 to find Urban II pronouncing a sentence of excommunication not only on laity who participated in investiture but on clergy who accepted the symbols of office from lay hands.

Anselm was conscientious to a fault, and now that he understood his duty, he was uncompromising in carrying it out. When he returned to England at the invitation of the new king, Henry I, he refused to do homage to Henry, and he refused to consecrate bishops whom Henry had invested. Henry would not relinquish what he regarded as a royal prerogative. So in 1103 Anselm went to Rome in company with a royal messenger to seek advice from the pope about how to satisfy both the claims of the king's honor and the demands of Anselm's conscience. The new pope, Paschal II, took Anselm's side and sent him back to England, but Henry would not allow him back unless Anselm submitted to the king's terms and renounced his obedience to the pope. When Anselm, predictably, refused, Henry seized the possessions of the archbishopric. After a year and a half of tense negotiations, a compromise was reached: Anselm would do homage to Henry for the temporal possessions associated with the archbishopric, and Henry would give up any role in investing bishops with the symbols of their spiritual authority. On the strength of that compromise Anselm returned to England in 1106.

Anselm had not managed to do any writing during his second exile. After his return, however, he completed one more work: *De concordia* (1107–08), in which he attempted to reconcile human free choice with divine foreknowledge, predestination, and grace. By this time he had become seriously ill and was so weak that he had to be carried around on a litter. It was becoming clear that he would not live to write a treatise on the origin of the soul, as he had hoped. On Tuesday of Holy Week, April 21, 1109, Anselm died peacefully, surrounded by the monks of Canterbury.

Part I

THE FRAMEWORK OF ANSELM'S THOUGHT

THE REASON OF FAITH

The published description for a course in the philosophy of religion taught at a major American university begins with these words: "There is a fundamental tension between Western philosophical thought, which emphasizes the import and efficacy of reasoned argument, and religious traditions, which stress the primacy of faith over reason." Many discussions of the relationship between faith and reason assume some such prima facie incompatibility between religious faith and philosophical reason, though few put the dichotomy in such stark terms. Even authors who wish to make room for both faith and reason in their systems are careful to delineate a distinctive role for each. In Thomas Aquinas, for example, certain truths are accessible to unaided reason, but others receive assent by faith alone; and one cannot have both faith and rationally grounded knowledge (*scientia*) with respect to one and the same truth.

Anselm does not assume any incompatibility, even a prima facie one, between faith and reason; nor does he assign a distinctive role to each. So rather than saying that Anselm has a view about the relationship between faith and reason, it is perhaps better to say that he has a view about "the reason of faith": the *ratio fidei*. "The reason of faith" is perhaps not idiomatic English, but the best idiomatic translations of *ratio fidei* are misleading. "The rational basis of faith" suggests something external: arguments in support of doctrinal formulations that have an apologetic or protreptic purpose. "The logic of faith" suggests something internal: the rational coherence of the doctrines of faith, the way they "all hang together" logically. Anselm's *ratio fidei* means both these things at once; it refers to the intrinsically rational character of Christian doctrines in virtue of which they form a coherent and rationally defensible system. This is what we will mean by "the reason of faith."

Anselm holds that the doctrines of the Christian faith are intrinsically rational because they concern the nature and activity of God, who is himself supreme reason[1] and exemplifies supreme wisdom[2] in everything he does. And because human beings are rational by nature, we can grasp the reason of faith. Anselm's central discussions of the reason of faith are found in the *Monologion* and *Proslogion,* the letter *On the Incarnation of the Word,* and *Cur Deus Homo.* We will look first at the boldness of Anselm's claims on behalf of the power of reason in the *Monologion* and their apparent tension with his insistence in the *Proslogion* that faith must precede understanding. We will then resolve this tension by examining two of Anselm's later works, *On the Incarnation of the Word* and *Cur Deus Homo,* in which Anselm is more open about the boldness of his project and about the grounds of his confidence in the ability of perfected human reason to discover the reason of faith.

The *Monologion* and *Proslogion*

In the prologue to the *Monologion* Anselm tells us that he wrote the work in response to the requests of his monks: "Some of the brethren have often eagerly entreated me to write down some of the things I have told them in our frequent discussions about how one ought to meditate on the divine essence, and about certain other things related to such a meditation, as a sort of pattern (*exemplum*) for meditating on these things."[3] Thus in an important way the work is addressed to those who are already Christians and wish to meditate on what they already believe. Anselm's monks wanted a sort of road map for thinking about God. But, as Anselm goes on to tell us, they asked for a guide that did not presuppose belief: "They prescribed the following form for me in writing this meditation: absolutely nothing in it would be established by the authority of Scripture; rather, whatever the conclusion of each individual investigation might assert, the necessity of reason would concisely prove, and the clarity of truth would

manifestly show, that it is the case, by means of a plain style, unsophisticated arguments, and straightforward disputation. They also insisted that
I not disdain to answer even the simple and almost foolish objections that
would occur to me."[4] In other words, the monks of Bec were asking for a
template for philosophical reflection on God, starting from premises that
were (in principle at least) accessible even to those who do not accept the
authority of Scripture or the fathers of the Church. And that is what
Anselm provided.

This template for philosophical reflection includes more than arguments for the existence of God and accounts of the divine attributes. It
includes extensive discussion of the Trinity, including arguments that
clearly seem to be intended as philosophical *proofs* that God is triune. The
evidence from within Anselm's works that these arguments are indeed
meant as philosophical proofs of the doctrine of the Trinity is overwhelming. Not only does Anselm say in the *Monologion* that he wrote the
work in accordance with his monks' demand that "absolutely nothing in it
would be established by the authority of Scripture,"[5] but in *De incarnatione
Verbi* he says that both the *Monologion* and the *Proslogion* were written
"mainly so that what we hold by faith concerning the divine nature *and
persons,* leaving aside the Incarnation, could be proved by necessary reasons, independently of the authority of Scripture."[6] So the reluctance of
some commentators to take Anselm at his word must rest entirely on
external considerations. Their incredulity most likely derives from the fact
that Anselm's program runs afoul of the familiar distinction between what
Aquinas called "preambles to faith," doctrines that can be proved by
reason alone, and "mysteries of the faith," doctrines that must be taken on
faith. As William E. Mann puts it, "That God is triune in nature is a
'mystery' in a special, theological sense of the term: it is communicated to
humans by divine revelation, it is beyond the powers of natural human
reason to demonstrate, and so if it is to be accepted, it must be accepted as
an item of religious faith.... Despite operating under a number of con-
straints that may appear to us to preclude successful completion of his
project, he proceeds self-assuredly, confident that reason can demonstrate,
not that the doctrine is true (for then it would not be a mystery) but that it
is free from contradiction—more than that, that It All Makes Sense."[7]

But the distinction between mysteries and preambles—at least in its
most familiar, Thomist form—rests on an Aristotelian epistemology that
is foreign to Anselm. For Aquinas, because we come to know God (as we

come to know anything) on the basis of sense-experience, we can know philosophically only those things about God that show up somehow in the objects of the senses; and sense objects do not tell us that God is triune, any more than a painting tells us that its creator was married. Since Anselm does not embrace this Aristotelian view of knowledge, he has no reason to embrace the distinction between preambles and mysteries that Aquinas's Aristotelianism supports. Someone who is inclined to accept some version of that distinction will of course think that Anselm's constructive Trinitarian project in the *Monologion* was misguided and doomed to failure, but that is no good reason to think that Anselm was not trying to do exactly what he claimed to be doing.

Though he is cagey about admitting it in the *Monologion,* Anselm is aware that in making a constructive rational case for the doctrine of the Trinity, he is abandoning the method (though certainly not the content) of Augustine's *De Trinitate.* Augustine had stated explicitly that one must first appeal to Scripture in order to establish that God is a Trinity; only then can one provide rational defenses of Trinitarian doctrine for those windbag argument-mongers (*istis garrulis ratiocinatoribus*) who demand them.[8] Anselm knew *De Trinitate* well, so it is reasonable to assume that he was fully aware that his own Trinitarian arguments violated Augustine's strictures, though his deference to Augustine prevented him from acknowledging this fact openly. Even in *De incarnatione Verbi,* where he acknowledges his innovations, he tries to play down their extent and significance:

> if anyone will think it worth his while to read my two little works, the *Monologion* and *Proslogion* ... I think he will find in them discussions of this matter that he will not be able to refute and will not wish to belittle. If in those books I have said anything that I did not read elsewhere (or do not remember having read elsewhere) ... I do not think I should be reproached in any way. For I have not said it as if I were teaching something that our teachers did not know or correcting something they did not say well, *but as saying something that they were silent about—* something that nevertheless does not contradict what they said, but harmonizes with it.[9]

While Anselm is correct that his *conclusions* do not contradict anything Augustine said, he is arguably disingenuous in suggesting that his method of reaching those conclusions is harmonious with that of Augustine.

Nonetheless, Anselm does not think his unparalleled boldness is hubristic. As we noted earlier, Anselm's unusually high estimate of the power of human reason ultimately derives not from his confidence in human beings, but from his confidence in God—from his conviction that God, who is supreme wisdom and exercises supreme reason in everything he does, has made human beings rational by nature. Furthermore, even though Anselm's constructive arguments for Trinitarian doctrine are not drawn from Scripture, as Augustine's were, he would insist that his rational investigation remains under the control of Scripture. For Anselm believes that "Holy Scripture contains the authority of every conclusion of reason"[10] and "gives aid to no falsehood";[11] consequently, he is confident that if his rational arguments go astray in some way, Scripture will provide the materials to correct them.

Though Anselm tried not to draw attention to the boldness and innovation of his philosophical project in the *Monologion,* one of the work's earliest readers saw very clearly what Anselm had done, and he was not at all happy with it. Anselm submitted the work to Lanfranc, by then Archbishop of Canterbury, for his approval. We do not have the text of Lanfranc's assessment, but we do know that he took a dim view of Anselm's avoidance of Scriptural authority. One can imagine that he was especially put off by the way in which Anselm occasionally gives reason the job of approving the text of Scripture. For example, in chapter 33, after reaching some philosophical conclusions about the Word, Anselm comments that "he is not improperly called ... [God's] image and figure and character"[12]—as though philosophical approval were needed for the language of Colossians 1:15 ("He is the image of the invisible God") and Hebrews 1:3 ("He is the splendor of his glory and the figure [in Greek, *charactēr*] of his substance"). Anselm's reply to Lanfranc is very telling. He assured his former superior that the *Monologion* contained nothing that could not be found in Scripture or in Augustine. But he made no changes to the *Monologion* itself, and he never submitted another work for Lanfranc's approval. He was unwavering in his conviction that it is legitimate for the Christian to explore the reason of faith without reliance on authority.

Although in one obvious sense Anselm was writing the *Monologion* for Christians, he did not mean for the arguments to be accessible or persuasive only to believers. Instead, he begins the work by announcing that he is addressing "anyone [who] does not know, either because he has not heard or because he does not believe," the doctrines about God and cre-ation that Anselm sets out to prove—provided only that he is at least "moderately intelligent." He sets out to offer arguments by which a reader can "convince himself...by reason alone."[13] So Anselm clearly supposes that any reasonably intelligent person, Christian or not, can follow the pattern for philosophical reasoning that he lays out in the *Monologion*. But there is no reason to suppose that Anselm believes just anyone could have done the thinking without being told the pattern. It is only later, however, that Anselm will explain why not everyone can produce the reasoning that everyone can follow.

In some ways the *Proslogion* appears to be engaged in a rather different enterprise from the *Monologion*. It takes the form of a prayer addressed to God, so it explicitly adopts the attitude of someone who already believes and is "trying to raise his mind to the contemplation of God and seeking to understand what he believes,"[14] as Anselm says in the prologue. Whereas the first chapter of the *Monologion* assures us that the arguments to come will be accessible and persuasive to any reasonably intelligent person, the first chapter of the *Proslogion* is a "rousing of the mind to the contem-plation of God" that relies heavily on Scripture and could be uttered sincerely only by a believer, concluding with an affirmation that "Unless I believe, I shall not understand."[15]

Yet before we conclude that the arguments of the *Proslogion* were intended only for believers, we must also take into account the ways in which the project of the *Proslogion* parallels that of the *Monologion*. An-selm suggests that the *Proslogion* differs from the *Monologion* only in the greater simplicity and unity of its arguments.[16] Moreover, it is quite clear that Anselm meant his argument to be persuasive to the unbeliever, the Psalmist's fool who "has said in his heart, 'There is no God.'"[17] For the fool understands that than which nothing greater can be thought, and no one who genuinely understands that being can fail to see that it "exists in such a way that it cannot, even in thought, fail to exist."[18] Thanks to the argument of *Proslogion* 2, God's existence is "so evident to the rational mind"[19] that Anselm could not fail to understand that God exists even if (like the fool?) he did not want to believe in God.[20] And in fact Anselm expressly says in a later work that he wrote both the *Monologion* and the *Proslogion* "mainly so that what we hold by faith concerning the divine nature and persons, leaving aside the Incarnation, could be proved by necessary reasons, independently of the authority of Scripture."[21]

Yet if Anselm does indeed mean for the arguments of the *Proslogion* to be persuasive even to unbelievers, why does he begin with an impassioned "rousing of the mind to the contemplation of God" and the declaration, "Unless I believe, I will not understand"? The *Proslogion* itself offers no clear answer to this question. We will return to it after examining *On the Incarnation of the Word* and *Cur Deus Homo*, which provide the materials for an elegant solution.

On the Incarnation of the Word

In *On the Incarnation of the Word* Anselm's primary target is the heresy of Roscelin.[22] But before he settles into his refutation of Roscelin, Anselm "preface[s] a few words in order to curb the presumption of those who with abominable insolence dare to raise as an objection to one of the articles of the Christian faith the fact that they cannot grasp it by their own intellect."[23] It is crucial to understand that these words are not addressed to unbelievers but to professing Christians. Anselm thinks it is perfectly legitimate for *unbelievers* to raise objections against the truth or intelligibility of Christian belief, and it is incumbent on the philosophically capable believer to answer those objections—that, after all, is why Anselm will write *Cur Deus Homo*. Anselm had delineated the different epistemic responsibilities of believers and unbelievers with exceptional clarity in a letter written to Fulk, Bishop of Beauvais, not long after he first learned of Roscelin's heresy:

> It is utterly foolish and silly to fall into wavering and doubt about what has been most firmly established on the solid rock, simply on account of one person who does not understand it. Our faith should be defended by reason against the impious, not against those who profess to rejoice in the name of Christian. It is just to demand from [professing Christians] that they hold unshaken the pledge made in baptism, whereas [unbelievers] should be shown rationally how irrationally they scorn us. For a Christian ought to progress through faith to understanding, not reach faith through understanding—or, if he cannot understand, leave faith behind. Now if he can achieve understanding, he rejoices; but if he cannot, he stands in awe of what he cannot grasp.[24]

In Anselm's view, Roscelin is a professing Christian who has sinfully left faith behind because he could not understand. So before Anselm diagnoses

Roscelin's metaphysical errors, he must rebuke the spiritual failures that allowed Roscelin to go astray.

A Christian must begin with faith. And faith, Anselm thinks, is not simply an epistemic attitude but a spiritual discipline marked by an obedient will: "First our heart must be cleansed by faith; Scripture describes God as 'cleansing their hearts by faith.' And first our eyes must be enlightened by our keeping God's commandments, since 'the command of the Lord is bright, enlightening the eyes.' And first we ought to become little children through our humble obedience to the testimonies of God, in order that we might learn the wisdom that the testimony of the Lord gives, for 'the testimony of the Lord is sure, giving wisdom to little children.' "[25] An important part of this obedient faith is meditation on Scripture: "the more abundantly we take nourishment in Holy Scripture from those things that feed us through obedience, the more acutely we are brought to those things that satisfy us through understanding."[26]

Such spiritual formation enables the Christian to "experience" the truth of Christian doctrine: "There is no room for doubt about what I say: one who has not believed will not understand. For one who has not believed will not experience, and one who has not experienced will not know. For as much as experiencing a thing is superior to hearing about it, so much does the knowledge of someone who has experience surpass that of someone who merely hears."[27] As Anselm uses the word, to experience (*experior*) something is to have firsthand acquaintance with it.[28] Somehow, then, believers who have "developed spiritual wings through the firmness of their faith" will be able to know the truths of Christian doctrine as matters of lived experience. They have "set aside the things of the flesh" and are living according to the spirit, and Scripture promises that "the spiritual man judges all things, and he himself is judged by no one."[29]

In dealing with the loftiest matters, reason can go astray more easily than it can make progress; "let no one, therefore, be in a hurry to plunge into the thicket of divine questions unless he has first sought in firmness of faith the weight of good character and wisdom, lest he should run carelessly and frivolously along the many side-roads of sophistries and be snared by some obstinate falsehood."[30] Anselm emphasizes three aspects of faith that keep reason from going astray: humility, obedience, and spiritual discipline. In humility we recognize the lowliness of our own minds and the loftiness of divine truth; such a recognition makes us appropriately cautious in our reasoning and saves us from groundless obstinacy in defending our positions. In obedience we accept Scripture and the teachings of the Church, which provide a determinate goal at which all our thinking must aim; this goal keeps reason from jumping the tracks. And through spiritual discipline we clear our minds of "bodily imaginations" so that we can "discern those things that ought to be contemplated by reason itself, alone and unmixed."[31]

Anselm's thesis in these prefatory remarks is as clear and emphatic as one could possibly want: Christians must have faith before they can have understanding. Because Roscelin sought understanding without submitting to faith, his reason failed. Yet Anselm does not suppose that his only recourse is to point out Roscelin's spiritual failures or to recite the authoritative texts that he will then call on Roscelin to accept. Bad reasoning occasioned by sinful conduct is still bad reasoning, and it is to be counteracted by good reasoning. Indeed, as Anselm clearly recognizes, an appeal to authority would be useless in this case: "The reply to this man should not be made using the authority of Holy Scripture, since either he does not believe Scripture or he interprets it in some perverse sense: for what does Holy Scripture say any more clearly than that there is one and only one God? Instead, his error should be exposed on the basis of reason, which he tries to use to defend himself."[32] Of course, even if Anselm makes the truth "so evident . . . that anyone with understanding will see that nothing that is said against it has any power of truth,"[33] Roscelin might still reject it out of a sinful, arrogant attachment to his own views. But Anselm clearly seems to think Roscelin is capable of following a rational argument that exposes his error. The heretic's reason is untrustworthy because it is not steered by faith, but it is not disabled altogether.

Cur Deus Homo

Both *On the Incarnation of the Word* and *Cur Deus Homo* were written in part to provide intellectual support for faithful Christians who wanted to know how to respond to objections to Christian orthodoxy. In *On the Incarnation of the Word* the objections came from Roscelin, who as a Christian ought to have begun with faith. In *Cur Deus Homo,* by contrast, they come from unbelievers. In both cases, however, Anselm is confident that reasoned argument can meet the objections.

If anything, *Cur Deus Homo* shows a greater confidence in the power of reason than *On the Incarnation of the Word*. The project of *On the Incarnation of the Word* is largely negative: it shows that Roscelin's objections to Christian orthodoxy rest on philosophical confusions and have no rational force. By contrast, *Cur Deus Homo* purports not only to neutralize the objections of unbelievers but to offer conclusive positive arguments in support of the contested Christian doctrines. Since those arguments "proceed as though nothing were known of Christ,"[34] there is nothing in them that unbelievers are entitled to reject.

One might explain the primarily negative or defensive character of *On the Incarnation of the Word* by noting that Anselm had provided positive arguments elsewhere for the Trinitarian doctrine that Roscelin was denying. But those arguments appear in the *Monologion,* another work whose arguments are purportedly accessible to unbelievers; so it begins to look as if Anselm thinks reason works more powerfully on unbelievers than on heretics. It is not difficult to imagine why this might be. Unbelievers lack the direction and insight conferred by faith, so they cannot discover the reason of faith on their own; but if they are patient and honest, they can at least follow the reasoning of a believer. Heretics, by contrast, have the guidance of faith available to them but actively repudiate it; they are, by definition, neither patient nor honest. The best the believer can do is expose the heretic's errors in reasoning. One can only hope that the heretic will acknowledge the error and start the search for understanding all over again, this time in the right way: having "first sought in firmness of faith the weight of good character and wisdom."[35]

In one striking respect what Anselm says in *Cur Deus Homo* about his own exploration of the reason of faith goes beyond what he had been willing to admit not only in *On the Incarnation of the Word* but in the *Monologion* and *Proslogion* as well. In the *Monologion* Anselm had professed an unwillingness to say anything new. He assured Lanfranc that everything in the *Monologion* could be found in Scripture or in Augustine, and he stated that readers should treat as merely tentative or provisional any conclusions that cannot be found "in a greater authority."[36] In *On the Incarnation of the Word,* as we have seen, he gingerly acknowledges that he may in fact have said things in the *Monologion* and *Proslogion* that had not been said before; but he is not quite ready to claim openly that he has developed arguments that had never occurred to the fathers of the Church. By the time he writes *Cur Deus Homo,* however, he unabashedly acknowledges that he is doing something altogether new. True, the fathers of the Church thought so deeply and wrote so well that "we cannot hope for anyone in our day or in the years to come who will be their equal in the contemplation of the truth." But that is no reason to confine ourselves to repeating what they have already said: "For 'brief are the days of man,' so even our holy fathers and teachers were not able to say everything they could have said had they lived longer; and the reason of truth is so abundant and so deep that mortals cannot come to the end of it."[37] Anselm does not go so far as to say that it is permissible to *contradict* the fathers, as opposed to merely supplementing them; but he does in fact reject a venerable patristic view through the arguments against the ransom theory that he puts into the mouth of Boso.[38] He just avoids saying outright that that is what he is doing.

What one must never do is contradict Scripture or the teachings of the Church. Yet even this restriction leaves considerable room for intellectual exploration. In some cases multiple interpretations of Scripture are possible.[39] Moreover, "there are matters in which it is possible to hold any of a number of views without danger ... If in such matters we expound the divine writings in such a way that they support different views, and we find no passage that settles what we must unhesitatingly hold, I do not think anyone ought to find fault with us."[40] Accordingly, Anselm puts forward one explanation of the reasonableness of the Incarnation in *Cur Deus Homo,* but because the reason of faith is inexhaustible, other explanations—equally true, equally sufficient—are possible;[41] and in fact Anselm will offer one of his own in *On the Virginal Conception.* Finally, just as the reason of faith is inexhaustible, so too are the gifts of grace that God provides for those who seek to explore it.[42]

Discovery and Demonstration

Recall our earlier perplexity about the *Proslogion.* On the one hand, both internal and external evidence shows that Anselm meant his arguments in that work to be persuasive to the unbeliever. On the other hand, he prepares for those arguments in a way that seems to exclude the unbeliever, with a passionate cry to God and an acknowledgment that "Unless I believe, I will not understand." In light of Anselm's methodological reflections in *On the Incarnation of the Word* and *Cur Deus Homo* we can now make sense of both aspects of the *Proslogion.* As we have seen, Anselm thinks that Christians must start from faith in order to progress to understanding. It is no accident, therefore, that Anselm changes the second-person plural of the Old Latin text of Isaiah 7:9, "Unless you believe, you will not understand," to a first-person singular. It is Anselm, the author of the work, who as a Christian must have faith in order to achieve understanding. Not every reader of the work will be in same position as its author. The first chapter of the *Proslogion* both represents and enacts the humility, obedience, and spiritual discipline that are necessary for discovering the reason of faith. No unbeliever can achieve such discovery, but a patient, honest, and "moderately intelligent" unbeliever can follow and appreciate the demonstration or defense of the reason of faith that is discovered by the faithful believer. Thus, the fool cannot grasp the reason of faith in the same way as someone who has the "experience" that comes from belief; yet there is always something the believer can say to the fool that the fool can understand. And (although Anselm does not say this explicitly) the fool who is convinced by the demonstration has not attained understanding of the same kind, or in the same degree, as the believer who formulated the proof. The convinced fool, no longer a fool, has simply been brought to a state in which faithful inquiry is possible for him. He can now retrace not only the believer's reasoning, but the spiritual discipline that made such reasoning possible by yielding an understanding born of experience.

But the first chapter of the *Proslogion* does more than represent, in a generic sort of way, the attitudes of heart and mind that are necessary to discover the reason of faith. It also ponders the very features of the believer's spiritual life that lead Anselm to his discovery. Anselm loves God and desires to know him, yet God seems distant, absent, and inaccessible. Anselm experiences the problem of divine hiddenness as both an epistemic and a moral challenge: God is the only object of knowledge that would both fully occupy his intellect and fully unify his thinking, and knowing God would fully satisfy his desire and achieve the purpose for which he was created. Out of his reflection on these challenges arises a single conception of God that accommodates and indeed accounts for all the data of his experience as a believer. Because God is that than which nothing greater can be thought, he is both present to Anselm's mind and immeasurably distant from it. He both inspires Anselm's search and frustrates it, resisting any easy resolution but promising ultimate fulfillment.

So the first chapter of the *Proslogion* records a pattern of reflection on the inner life of a believer engaged in the spiritual formation that, Anselm argues, gives rise to a kind of firsthand insight that can appropriately be called "experience." The chapter also invites other believers into that same reflection so that they too can experience God as that than which nothing greater can be thought and thereby come to understanding, which is "intermediate between faith and vision."[43] Yet such understanding is not an incommunicable mystical epiphany. It is a rational grasp of the intrinsically rational character of the one who is supreme reason, and so it can be conveyed to anyone who has the power of reason, regardless of whether such a person has had the experience of faith. Thus, although the fool cannot pray chapter 1 of the *Proslogion,* he can, if he makes the effort, appreciate the compelling argument of chapter 2. Anselm never raises the further question of whether the fool actually *can* make such an effort without a willing spirit that is already a gift of grace, a first spark of the fire of faith.[44]

THOUGHT AND LANGUAGE

Language and thought both involve what Anselm calls *locutio:* a saying or uttering. We know from frequent experience, Anselm says, that there are three ways in which we can "say"—that is, express—one and the same thing: "We say a thing either by making perceptible use of perceptible signs, i.e., signs that can be perceived by the bodily senses; or by thinking imperceptibly within ourselves the very same signs that are perceptible when they are outside ourselves; or by not using these signs at all, whether perceptibly or imperceptibly, but rather by saying the things themselves inwardly in our mind by either a corporeal image or an understanding of reason that corresponds to the diversity of the things themselves."[1] Corresponding to these three ways of saying a thing, Anselm says, there are three kinds of words. We shall call them perceptible words, imperceptible words, and mental words, respectively. Perceptible and imperceptible words are linguistic items: Latin (say) or English words, whether actually written down or vocalized, in the case of perceptible words, or merely imagined, in the case of imperceptible words. Mental words, however, are nonlinguistic; they are thoughts, not items of vocabulary.

Anselm has nothing more to say about imperceptible words. Perceptible words and mental words, on the other hand, receive a good deal of attention. In effect, Anselm's theory of perceptible words is his philosophy of language, and his theory of mental words is his philosophy of thought. And the philosophy of language rests on the philosophy of thought, because mental words are the fundamental and indispensable words: "And because all other words were discovered on account of [mental] words, where they are present, no other word is necessary for knowing a thing; and where they cannot be present, no other word is useful for making a thing known."[2] So we will first examine Anselm's account of thought: that is, his theory of mental words.

Thought

The account of thought as a kind of mental speech—that is, as the utterance of mental words—coexists in Anselm's work with another analogy; thought is also a kind of mental vision. One might well take the two analogies to suggest somewhat different accounts of thought, but Anselm obviously intends both of them as illustrations of a single, consistent theory. He even shifts from one analogy to the other in the space of a single sentence: "by an utterance of the mind or reason I mean ... [what arises] when things themselves ... are examined within the mind by the gaze of thought."[3] Generally speaking, he uses the analogy from vision when he is interested in the *objects* of thought and the analogy from speech when he is interested in the *act* of thinking or the *mental state* by means of which the object of thought is present to the mind.

The objects of thought, then, are things we can (metaphorically speaking) see in the mind's eye. Anselm has no theory to explain what is going on when we see things that aren't there, but he assumes we can. We can, for example, think things[4] that do not yet exist, and he is perfectly happy to talk about such thought as a kind of mental vision of the not-yet-existent: "the things themselves, whether they already exist or are yet to exist, are examined within the mind by the gaze of thought."[5] We can even think things that are completely imaginary.[6] We cannot, however, think something that is impossible. This last point is extremely important, not least because (as we shall see in chapter 5) it plays a crucial role in the argument of the *Proslogion*. Anselm does hold that we can think impossibilities in a diminished sense. We can say the words "round square," for example. But we cannot examine round squares within our minds by the gaze of thought, which is what constitutes thinking in the fullest sense. So "it cannot be thought" is practically synonymous in Anselm's writings with "it is impossible" and "it can be thought" with "it is possible."[7]

Anselm's theory of thought therefore allows for the possibility that thought can, in a sense, misfire. I can suppose myself to be thinking something when in fact I am not, because I have not succeeded in getting before my mind the thing I intend to "examine by the gaze of thought." In his letter *On the Incarnation of the Word* Anselm speculates that such a thing has happened to Roscelin: "But if this man has been called back from positing a multiplicity of gods and now denies a plurality of persons in God, he is doing this because he does not know what he is talking about. He is not conceiving God or his persons, but something along the lines of a plurality of human persons; and since he sees that one human being cannot be a plurality of persons, he says that God too cannot be a plurality of persons."[8] If Roscelin were actually thinking God, he would see that the divine nature, unlike human nature, does admit a plurality of persons within a single substance. As it is, however, he has not even managed to think God, though he uses the word 'God' and takes himself to have God before his mind.

Thus, Anselm uses the analogy from vision primarily to characterize the objects of thought: they are the actual or merely possible things about which we think. But our thinking these things is a mental act and necessarily involves a mental state, and Anselm uses the analogy from speech to explain what the mind is doing when it engages with the objects of thought. Mental words can be either mental pictures or concepts: "I say a man . . . when my mind sees the man himself either through an image of a body (as when it imagines his sensible appearance) or through reason (as when it thinks his universal essence, which is rational, mortal animal)."[9] Yet even concepts, though they are clearly not pictorial in any way, are a kind of image or likeness: "all words of this sort, by which we say any given things in the mind (in other words, think them), are likenesses and images of the things whose words they are."[10]

Now it is not immediately obvious how the concept *rational, mortal animal* is in any way a "likeness" or "image" of a human being. Certainly a mental picture of a man resembles the man in a more obvious way than *rational, mortal animal* does. (Indeed, can any real sense be made of the question "How closely does *rational, mortal animal* resemble a man"?) But this point merely emphasizes the fact that for Anselm a mental word's being a likeness or image is not a matter of its resembling anything. Instead, a mental word is a likeness insofar as it is a means by which the object of thought is made present to the gaze of the mind. Anselm always says that we think things "through" or "by" a mental word;[11] that is, the mental word, whether a picture or a concept, is not the object of thought but the means by which the extramental object is made present to the mind so that it can be "examined by the gaze of thought." As Peter King notes, in order to think something "we use a variety of more or less accurate means, ranging from mental images to rational conceptions. Hence likeness is a matter of accuracy, not pictorial resemblance, in the means we use to conceive something."[12]

Although we can, and indeed very often do, successfully use mental pictures to get things before our minds, they are the least accurate mental words. Though they fix the direction of our mental gaze, they also provide distractions that can easily lead us astray. And the further removed an object of thought is from corporeality, the less satisfactory a mental picture of that object will be. A mental picture of even a purely physical object will be less "like" the object than a definition is, because the content of the mental picture includes extraneous information. My mental picture of a rock, for example, will include a particular color, but no particular color is part of what it is to be a rock. My mental picture of a human being is worse, since not only does it include extraneous information, it fails to include some essential information. *Animal* is picturable, more or less; *rational* certainly is not. So a mental picture of a human being is a very clumsy instrument by which to fix the mind's gaze on a human being.

When the object of thought is completely incorporeal, mental pictures are positively dangerous. Anselm argues in *De incarnatione Verbi* that certain "heretics of dialectic"[13] in his day had gone hopelessly astray because they were relying entirely on mental pictures in trying to think about incorporeal realities: "In their souls, reason, which ought to be the ruler and judge of everything in a human being, is so covered up by bodily imaginations that it cannot extricate itself, and they cannot discern those things that ought to be contemplated by reason itself, alone and unmixed."[14] Now this sounds as though Anselm means to ban mental pictures altogether when we are thinking about incorporeal realities, but in fact his approach is not quite so austere. Though we must not let the content of our mental pictures drive our thinking about incorporeal realities, it is often helpful for us to draw on mental pictures (or at least on conceptions of picturable things) in contemplating what reason has discerned. Even in *De incarnatione Verbi* Anselm looks for a model in created things of the trinity-in-unity that reason discovers in the Creator. Yet he is quite careful to limit the role of such models. "Reason itself, alone and unmixed" must go first; only after reason has shown that trinity-in-unity is possible in the Godhead can we look for a sensible analogy that illustrates and makes concrete what reason has discovered. If we fail to find such an analogy, our failure in no way casts doubt on the conclusions of reason, though perhaps our grasp of those conclusions will be shakier or more tentative than it would otherwise have been. And if we do find a suitable analogy, it will be inadequate and misleading in ways that reason itself will be able to discern.

Language

Words are signs. That is, in addition to whatever intrinsic character they have as bits of vibrating air or marks on a page, they also have the causal power to bring something to mind. In the terminology that Anselm shares with many medieval thinkers, both before and after him, words are said to "signify" or to "have signification." Anselm's philosophy of language is primarily an account of the signification of words.

As a rule, when Anselm says that a word signifies, he means two things: first, that the word functions as a sign; and second, that it has a significate. The significate is the item that is signified by the sign; it is what the sign is a sign *of*. Both aspects of signification raise philosophical challenges, but Anselm devotes particular attention to two challenges posed by the second. The first challenge concerns the signification of so-called denominative terms; the second concerns the signification of negative terms such as 'nothing' and 'nonhuman'. We will look at both in turn.

The Signification of Denominative Terms

Surprisingly large stretches of medieval philosophy take off from throwaway remarks by Aristotle, and one particularly good example of this phenomenon is the energetic discussion of what Aristotle called "paronyms" and medieval Latin writers called "denominatives." Aristotle wrote, "Whatever get from something the names by which they are called, but differ in ending, are called 'paronyms.' For example, a literate [person is so called] from literacy and a brave [person is so called] from bravery."[15] Whatever exactly Aristotle had in mind by this remark, a debate arose over the signification of such paronymous or denominative terms. Now it helps to keep in mind that in Latin one can use a word like 'literate' or 'brave' by itself, without a noun, as a predicate. For example, in Latin one can say, "Thomas is a literate," just as in English one can say, "Thomas is an illiterate." The question is what is signified by 'literate' in "Thomas is a literate." Aristotle, again in the *Categories,* casually lists 'literate' in the category of quality, so presumably for Aristotle, 'literate' signifies a quality—the quality of literacy that Thomas possesses or exemplifies. But Priscian, the great Latin grammarian, gives 'literate' as an example of something that signifies a substance.

In the great tradition of medieval philosophy, the ideal is to show how both authorities are right, so long as we make the proper distinctions. And that is what Anselm undertakes to show in his dialogue *De grammatico.* One of his main expository devices is to contrast the signification of 'man' with the signification of 'literate', and we will follow him in using that device.

To begin with, 'man' signifies man—a substance. That is straightforward enough, at least apparently. (Later, when we come to discuss the signification of common names, we will see that it is not quite so straightforward as it appears.) 'Literate', by contrast, signifies both a substance (with a nod to Priscian) and a quality (with a nod to Aristotle). It signifies the man who possesses literacy, and since that man is a substance, 'literate' signifies a substance. But it also signifies the literacy the man possesses, and since that literacy is a quality, 'literate' also signifies a quality.

So 'literate' signifies both man and literacy. But it does not signify them both in the same way. 'Literate' signifies literacy *per se* (through itself); it signifies man *per aliud* (through another). To illustrate the distinction between signification *per se* and signification *per aliud,* Anselm offers the following example:

T: Suppose you see a white horse and a black ox standing opposite each other, and someone says to you, "Strike it"—meaning the horse, but not giving any sign to indicate which one he means. Would you know he meant the horse?

S: No.

T: But if, not knowing what he meant, you were to ask him, "Which one?" and he replied, "The white one," would you understand which one he meant?

S: I would understand the horse by means of the name 'white'.[16]

"The white one" in Latin is simply the one word *album,* 'white'. In this usage, the student says, 'white' signifies the horse. But obviously 'white' doesn't by itself—*per se*—signify the horse. The only thing 'white' signifies *per se* is whiteness. But given the additional knowledge you have in light of the situation in which you find yourself, 'white' signifies the horse. This is a case of signification *per aliud.*

To pin the point down a little better, we need to introduce the standard medieval definition of signification, which derives from Aristotle's *De interpretatione* in the translation of Boethius. "To signify," according to this definition, "is to establish an understanding" (*constituere intellectum*).[17] That is, a word signifies because it makes you think of something; and what it signifies is what it makes you think of. A word signifies *per se* whatever it makes you think of without, as it were, extra goosing from the context of utterance or some additional knowledge that isn't conveyed by the term itself. Thus, 'white' *per se* signifies whiteness. But given such context or knowledge, the word can also make you think of something else; so we will say that the word also signifies that something else, only *per aliud,* not *per se.* Thus, in the example from *De grammatico,* the word 'white' makes you think of the horse, though only given the context; and so it signifies the horse, though only *per aliud.* In the same way, 'literate' signifies literacy *per se;* but because it makes a sort of oblique reference to the man who possesses literacy, it also signifies the man *per aliud.* Here the *per aliud* signification is less contrived than in the white horse case, since we never run across literacy except in human beings, although Anselm notes that a literate nonhuman animal is at least conceivable. Anselm also notes that this is a further reason we wouldn't want to say that 'literate' signifies man *per se.* If it did, "literate nonhuman" would be an internally contradictory expression like "round square." Moreover, if 'literate' signified man *per se,* you couldn't properly say "literate man." 'Literate' would have the same signification as 'man having literacy', so 'literate man' would be equivalent to 'man having literacy man'.

The Signification of Negative Terms

Both of the main sources of the medieval doctrine of signification seem to suggest that since every word is a sign, every word has a significate. We have already noted one of these sources: the Aristotelian-Boethian view according to which a word has a signification because it "establishes an understanding." Now ordinarily a sign "establishes an understanding" by establishing an understanding *of something;* the word 'chair' does not establish just any old understanding, but an understanding of a chair. But then how can we account for the signification of a word like 'nothing'? If 'nothing' signifies, it establishes an understanding of something; yet if it establishes an understanding of something, it seems to fail in its proper job, since it ought to establish an understanding of *nothing.* Yet it is an equal failure if it establishes an understanding of nothing, since in that case it seems to have no signification at all.

The same problem arises in Augustine, who was the other main source of the medieval doctrine of signification. In his dialogue *On the Teacher* Augustine asks, "Can a sign be a sign if it doesn't signify something?" His son Adeodatus gives the expected answer, "It cannot."[18] But they very quickly run into problems applying this doctrine. Augustine quotes a line of Vergil that consists of eight words—and therefore of eight signs, as they agree. Since they understand this line, they ought to be able to say, for each of the eight words, what that word signifies. Unfortunately, the first word is 'if', and it is not altogether clear what 'if' signifies. The second word is 'nothing', which causes an even bigger problem. Adeodatus proposes that 'nothing' signifies that which does not exist, but Augustine remarks, "Perhaps so, but something you granted earlier makes me disinclined to accept this definition. There is no sign that does not signify something; but what does not exist, cannot in any way be something. So the second word in this line is not a sign, because it does not signify something. And so either we were wrong to hold that all words are signs, or else it is not true that all signs signify something."[19] Augustine offers the bizarre suggestion that 'nothing' signifies "the disposition of the mind when it does not see a thing and discovers, or thinks it has discovered, that it does not exist." Without either accepting or rejecting this account, he moves the discussion along with a painful bit of wordplay (" 'Nothing' hinders us, yet we suffer delays") and quickly brings Adeodatus to the point of giving up on the project of identifying the "something" that is signified by each of the signs in the text he had quoted.[20]

So both ways of thinking about signification encourage us to suppose that every sign is the sign of something. Following Peter King, we can distinguish three kinds of names that pose a challenge to such an account.[21] There are privative names, such as 'injustice' and 'blindness', which name an absence rather than a positive quality; indefinite names, such as 'non-human', which function as names by negating rather than affirming; and empty names, such as 'nothing', which necessarily do not name anything at all.[22] Anselm believes that the Aristotelian-Boethian account of signification has the resources to accommodate privative, indefinite, and empty names. His strategy is to assimilate both privative and empty names to indefinite names, and to explain the signification of indefinite names by arguing, in effect, that a sign can establish an understanding—and thus, according to the Boethian definition, signify—even though it does not establish an understanding *of* anything. To put the point in more contemporary language, some words convey informational content even though they do not refer to any actual or possible object.

Since Anselm gives a single account of the semantics of privative, indefinite, and empty names, we shall refer to all three sorts by the general expression "negative names." The most sustained discussion of negative names is found in *De casu diaboli*. Anselm has concluded in the standard Augustinian way that evil "has no being"[23] and is simply a privation of good. The student who is Anselm's interlocutor in the dialogue wearily runs through the standard arguments that purportedly prove that evil is nothing, but he complains that he cannot endorse them unless Anselm refutes his counterargument for the claim that evil is in fact something: "if the word 'evil' is a name, it surely has a signification; and if it has a signification, it signifies. But then it signifies *something*. How, then, is evil nothing, if what the name 'evil' signifies is something?"[24] Anselm tries to dismiss the student's question by noting that 'nothing' is clearly a name, yet no one would dream of arguing that 'nothing' names something, and therefore nothing is something. The student, quite properly, objects that 'nothing' is as problematic as 'evil'. In effect, the student poses a dilemma. 'Nothing' either signifies something or it doesn't. We can't say that 'nothing' signifies something, because "if what is signified by this name is not nothing but instead is something... then it is falsely and inappropriately called by that name."[25] But we also can't say that 'nothing' signifies nothing, because that would mean that the word does not signify anything and so isn't in fact a name at all.

Anselm solves the student's problem by using one of his favorite techniques: showing that there are two ways of understanding the word. Taken in one way, he says, 'nothing' signifies something; taken in another way, it signifies nothing. He first claims that 'nothing' "does not differ in signification" from 'not-something'. And "nothing is more obvious than this: 'not-something' by its signification requires that every thing whatsoever, and anything that is something, is to be excluded from the understanding; and that no thing at all, or what is in any way something, is to be included in the understanding. But since there is no way to signify the exclusion of something except by signifying the very thing whose exclusion is signified—for no one understands what 'not-human' signifies except by understanding what a human is—the expression 'not-something' must signify something precisely by eliminating that which is something."[26] Thus, when we look at 'nothing' in one way, 'nothing' signifies something. It signifies the same thing 'not-something' does, namely, everything that is something—although it signifies this "by excluding" (*destruendo*) rather than in the more usual way, "by including" (*constituendo*). But when we ask what the significate of 'nothing' is—that is, what thing or essence is to be included in a person's understanding as a result of hearing or reading the word 'nothing'—we find that 'nothing' has no significate. 'Nothing' does not name anything in particular, and so it signifies nothing.

The student in *De casu diaboli* is willing to accept this account of how 'nothing' signifies both something and nothing, but he still finds Anselm's answer incomplete. After all, the student argues, if 'nothing' signifies something only "by excluding," it is hard to see how 'nothing' qualifies as a name. If 'nothing' is indeed a name, it must be the name of *something*. Yet that something of which 'nothing' is the name somehow needs to be both something and nothing. For if it is not something, 'nothing' is not a name at all; but if it is not nothing, 'nothing' is not the right name for it.

Anselm's reply, to put it in contemporary terminology, is that the logical form of sentences containing negative names is not to be ascertained by looking at their surface grammar. As he puts it, "the form of an expression often doesn't match the way things are in reality."[27] 'Nothing' functions grammatically like a name, but it does not name anything; it has no significate. (If *nomen* did not have to do duty in Latin for both "name" and "noun," Anselm could say that 'nothing' functions like a noun but is not a name.) We can say that the "things" they signify are "quasi-something" because "we speak of them as if (*quasi*) they were something,"[28] but this is simply a contrived way of saying that words like 'nothing', 'evil', and 'blindness' function like names without naming anything. We understand the logical form of sentences in which negative words appear by paraphrasing them away. The possibility of such paraphrases shows that negative words are not indispensable; they are, however, useful shorthands, and so they are permissible, so long as we understand them properly.

In the Lambeth Fragments Anselm offers a distinction that enables him to make this account clearer and to show how it fits into the broadly Boethian semantics that he accepts: "To establish an understanding is not the same as to establish something in the understanding. 'Not-man' establishes an understanding because it makes someone who hears it understand that man is not contained in, but excluded from, the signification of this word. It does not, however, establish something in the understanding that is the significate of this word, in the way that 'man' establishes a certain conception of that which this name signifies. In this way 'injustice' excludes required justice and does not posit anything else, and 'nothing' excludes something and does not posit anything in the understanding."[29] To establish something in the understanding is to cause a conception of the thing that is the significate of the term. Negative names do not do this, for those names have no significate and therefore no corresponding conception in the mind. Yet they do establish an understanding: they convey informational content. In this way there can be signification without a significate.

The Signification of Common and Proper Names

Common names signify common natures. Anselm writes, "When 'human being' is uttered, only the nature that is common to all human beings is signified."[30] More precisely, 'human being' signifies "those things of which the whole human being consists"—including, apparently, "animal, rationality, and mortality."[31] It signifies them all *per se,* in the sense already explained, and *ut unum,* in the sense that it signifies all of them as unified or as a unity. So when we hear the expression 'human being', human nature is brought to mind as a single, though metaphysically complex, thing. But 'human being' signifies no more than this: it does not bring to mind the features that distinguish one human being from another, and thus it does not signify individuals *qua* individuals.[32]

Proper names, by contrast, do signify individuals. Anselm is very clear that, metaphysically speaking, individuals are made up of a common nature and a collection of distinguishing characteristics.[33] In order for a proper name to signify an individual, it just needs to bring that individual to mind; and it can do this by bringing to mind the common nature plus some feature unique to that individual. For example, Anselm suggests (roughly) that the name 'Jesus' brings Jesus, and no one else, to mind because it makes us think of "the human being whose birth was announced by an angel to the Virgin Mary."[34]

Signification and Appellation

In addition to signification, Anselm employs the notion of "appellation." A name is said to appellate anything of which it can be said in nondeviant ordinary usage. A common name signifies a common nature, but it appellates not only the common nature but also any individual that exemplifies the nature (as in "Socrates is a human being"). The denominative 'literate' signifies literacy *per se* and the literate person *per aliud,* but it appellates literate people, not literacy: for one can say "Socrates is literate" but not "Literacy is literate."[35]

The Signification of Verbs

Verbs are signs, too, but their signification differs from that of names. Anselm notes two distinctive features of the signification of verbs. He takes over the first from Aristotle. Aristotle noted that verbs, unlike names, are tensed; they involve time in some way. In the translation of Boethius, Aristotle says that verbs "consignify" time. Anselm has no interest in working up a theory of "consignification" as some special semantic relation, so he prefers to say that verbs signify "with" time. And indeed Anselm is not especially interested in this feature of verbs, apart from noting the ways in which it can be misleading in the context of talking about God, who is not a temporal being.[36]

The feature that he finds much more interesting is the way in which verbs combine with nouns to make statements. Merely setting one name next to another name does not produce a statement: "a literate man" does not have a truth value any more than 'man' by itself does. But setting a verb next to a name can produce a statement: "a man reads" does have a truth value. (To be more precise, the Latin sentence that we translate as "a man reads" involves setting a verb next to a name in order to produce a statement with a truth value. Latin has no articles, so "a man reads" is simply the name *homo* next to the verb *legit*. And by convention, indefinite categorical propositions like "a man reads" were treated as particular statements. Thus, *homo legit* would be construed as "Some man reads," which does have a truth value.) Verbs have this statement-making power, Anselm thinks, because they signify actions or doings; in combination with a name they signify further that what is signified by the name performs the action signified by the verb. As Anselm puts it, "whenever a verb is predicated of any thing at all, what is signified is that the thing brings about [*facit*] what is expressed by that verb."[37]

Since Anselm takes this account of the predicative force of verbs to be perfectly general, he has to interpret "doings" quite broadly. He finds support for this interpretation in ordinary usage. 'To do' (*facere*), he says, is the most general verb and can substitute for any other verb, whether positive or negative. If someone asks, "What is he doing?" any verb at all can legitimately appear in the reply (provided, he says, "that there is someone who knows how to do this properly"[38]). And if any verb can be used to say what someone is doing, it is clear that every verb signifies a doing—even verbs that do not at first glance seem to describe causal activity:

> Everything of which some verb is said is a cause that what is signified by the verb is the case; and in our common way of speaking, every cause is said to "bring about" [*facere*] that of which it is the cause. Hence, everything of which any verb is predicated brings about what is signified by that verb. I will pass right over those verbs that according to their signification are properly cases of bringing about, such as 'to run' and similar verbs; what I am saying can be recognized even in other verbs that seem foreign to this property of bringing about. For in this way someone who sits brings about sitting, and one who undergoes brings about an undergoing.[39]

Even *esse*, 'to be', signifies a kind of bringing about, although the account arguably begins to break down when Anselm tries to apply it to *esse*. There doesn't seem to be any plausible way for Anselm to analyze "An animal exists" in terms of an animal's "bringing about" anything—even stretching *facere* to its uttermost limits—and he doesn't really try. Instead, he says that it is the *conception* of the animal, which is presupposed by the utterance of "An animal exists," that is a cause of the animal's being *said* to exist.[40] But even if we grant for the sake of argument that the conception of the animal is a cause of the animal's being said to exist, this claim will not serve as an instance of the more general theory of predication that Anselm is trying to defend—not least because if it *were* intended as an instance of the more general theory, it would entail that "An animal exists" is semantically equivalent to "The conception of an animal is a cause of the statement 'An animal exists,'" which is patently false and generates a vicious regress to boot. In order for Anselm's theory of predication to be perfectly general, he would need a metaphysical doctrine according to which existing could plausibly be described as something an existent thing *does*. Lacking this, he would have to treat *esse* as a special case, to be explained differently from all other verbs. Since in fact Anselm does treat *esse* as a special case, by analyzing existential statements in terms of a conception's causing a statement rather than in terms of an extramental thing's bringing about the action signified by a verb, perhaps we can read Anselm most charitably as recognizing that it is impossible to give a wholly general account of predication in terms of a causal relation holding between the significates of the subject and predicate. Anselm, then, does not treat 'exists' as a predicate on a par with other predicates. Kant's charge that Anselm does so can therefore be seen as misplaced, even apart from any analysis of the ontological argument.

TRUTH

Verbs combine with nouns to make statements, and statements have truth-values. So, having considered the signification of nouns and verbs, we should now turn to Anselm's account of truth. At first glance Anselm appears to embrace a straightforward, commonsensical view of the sort suggested by Aristotle's famous definition of truth from *Metaphysics* 4: "What is false says of that which is that it is not, or of that which is not that it is; and what is true says of that which is that it is, or of that which is not that it is not."[1] In much the same spirit, Anselm says that a statement is true "when it signifies that what-is is."[2] But the theory of truth that Anselm builds on this observation is one that would surely have confounded Aristotle. For no matter what the topic, Anselm's thinking always eagerly returns to God; and the unchallenged centrality of God in Anselm's philosophical explorations is nowhere more in evidence than in his account of truth. Indeed, we see in the student's opening question in *De veritate* that the entire discussion has God as its origin and its aim: "Since we believe that God is truth, and we say that truth is in many other things, I would like to know whether, wherever truth is said to be, we must acknowledge that God is that truth."[3] The student then reminds Anselm that in the *Monologion* he had argued from the truth of statements to an eternal supreme Truth. Does this not commit Anselm (the student seems to be asking) to holding that God himself is somehow the truth of true statements? But what definition of truth could make sense of such an odd claim? Anselm is happy to take up the challenge of showing that his description of God as "supreme Truth" is no mere metaphor, but the expression of the deepest insight into the nature of truth. An account of truth, Anselm thinks, is just theology under a different name.

This first distinctive characteristic of Anselm's theory, the centrality of God as supreme Truth, helps account for a second distinctive character-istic: its strong insistence on the *unity* of truth. All truth either is God or somehow reflects God; thus, one simple being provides the norm by which all truth claims must be judged. As G. R. Evans rightly notes, "When Anselm makes distinctions, as he frequently does, he intends to show more clearly the underlying unity of what is being subdivided."[4] As we shall see, Anselm will deploy the concept of *rectitude* to assimilate all the various manifestations of truth—in statements, opinions, wills, actions, the senses, and the being of things—to each other and, in the end, to the supreme Truth. Indeed, it will turn out that truth is so much the same thing in each of its manifestations that it is not strictly correct to speak of the truth *of* this or that thing. There is just truth, period; instead of speaking of the truth *of* action *a* and statement *s,* we should say that both action *a* and statement *s* are in accordance with truth, period.

Truth and Rectitude

In their search for a definition of truth, the teacher and student who are the interlocutors in *De veritate* begin with the most common sort of truth: the truth of statements. Anselm's account of truth in statements is a kind of correspondence theory. But unlike a standard contemporary corre-spondence theory that appeals to one correspondence, that between a statement and reality, Anselm's theory invokes *two* correspondences. A statement is true when it corresponds *both* to the way things are *and* to the purpose of making statements. Now Anselm holds that the purpose of making statements *just is* to signify the way things are, so the two corre-spondences cannot pull apart. But Anselm clearly takes the function of statements to explain why we should call them true when they corre-spond to reality; their corresponding to reality would not be reason to call statements true unless such correspondence were what statements were *for:*

TEACHER: For what purpose is an affirmation made?

STUDENT: For signifying that what-is is.

T: So it ought to do that.

S: Certainly.

T: So when it signifies that what-is is, it signifies what it ought to.

S: Obviously.

T: And when it signifies what it ought to, it signifies correctly (*recte*).

S: Yes.

T: Now when it signifies correctly, its signification is correct (*recta*).

S: No doubt about it.

T: So when it signifies that what-is is, its signification is correct.

S: That follows.

T: Furthermore, when it signifies that what-is is, its signification is true.

S: Indeed it is both correct and true when it signifies that what-is is.

T: Then its being correct is the same thing as its being true: that is, its signifying that what-is is.

S: Indeed, they are the same.

T: So its truth is nothing other than its correctness (*rectitudo*).

S: Now I see clearly that this truth is correctness.[5]

So for statements, at least, rectitude (correctness) is a fundamentally teleological notion: statements are correct when they do what they were "made for."

But made by whom? Anselm goes on to make a distinction that shows clearly that it is not the one who *utters* a statement who "makes" it in the sense that is relevant to determining its rectitude or truth. The distinction arises out of a clever observation by the student:

S: A statement...has received the power to signify (*accepit significare*) both that what-is is, and that what-is-not is—for if it had not received the power to signify that even what-is-not is, it would not signify this. So even when it signifies that what-is-not is, it signifies what it ought to. But if, as you have shown, it is correct and true by signifying what it ought to, then a statement is true even when it states that what-is-not is.[6]

To this the teacher responds that we do not customarily call a statement true just because it signifies what it received the power to signify: but we *could*. Statements have two truths or two rectitudes. A statement's signifying what it received the power to signify is "invariable for a given statement": "It is day," for example, always signifies that it is day, and so it has that sort of rectitude "naturally." But a statement's signifying what is the case is "variable": "It is day" does not always signify that what-is is, and so it has this second sort of rectitude "accidentally and according to its use." This accidental rectitude is what a statement has "because it signifies in keeping with the purpose for which it was made." And here is where Anselm makes it clear that it is not made by a particular speaker:

> T: For example, when I say "It is day" in order to signify that what-is is, I am using the signification of this statement correctly, since this is the purpose for which it was made; consequently, in that case it is said to signify correctly. But when I use the same statement to signify that what-is-not is, I am not using it correctly, since it was not made for that purpose; and so in that case its signification is said not to be correct.[7]

Note first that this speech makes it clear that a statement (*oratio*) is a type, not a token.[8] The token is a *use* of the type, and such a use is correct—or true—when the speaker uses the type in accordance with the purpose for which the type was made. Now the purpose of every statement-type is to signify that what-is is, so a given statement-token is correct when it signifies that what-is is. The statement-token as such has no further purpose, beyond that of the type, by which it can be evaluated as correct or incorrect, true or false.

One might be tempted to think that the token does have a purpose of its own, namely, the speaker's purpose. But Anselm's understanding of truth as rectitude precludes him from identifying the purpose of a statement-token with the speaker's purpose in uttering that token. For if the purpose of the token really is the speaker's purpose, then every token (except perhaps those that involve Freudian slips and other kinds of misspeaking, in which the speaker fails to utter the words he intended to utter) will achieve its intended purpose. Now whatever achieves its intended purpose has rectitude and, therefore, truth. So if the purpose of the token is the speaker's purpose, almost every sentence-token will turn out to be true. Strictly speaking, then, the token does not have a purpose. The *tokening* (the act of uttering the token) has a purpose, but the token itself is simply an instance or use of the type, and it is the type that has a purpose. Using the type correctly is using it for its proper purpose.

Of course, the tokening is an act, and, as we shall see, acts have rectitude and truth as well. Once again, Anselm cannot hold that the speaker's
purpose in uttering the token establishes the purpose of acts of tokening.
For in that case, an act of lying would have rectitude if the speaker
succeeded in the deception he intended, but an act of truth telling would
lack rectitude if the speaker failed in, say, the persuasion he intended to
produce in his audience. Here again, therefore, it seems that action *types*
have purposes (in this case, the purpose of the type *tokening statement-types*
is that of using signification correctly), and particular actions are right
when they accord with the purpose of the action-type. Thus, speaker's
purpose and agent's purpose do not matter for rectitude. Rectitude is a
matter of natures or types, and it is God who makes natures and thus gives
them their purpose. Creatures have no genuine power to confer purposes.[9]

So it is statement-types, not tokens, that were "made" in order to signify that what-is is. We asked earlier: made by whom? By now it has
become clear that Anselm's answer is: by God.[10] This answer certainly
appears strange, since the statement-types that Anselm is talking about
here are *natural-language* statements, not the denatured propositions of
contemporary philosophy.[11] Indeed, Anselm does not have our notion
of proposition, in the sense of whatever it is that is equally "expressed" by
the Latin "Dies est" and the English "It is day"—or, for philosophers
worried about the indexical "now" implicit in "It is day," whatever is
equally expressed by the Latin "Omnis homo animal est" and the English
"Every human being is an animal."

The strangeness of the view lies not in the mere claim that God makes
natural-language statement-types. God's making those is in itself no odder
than his making any other type. The strangeness lies instead in the *teleological* element of Anselm's claim. God not only makes the type "It is
day" but confers on it its purpose of signifying that it is day (when, in fact,
it is day). So if the English language had developed in such a way that we
all used "It is day" to express what we now mean by saying "It is oblig-
atory," we would all be misusing that statement-type. We would be violating God's will for our linguistic practices. On this view, since English is
not something we are making up, we can get it wrong.

Now there are ways of mitigating the strangeness of this view, but we
will not pursue them here, since they all involve a platonism so lush and
giddy that even Anselm ought to blanch at them.[12] The important point
is that there is no need to go to such lengths in order to preserve the

teleological notion of truth to which Anselm is committed. One can build the teleology into our God-given power to use language, rather than into the statement-types themselves. Such a move allows one to recognize the conventionality of natural languages—to acknowledge, in other words, that it is human beings who make natural-language statement-types—but insist that our ability to make and use such languages was given to us by God for the purpose of signifying that what-is is. Thus, we use our power of speech correctly when we use conventional natural-language statement-types in order to signify that what-is is. Unfortunately, Anselm himself cannot take this approach, since it involves conceding that creatures do have a limited power to create natures and confer purposes on them.

In any event, the truth of statements (which Anselm also calls the "truth of signification") is only the first manifestation of truth that the teacher and student consider. They turn next to the truth of thought or opinion, which is also identified with rectitude, again understood teleologically:

> S: According to the reasoning we found persuasive in the case of
>   statements, nothing can be more correctly called the truth of a
>   thought than its rectitude. For the power of thinking that some-
>   thing is or is not was given to us in order that we might think that
>   what-is is, and that what-is-not is not. Therefore, if someone
>   thinks that what-is is, he is thinking what he ought to think, and so
>   his thought is correct. If, then, a thought is true and correct for
>   no other reason than that we are thinking that what-is is, or that
>   what-is-not is not, its truth is nothing other than its rectitude.[13]

Scripture also requires that we speak of truth in the will and in action,[14] and these are analyzed in the same way. There is truth in a will so long as a rational creature wills "what he ought—i.e., that for the sake of which he had received a will";[15] there is truth in an action so long as the agent (whether rational or irrational) does what it ought to do, which is what-ever it was created by God to do. Thus, as the student notes, truth in the will is just a special case of the truth of action.[16] There is also a close con-nection between the truth of action and the truth of signification, as the teacher argues in chapter 9: "since no one should do anything but what he ought to do, by the very fact that someone does something, he says and signifies that he ought to do it. And if he ought to do it, he says something true; but if he ought not, he lies."[17]

Thus far, Anselm's discussion of truth poses no special philosophical difficulties (apart from the strangeness of the suggestion that natural-language statement-types are created by God). Truth is rectitude—in fact, Anselm defines truth as "rectitude perceptible by the mind alone."[18] Rectitude, in turn, is a matter of something's doing or being what it ought to do or be. As applied to statements, thoughts, wills, and actions, this account of truth seems straightforward enough. But two further applications of the account will reveal deep philosophical puzzles beneath the superficial simplicity. When Anselm turns to the truth that is in the being of things, he finds that the notion of "what something ought to be" is unexpectedly complicated. And when he finally turns to the supreme Truth, God, he insists that God is rectitude but denies that we can ever correctly say that God "ought to be" anything whatever.

The Truth in the Being of Things

Having analyzed the truth that is found in statements, opinion, the will, action, and the senses, Anselm turns in chapter 7 of *De veritate* to a consideration of what he calls "the truth of the being of things." The teacher asks, "Do you think anything is, in any time or place, that is not in the supreme Truth and did not receive its being, insofar as it has being, from the supreme Truth; or that it can be anything other than what it is in the supreme Truth?" The student replies, "That is unthinkable."[19] Now 'is' and 'being' are used very broadly here: Anselm has in mind not merely the existence of things (their being such as to come within the scope of the existential quantifier), but their being the way they are, having the characteristics they have, and so forth. On this understanding of 'is' and 'being', we can identify at least two distinct claims to which the student is agreeing:

(1) Everything that exists (is a certain way, is the case) received its existence (its being that way, its being the case) from the supreme Truth.

(2) Necessarily, everything that exists (is a certain way, is the case) exists (is that way, is the case) in the supreme Truth.

(1) is simply an emphatic affirmation of God's sovereignty and providence. Anselm's formulation is, as always, very careful. He does not say that God *causes* the being of all things, but that all things receive their being from

God. For there are evils that God permits but does not bring about; but it is nevertheless legitimate, Anselm argues, to say that those evils are received from God.[20]

What (2) means is less clear. What exactly is it for something to "exist in" or to "be a certain way in" the supreme Truth? By way of an example, suppose John is young. According to (2), John is young in the supreme Truth. This cannot simply mean that God knows that John is young, or even that John's youth exists as an object of awareness for the divine mind. For Anselm will argue that John's being young is *correct* or *right*—that it is as it ought to be, and hence is *true*—because it is in the supreme Truth. Now it would make no sense to say that John's being young is as it ought to be because God knows that John is young or because John's youth is an object of awareness to the divine mind. The notion seems to be, rather, that John's being young is in accordance with God's plan or purpose. If this is a correct understanding of (2), then there is a close connection between (1) and (2). (1) says that things received their existence and their characteristics from God; (2) says that what they received from God necessarily accords with his plan for them. Thus, according to (2), there is rectitude in all things, because all things accord with God's plan for them. Whatever is, is right.

In chapter 8 Anselm addresses an obvious objection. Both what God permits and what God causes equally ought to be, according to Anselm, because God in his perfection would not allow or cause anything that ought not to be. And yet among the things that God permits are evil actions. Hence, the student asks, "But how can we say, with respect to the truth of a thing, that whatever is ought to be, since there are many evil deeds that certainly ought not to be?" Anselm argues that such things both ought to be and ought not to be:

T: I know you do not doubt that nothing is at all, unless God either causes or permits it . . . Will you dare to say that God causes or permits anything unwisely or badly?

S: On the contrary, I contend that God always acts wisely and well.

T: Do you think that something caused or permitted by such great goodness and wisdom ought not to be?

S: What intelligent person would dare to think that?

T: Therefore, both what comes about because God causes it and what comes about because God permits it ought equally to be.

S: What you are saying is obviously true.

T: Then tell me whether you think the effect of an evil will ought to be.

S: That's the same as asking whether an evil deed ought to be, and no sensible person would concede that.

T: And yet God permits some people to perform the evil deeds that their evil wills choose.

S: If only he did not permit it so often!

T: Then the same thing both ought to be and ought not to be. It ought to be, in that God, without whose permission it could not come about, acts wisely and well in permitting it; but if we consider the one whose evil will instigates the action, it ought not to be.[21]

Anselm's position has some apparently unwelcome consequences. First, Anselm cannot argue that one of the ways of looking at a situation is privileged and thus mitigate the awkwardness of saying that the same action both ought to be and ought not to be. If there were a privileged way of looking at the situation, it would surely be God's way. But God looks at every situation in at least the same variety of ways that humans do. (To speak anthropomorphically, he must ask "Ought John to kill Samantha?" in one way when assessing his providential plan, and in quite another way when assessing the punishment that might be due to John.) Which way is relevant depends entirely on the circumstances in which, or the reasons for which, we want to know the answer to the question, "Ought S to have done X?" or "Ought S to do X?"

Since Anselm applies this analysis to "can" statements as well as to "ought" statements, the view has a second unwelcome consequence. Not only whether someone *ought to* perform a certain action, but also whether someone *can* perform a certain action, depends on the way in which one is considering the "can"-statement. It might be true, for example, that Gertrude can wash her car tomorrow and can also refrain from washing her car tomorrow, when we ignore God's eternal plan. But when we assess the same thing while considering his plan, Gertrude can only do one or the other, depending on what God planned to permit.

One might object that Anselm need not embrace these consequences. Contrary to what Anselm seems to think, one might argue, in such cases we are not considering the same action in two different ways. Instead, we are considering two different actions. In the first example, we are not evaluating John's murdering (considered morally) and John's murdering (considered in terms of providence); rather, we are evaluating John's murdering and God's permitting John to murder, which are clearly distinct actions. Unfortunately, Anselm cannot dissolve the apparent paradox so easily. For he is interested in whether these two actions ought to have occurred, and here we cannot assess God's action of permitting without considering what it is that he is permitting, namely, John's murdering of Samantha. And since whatever God permits ought to be, John's murdering of Samantha ought to be.[22] Yet, looked at in another way, it ought not to be. The requirement that we assign different truth-values to one and the same statement depending on the ways in which the statement is considered cannot be eliminated after all.

So what is it to consider the truth of one and the same statement in different ways? It is to take into account different features or aspects of reality when assessing a sentence. One might want to argue that if this is all that is meant by "ways" of considering the truth of statements, then it is clear that there *is* a privileged way: the one in which we consider everything about how the world is. But Anselm cannot go along with this suggestion, since it implies that any judgment of the form "*X* ought not to be" (where *X* is anything that is actually the case) is, if considered in the privileged way, false. For if we consider everything, then we consider God's plan; and if we do that, then whatever is the case ought to be the case. But then there seems to be little sense left in saying that one ought not to have murdered or lied or been spiteful to one's friends, because whatever one did is what God permitted one to do and therefore what—taking everything into account—one ought to have done. And clearly Anselm is not willing to strip moral judgments of their force in this way. So we are left with a theory of truth according to which one and the same statement is true or false depending on the context of assessment.[23]

In the end, this odd feature of Anselm's view is almost invisible in *De veritate*. He rarely refers explicitly to the context in which he assesses the truth of normative and modal claims—perhaps because it is typically obvious which context is the relevant one given the discussion at hand. When there is ambiguity, Anselm is quick to let us know what the relevant context is. Nonetheless, Anselm's contextualism (as we shall call his view that the truth-value of some statements varies depending on the context of assessment) has important implications for other areas of his thought. We shall meet it again in his account of the relationship between divine eternity and creaturely time, as well as in his theory of the Trinity.

The Supreme Truth

In *De veritate* 2–9 Anselm examines a variety of truths and finds that each of them can be identified as rectitude. It is therefore no surprise that when he comes to God, the supreme Truth, at the beginning of chapter 10, Anselm easily wins his student's agreement that the supreme Truth is rectitude. But Anselm immediately makes it clear that God cannot be rectitude in the same sense as all the other rectitudes:

> T: You will surely not deny that the supreme Truth is rectitude.
>
> S: Indeed, I cannot acknowledge it to be anything else.
>
> T: Note that, while all the rectitudes discussed earlier are rectitudes because the things in which they exist either are or do what they ought, the supreme Truth is not a rectitude because it ought to be or do anything. For all things are under obligations to it, but it is under no obligation to anything.[24]

By affirming that the supreme Truth is rectitude, Anselm completes his assimilation of all truths to rectitude. But by insisting that the rectitude of the supreme Truth is not the same as the rectitude of all inferior truths, he seems to run up against two problems. The first is what we shall call *the problem of significance:* What can Anselm *mean* by calling God the supreme Truth or rectitude? He cannot avoid such language, since both Scripture and the arguments of the *Monologion* require him to call God "Truth," and the earlier arguments of *De veritate* require him to identify truth with rectitude. And yet the earlier sense of rectitude, according to which a thing has rectitude in virtue of its being what it ought to be or doing what it ought to do, cannot apply to God. So it is hard to see what significance Anselm can attach to this language that he now has no choice but to use.

The second problem is what we shall call *the problem of unity:* By insisting that God is not a truth or a rectitude in the same sense as all other truths or rectitudes, Anselm appears to abandon his stated aim of showing that "there is one truth in all true things." For the truth that we identify with God is not the same as the truth of statements, actions, and the other true things analyzed in the earlier chapters. Now recall the student's opening question: "Since we believe that God is truth, and we say that truth is in many other things, I would like to know whether, wherever truth is said to be, we must acknowledge that God is that truth." It appears that Anselm has now backed himself into such a corner that he must deny that God is the truth "wherever truth is said to be."

We shall begin with Anselm's solution to the problem of significance. Immediately after pointing out that the supreme Truth is rectitude, but a rectitude of quite a different sort from all the others, the teacher continues:

T: Do you also see that this rectitude is the cause of all other truths and rectitudes, and nothing is the cause of it?

S: I see that, and I notice that some of these other truths and rectitudes are merely effects, while others are both causes and effects. For example, the truth that is in the being of things is an effect of the supreme Truth, and it is in turn a cause of the truth of thoughts and statements; and the latter two truths are not a cause of any other truth.[25]

This exchange strongly suggests that what we mean when we call God "Truth" is that he is the cause of the other truths.

This suggestion is confirmed by the new spin Anselm gives to the argument from *Monologion* 18 with which the student had confronted him at the beginning of *De veritate*. Anselm had argued from the truth of statements to the existence of a supreme Truth without beginning or end: "Let anyone who can do so think of this: when did it begin to be true, or when was it not true, that something was going to exist? Or when will it cease to be true, and no longer be true, that something existed in the past? But if neither of these can be thought, and neither statement can be true apart from truth, then it is impossible even to think that truth has a beginning or end."[26]

Now that the student understands that the supreme Truth is the cause of other truths, Anselm says, he is in a position to appreciate the true force of that earlier argument: "[W]hen I asked, 'when was it not true that something was going to exist?' I didn't mean that this statement, asserting that something was going to exist in the future, was itself without a beginning, or that this truth was God." Instead, what he meant was that no matter when the statement "Something is going to exist" might have been uttered, it would have been true. Therefore, the cause of its truth must always have existed. And, Anselm continues, "The same reasoning applies to a statement that says something existed in the past. Since it is inconceivable that this statement, if uttered, could lack truth, it must be the case that the supreme cause of its truth cannot be understood to have an end. For what makes it true to say that something existed in the past is the fact that something really did exist in the past; and the reason something existed in the past is that this is how things are in the supreme Truth."[27] So to argue that the supreme Truth is eternal is not to argue that some feature of statements is eternal, but that the cause of their truth is eternal. God is the supreme Truth because he is the cause of the truth of all other true things.

Having thus solved the problem of significance, Anselm turns to the problem of unity: "Let's ... ask whether there is only one truth in all the things in which we say there is truth, or whether there are several truths, just as there are several things in which (as we have established) there is truth."[28] Suppose, for example, that "the rectitude of signification differs from rectitude of will because the one is in the will and the other in signification." It would follow that "rectitude of signification has its being because of signification and varies according to signification." The student replies, "So it does. For when a statement signifies that what-is is, or that what-is-not is not, the signification is correct; and it has been established that this is the rectitude without which there is no correct signification. If, however, the statement signifies that what-is-not is, or that what-is is not, or if it signifies nothing at all, there will be no rectitude of signification, which exists only in signification. Hence, the rectitude of signification has its being through signification and changes along with it."[29]

The teacher quickly rejects this commonsensical position. The rectitude or truth of signification does not have its being through signification, but in fact is altogether independent of signification. For suppose (the teacher argues) that no one wills to signify what ought to be signified. Then there will be no signification, but "the rectitude in virtue of which it is right for what-ought-to-be-signified to be signified, and by which this is demanded, does not cease to exist." The teacher concludes:

> T: So when rectitude is present in signification, it's not because rectitude begins to exist in signification when someone signifies that what-is is, or that what-is-not is not; instead, it's because at that time signification comes about in accordance with a rectitude that always exists. And when rectitude is absent from signification, it's not because rectitude ceases to exist when signification is not what

> it should be or there is no signification at all; instead, it's because at
> that time signification falls away from a rectitude that never fails.[30]

Thus, the rectitude of signification does not depend on signification. And there is nothing distinctive about signification in this regard: rectitude of will does not depend on the will or rectitude of action on action. Rectitude does not depend on the things in which there is rectitude: there is one never-failing, unchangeable rectitude for all things in which we say there is truth or rectitude.

The conclusion that there is only one truth in all true things seems to come too quickly, since it is possible that the never-failing rectitude that makes it right for what-ought-to-be-signified to be signified is distinct from the never-failing rectitude that makes it right for what-ought-to-be-done to be done, and so on for each of the other sorts of rectitude discussed in *De veritate*. In other words, the original question about whether there are distinct *species* of truth, corresponding to the distinct species of true things, is not answered by the teacher's discussion of the rectitude of signification, which seems designed to show that there are not distinct *instances* of a given species. Nonetheless, given what he has already said in discussing God as supreme Truth, Anselm is entitled to this conclusion. For we know that God is the cause of *all* the truths:

T: Do you also see that this rectitude is the cause of all other truths and rectitudes, and nothing is the cause of it?

S: I see that, and I notice that some of these other truths and rectitudes are merely effects, while others are both causes and effects. For example, the truth that is in the being of things is an effect of the supreme Truth, and it is in turn a cause of the truth of thoughts and statements; and the latter two truths are not a cause of any other truth.[31]

So the one and only never-failing rectitude, in accordance with which whatever is right in signification, thought, action, or will comes to be, is God. The supreme Truth is in fact the only truth. As the student suggested at the outset, "wherever truth is said to be, we must acknowledge that God is that truth."

But then why, the student asks, "do we speak of the truth *of* this or that particular thing as if we were distinguishing different truths, when in fact there aren't different truths for different things?" The teacher replies that such language is not strictly correct:

T: Truth is said improperly to be *of* this or that thing, since truth does not have its being in or from or through the things in which it is said to be. But when things themselves are in accordance with truth, which is always present to those things that are as they ought to be, we speak of the truth of this or that thing—for example, the truth of the will or of action—in the same way in which we speak of the time of this or that thing despite the fact that there is one and the same time for all things that are temporally simultaneous, and that if this or that thing did not exist, there would still be time. For we do not speak of the time of this or that thing because time is in the things, but because they are in time. And just as time regarded in itself is not called the time of some particular thing, but we speak of the time of this or that thing when we consider the things that are in time, so also the supreme Truth as it subsists in itself is not the truth of some particular thing, but when something is in accordance with it, then it is called the truth or rectitude of that thing.[32]

Note that Anselm's solution to the problem of unity is not a standard Platonic maneuver of the sort that we see in his account of goodness. That is, he is not arguing that since various things are true, there must be something that is true in the highest degree and has its truth from itself rather than from another. Anselm in fact never argues in this way that God is true, as he argues that God is just, good, and so forth. (The expression "true God" appears in Anselm in Christological contexts, but he seldom uses 'true' of God predicatively.) God is Truth, but not true; other things are true, but not truths. So the unity of truth is not the unity of a property in its various instances, but strict numerical unity. There is one truth because Truth is God, who is one.

Conclusion

We now have a complete picture of Anselm's view of truth. "Wherever truth is said to be"—in statements, opinions, wills, actions, the senses, and the being of things—that truth is rectitude. Something has rectitude because it accords with its purpose. Something receives its purpose from whatever caused it. God causes all things. So whatever is said to be true is true in virtue of being caused by God in accordance with his will, and God is Truth because he causes all things and establishes the standards by which they are to be evaluated.

To a contemporary philosopher, Anselm's commitment to the unity of truth might well seem gratuitous. For one thing, we would not today speak of truth in wills, actions, the senses, and "the being of things," so the effort to try to capture all those uses of the word 'true' in a single theory seems needlessly strained. And even in the cases where we would speak of truth—in statements and opinions—the elaborate theory Anselm develops in the interest of a unified theory of truth adds unnecessary complexity to his promisingly commonsensical observation that a statement is true "when it signifies that what-is is."

But in fact it is not so difficult to see how Anselm's Grand Unified Theory of Truth emerges out of the deceptive simplicity of the Aristotelian commonplace. His first account of the truth of statements is that a statement's truth is its correctness, its getting things right. But its getting things right is not simply a matter of its corresponding to the way things are: it is a matter of the statement's *doing its proper job*. If a statement had some purpose other than saying that what-is is, its saying that what-is is would not be any reason to call the statement correct. (We call a clock "right" when the time it tells is the actual time, but only because clocks are meant for telling time.) Once Anselm starts attending to the notion of "getting things right" in this sense, however, it is perfectly natural for him to ask about the proper job of the will, of actions, and of all the other things whose rectitude he investigates in *De veritate*. In every case, the proper job is the job assigned by God. So all sorts of things—not just statements—can be said to be right or correct or true if they do the job assigned them by God.

Part II

GOD

THE *MONOLOGION* ARGUMENTS
FOR THE EXISTENCE OF GOD

The first fruits of Anselm's exploration of the reason of faith are his arguments for the existence of God in the first four chapters of the *Monologion*. These arguments have been almost completely eclipsed by the celebrated argument of the *Proslogion*—and not entirely without reason, as we shall see. Yet although these arguments lack the distinctively compelling character of the *Proslogion* argument, they do repay attention, since they reveal some of the metaphysical perplexities that would confront Anselm throughout his career.

The First *Monologion* Proof: The Argument for a Supreme Good

Anselm begins the *Monologion* with a forthright statement of his aim, method, and audience. His *aim* is to prove "that there is one nature, supreme among all existing things, who alone is self-sufficient in his eternal happiness, who through his omnipotent goodness grants and brings it about that all other things exist or have any sort of well-being, and a great many other things that we must believe about God or his creation." His *method* is to offer arguments by which a reader can "convince himself...by reason alone." And his *audience* is "anyone [who] does not know, either because he has not heard or because he does not believe," the doctrines about God and creation that Anselm sets out to prove—provided only that he is at least "moderately intelligent."[1]

Anselm notes that there are many ways in which he could accomplish his goal, but he will set forth the way that is "easiest" or "handiest" (*promptissimum*). It is the most accessible way to prove the existence of God because it takes off from the obvious and pervasive phenomenon of desire: "After all, everyone desires only those things that he thinks good. It is therefore easy for him to turn the eye of his mind sometimes toward investigating the source of the goodness of those things that he desires only because he judges that they are good. Then, with reason leading and him following, he will rationally advance toward those things of which he is irrationally ignorant."[2] The person who reflects on the good things that are the objects of desire can easily begin by asking this question: "Since there are countless goods, whose great diversity we both experience through our bodily senses and discern through the reasoning of our mind, are we to believe that there is some one thing through which all goods whatsoever are good? Or are different goods good through different things?"[3] It should be clear to "all who are willing to pay attention," Anselm says, that "all things whatsoever that are said to be more or less or equally a certain way as compared to each other are said to be so through something that is not understood as different but rather as the same in diverse things, whether it is detected equally or unequally in them." For example, we can compare just things as being more, less, or equally just. We have to understand them as all being just through one thing—justice—which is the same in all just things, though it is present in just things to varying degrees. Similarly, we can compare good things as being more, less, or equally good. So "it must be that [good things] are all good through something that is understood to be the same in diverse good things."[4]

Although Anselm takes himself to have established that all good things are good through some one thing, he recognizes that there remains an intuitive pull to say there are diverse sources of goodness for good things. Someone might object, for example, that "a horse is called good through one thing because it is strong and through another because it is fast. After all, though it seems that the horse is called good through its strength and good through its speed, it does not seem that strength is the same thing as speed."[5] But that, Anselm says, is the wrong way to think about the goodness of a good horse. Notice that while a strong and fast horse is good, a strong and fast robber is *bad*. Why is that? A strong and fast horse is good because it is *useful*; a strong and fast robber is bad because he is *harmful*. Whatever is good is good either because of its usefulness (*utilitas*) or because of its intrinsic value (*honestas*).

We would expect Anselm to argue at this point that usefulness is defined in terms of intrinsic value: what is useful is simply what tends to promote or bring about intrinsic value. So there is, after all, some one thing—namely, intrinsic value—that accounts for the goodness of everything that is good. But he does not argue in that way. Instead, he simply affirms the success of his earlier argument and applies its conclusion to utility and intrinsic value: "But since the argument we have already considered cannot be refuted in any way, it must also be the case that all useful or intrinsically valuable things, if they are genuinely good, are good through the very same thing—whatever that is—through which all goods must exist." Let us call this thing G. Who would doubt (Anselm asks) that G is itself a great good? So, since G is itself good, and all good things are good through it, it is good through itself: "It follows, therefore, that all other things are good through something other than what they themselves are, and it alone is good through itself."[6]

At this point Anselm introduces a new principle: whatever is good through something other than itself is less good than something that is good through itself. He takes this principle to be obvious and offers no defense of it—we will shortly come to see why he thinks it needs no defense. Since G is good through itself and all other things are good through G, the principle means that all other goods are less good than G. And since, by definition, "something is supreme if it surpasses others in such a way that it has neither peer nor superior,"[7] we can conclude that G is supremely good.

In chapter 2 of the *Monologion* Anselm says that we can substitute "great" for "good" in the first proof and thus obtain an argument for the existence of something supremely great. Since greatness is such an important notion for Anselm—one that will occupy center stage in the *Proslogion* proof—his explanation of the notion is worth quoting in full: "Now I do not mean great in size, as a given body is great; rather, I mean great in the sense that the greater something is, the better or worthier it is, as wisdom is great."[8] So degrees of greatness are correlated with degrees of goodness and worthiness. We have already seen that Anselm connects goodness with the notion of desire: we desire only those things that we think are good, and we desire them because we think they are good. But what does he mean by worthiness (*dignitas*)? It is the objective excellence of a thing. A nature that has greater worth is one that is more outstanding (*praestantior*)[9] and more fundamental (*principalior*),[10] one that ranks higher in the objective hierarchy of natures. And although goodness and worth are not quite the same thing conceptually speaking, since goodness connotes a relation to desire that worth does not, the two are quite closely connected, since *rational* desire will track the objective excellence of natures. What is intrinsically greater deserves to be loved more. Hence, Anselm is sometimes willing to switch back and forth between the language of worth and the language of goodness, as he does in *Monologion* 4: "If someone considers the natures of things, he cannot help realizing that they are not all of equal worthiness (*dignitas*); rather, some of them are on different and unequal levels. For anyone who doubts that a horse is by its very nature better (*melior,* the comparative of *bonum,* good) than wood, and that a human being is more outstanding (*praestantior*) than a horse, should not even be called a human being."[11] Accordingly, after telling us that the proof of a supremely good thing in chapter 1 can be used to infer the existence of a supremely great thing as well, Anselm assimilates the two conclusions: "And since only what is supremely good can be supremely great, there must be something greatest and best, that is, supreme among all existing things."[12] So we can regard the arguments of *Monologion* 1 and 2 as in effect a single proof of the existence of something supremely great and supremely good.

These considerations about goodness and greatness also explain Anselm's confidence in the principle that what is good through itself is a greater good than what is good through another. Anything that is good through something other than itself is, *qua* good thing, dependent and derivative. Something that is good through itself is a more fundamental good and therefore a greater good.

Though there are several points in Anselm's proof of a supreme good to which one could reasonably raise objections, we wish to focus on those that reveal the lacunae in Anselm's metaphysics. Consider first the principle that "all things whatsoever that are said to be more or less or equally a certain way as compared to each other are said to be so through something that is not understood as different but rather as the same in diverse things." We will call this the Single-Source Principle. Anselm offers no defense of this premise, but it is easy to construct one on his behalf. If there is no such thing, he might argue, then there is no ontological basis for our predicating 'F' of all the *F* things; such predications will depend on either linguistic accidents or metaphors. For example, there is no ontological basis for predicating 'green' of both a traffic light and an inexperienced co-worker, precisely because there is no feature that they have in common and that is the basis for our predicating 'green' of them. And for that reason we cannot sensibly compare their degrees of greenness. It would make no sense to say that one's inexperienced coworker is greener than a traffic signal, or vice versa, or that the two are equally green. Anselm's own example of justice encourages us to think along these lines. All just things are just through justice; justice is a property, and just things are just in virtue of exemplifying that property. The Single-Source Principle will thus be plausible on many understandings of what properties are. But then *G* will be a property—presumably the property of goodness—and Anselm is not trying to prove the existence of a property. *G* is supposed to turn out to be, not a property, but God.

Now one might note in Anselm's defense that he will go on to identify God with goodness; perhaps, then, the fact that Anselm's application of the Single-Source Principle encourages us to think in terms of the property of goodness is not an insuperable difficulty. But this defense simply relocates the problem. The Single-Source Principle is plausible only if we envision a relation between properties and property-bearers that Anselm does not think holds between God and creatures. As Anselm's own example sug-gests, just things are just because they *exemplify* justice or because justice is somehow *present in* them as a metaphysical constituent (while remaining "the same" even though it is "in diverse things"). But creatures do not exemplify the divine nature, and God is not present in creatures by way of being a metaphysical constituent.

What this argument brings out is that Anselm has two distinct and incompatible theories of properties, neither of which he develops beyond an intuitive level. On the one hand, he is inclined toward what we might think of as a Platonist (or perhaps, more generally, realist) understanding of properties as universals: unitary entities that are somehow "in" a plu-rality of things. Their being unitary is what grounds predication; we can properly say "Horses are good" and "Cats are good," without equivoca-tion, because goodness is one and the same thing in both horses and cats. On the other hand, as we will see in more detail in chapter 6 in this volume, Anselm holds that goodness, justice, and the like—any features that belong to the divine nature—are in fact identical with the divine nature. On this view, goodness is not a universal. Goodness is not realized in or exemplified by a plurality of things, because goodness is God, and there can be only one God. If we accept the first view of properties, Anselm's argument will at best establish the existence of a property or Platonic Form that is supremely good. If we accept the second, the Single-Source Principle is no longer plausible, and the argument does not even get off the ground. Only by switching from the first view to the second can Anselm give his argument the appearance of an argument for the existence of God.

The point in the argument at which Anselm attempts to make this switch comes when he asserts that G, the one thing in virtue of which all good things are good, is itself good. And it does not appear that he has any way to establish that claim. He offers no argument, but simply asks a rhetorical question: "Who would doubt that this thing, through which all goods exist, is itself a great good?"[13] Brian Leftow has suggested that Anselm may have had "some such thought as this in mind: delete this thing from reality, and all goodness goes with it."[14] Surely, we might think, if the removal of a thing entails the removal of all goodness, that thing itself must be good or exemplify goodness.

Unfortunately this intuitive consideration proves mistaken on closer inspection. Consider a parallel argument:

a. All dogs are dogs through some one thing—call it D.
b. Delete D from reality, and all dogs go with it.
c. Therefore, D is itself a dog.

Take any plausible candidate for D—the property *being a dog,* the Platonic Form of the Dog, the divine idea of dogginess, what have you— on which (a) and (b) might turn out to be true. The conclusion, (c), will turn out to be false on any of those interpretations. No property, no Platonic Form, no divine idea is a living organism of the species *canis domesticus.* The argument from (a) and (b) to (c) is therefore invalid, and the parallel argument that Leftow suggests for the claim that G is good is likewise invalid.

We might try a second way of marshaling intuitive considerations in favor of the claim that G is good. Causing, we might argue, is a kind of giving, and something cannot give what it does not have. Paint cannot make a wall yellow unless the paint is itself yellow; the electric burner cannot heat the food unless the burner is itself hot. Similarly, how could

G make things good unless G is itself good? But the principle on which this argument rests is notoriously vulnerable to counterexamples. The sun reddens skin even though the sun is not red; chemical reactions produce heat even though the chemicals are not hot. And in any event, although Anselm sometimes speaks as if he holds that causing is giving, he cannot consistently avail himself of that principle, for the reasons we have already seen. The goodness that God gives to creatures is not his own goodness— the goodness that God has—for God's goodness is identical with God himself. God gives creatures properties that he does not himself possess.

The Second *Monologion* Proof: The Argument for a Supreme Nature

In chapter 3 Anselm offers his second proof, an argument that there is a single supreme nature that is through itself whatever it is, and through which all other things are whatever they are. His first premise is simple:

>   (1) Whatever exists either exists through something or exists through nothing.[15]

As the *Monologion* unfolds, it becomes clear that Anselm prefers to use 'through' (*per*) to connote efficient causality and 'from' (*ex*) for material causality. But Anselm has a broad understanding of efficient causality, broad enough to include what we might think of as formal causality. In the Lambeth Fragments he says, "some causes are called 'efficient'—for example, an artisan (for he makes his product) and wisdom (which makes someone wise)."[16] So 'through' in this first premise can connote either agency (as a work of art comes to exist "through" the artist) or formal causality (as a wise person is wise "through" wisdom). Accordingly, (1) says that for anything that exists, either its existing has an explanation in terms of agency or formal causality or its existing has no such explanation.

The next premise rules out the second option:

>   (2) Nothing exists through nothing.[17]

(2) of course enunciates the familiar and venerable observation that we might call the Rodgers Principle: "Nothing comes from nothing. Nothing ever could."[18] It is a relatively weak version of the Principle of Sufficient Reason; it claims merely that nothing exists whose existence cannot be

accounted for in terms of either some agent or some formal feature. From (1) and (2) Anselm correctly goes on to infer

(3) whatever exists, exists through something.

But obviously "something" is not "some one thing." In the first proof Anselm took the unity of the ultimate source to be evident from the unity of the feature that was explained by that source, but in the second proof Anselm requires considerable additional argument to establish the desired claim that there is a single source for the being of everything that is. Note that if Anselm took existence to be a property on a par with other properties, he could have adopted the Single-Source Principle in chapter 3 just as he had in chapter 1, and the structure of the two arguments would have been exactly the same. We have here yet another indication that Anselm does not think existence is a property—a point that will be crucial for our interpretation of the argument of the *Proslogion*.[19]

Anselm continues by stating the two possible alternatives:

(4) Either (a) there is one thing, or (b) there is a plurality of things, through which whatever exists, exists.

In order to show that option (b) must be rejected, Anselm first notes the three possible ways in which this plurality of things might be related to each other.

(5) If there is a plurality of things through which whatever exists, exists, then either (b1) they are all traced back to some one thing through which they all exist, or (b2) each of them exists through itself, or (b3) they exist through each other.

Anselm then argues that if either (b1) or (b2) is true, there is really only one thing through which everything that exists, exists:

(6) If (b1), then there is really one thing through which all things exist (since "all things exist through that one thing through which the plurality of things exists"[20]).

(7) If (b2), then each of the plurality of things exists through one power or nature of self-existing.

Anselm offers no argument for the claim that this power or nature of self-existing must be one thing present in each of the plurality of things that are through themselves; perhaps the Single-Source Principle is his implicit justification. (If so, Anselm would be treating self-existence as a property in a way that existence is not.) And if there is some such power or nature of self-existing that all of them possess, in virtue of which each of them exists through itself, then—assuming, plausibly enough, that the "exists through" relation is transitive—it is more accurate to say that all things exist through that power or nature of self-existing. So once again we have only one thing through which everything that exists, exists. Accordingly,

(8) If each of the plurality of things exists through one power or nature of self-existing, then there is one thing through which whatever exists, exists.

Now whereas options (b1) and (b2) end up collapsing the alleged plurality of things back into a single thing, option (b3) can be rejected out of hand, "since it is irrational to think that something is through that to which it gives being."[21] So

(9) (b3) is absurd.

Having now closed off every possibility under option (b), Anselm is entitled to adopt option (a):

(10) There is one thing through which whatever exists, exists.

Let's call that one thing E. From (10) we know two things:

(11) E exists through itself.
(12) All other things that exist, exist through something other than themselves (namely, E).

Now just as what is good through something other than itself is inferior in goodness to what is good through itself, so, too, what exists through something other than itself is inferior in existence to what exists through itself:

(13) Whatever exists through something other than itself exists in a lesser way than what exists through itself.

From (11), (12), and (13) it follows that

(14) Everything that exists, besides E, exists in a lesser way than E.

And conversely,

(15) E exists most greatly and supremely of all things.

Anselm concludes, "That which exists most greatly of all things, and through which exists whatever is good or great—whatever, indeed, is anything at all—must itself be supremely good and supremely great and supreme among all the things that exist. Therefore, there is something— whether you call it an essence or a substance or a nature—that is the best and greatest and highest of all existing things."[22]

The Third *Monologion* Proof: The Argument for a Most Excellent Being

In chapter 4 Anselm offers his third proof, an argument for the claim that there is a single most excellent being, one that is preeminent in worthiness (*dignitas*). Anselm begins by observing that some natures are better than others. He is confident that no sensible person will deny this premise, since (as we have seen) "anyone who doubts that a horse is by its very nature better than wood, and that a human being is more outstanding than a horse, should not even be called a human being."[23] Now if, for any nature, there is a better, there are indefinitely many natures. But only "someone who is quite absurd" thinks that there are indefinitely many natures. (Why? Anselm here simply adopts the standard medieval view that there can be no actual quantitative infinity.)[24] So there must be some nature than which no other nature is better.

This is the conclusion that Anselm is seeking, but he realizes he must eliminate one more possibility. So he continues, "either the nature that is like this is the only one, or there are several like it and equal to it."[25] Given his argument up to this point, we might naturally interpret this as asking whether there is only one most excellent nature or instead several equally great natures, each of which is unsurpassed in excellence. For in the first part of the argument 'nature' has clearly meant "type" or "kind": the kind *human being* is greater than the kind *horse,* which is in turn greater than the kind *wood,* and there must be some kind than which no kind is greater. But now Anselm is asking, not about kinds, but about particular individuals. Notice that he says, "there are several *like* it and equal to it"— that is, several individuals of the same kind as it. So Anselm has equivocated on 'nature': instead of asking whether there is more than one kind at the top, he is asking whether there is more than one individual at the top.

To see how this equivocation proves fatal to the argument, we must follow the argument further. In order to show that there is only one individual of unsurpassed excellence, Anselm argues against the possibility that there is a plurality. Suppose there is a plurality. Are all these equally great individuals great through their shared essence-type, or through their distinguishing characteristics? They cannot all be equally great through their distinguishing characteristics ("through something other than what they are," as Anselm puts it) because then the distinguishing characteristic would be greater than the essence—for what is great through another is less great than that through which it is great. And we have already established that we are dealing with essences of unsurpassed excellence.

So Anselm examines the second alternative. Suppose instead that these equally great individuals are equally great through their essence—that is, through "the very thing that they are." If that is the case, Anselm says, they are not multiple individuals after all. They are all one, because they are all one essence. Here again Anselm is equivocating, this time on the word 'essence'. Anselm uses the word 'essence' interchangeably with 'nature'. But 'nature', as we have seen, has at least two distinct senses. It can mean "kind," but it can also mean "individual (of a kind)." 'Essence' likewise can have either of these meanings. In one sense of 'essence', two individuals of the same kind have the same essence without being one thing. In the other sense, two individuals of the same kind are two essences. In this argument Anselm infers that there is one essence in the second sense from the claim that there is one essence in the first sense—an inference that in general he does not accept.

He accepts it in this case, it seems, because he already has in mind that the thing at the top of the hierarchy is God. And it is true of God, as it is not true in any other case, that there cannot be multiple individuals with the same nature. Michael and Gabriel have the same nature but are distinct individuals, a plurality of angels. The Father, the Son, and the Holy Spirit have the same nature but are not a plurality of gods. As Anselm says in *De incarnatione Verbi* 2, "we do not say of two angels or two souls that they are numerically one anything, in the way that we do say of numerically one God that he is both Father and Son and of the Father and Son that they are numerically one God."[26] The move from "shared nature" to "numerically one nature" to "numerically one being that possesses the nature" is therefore legitimate only in the case of God. The fact that Anselm makes that move in this argument shows clearly that he is introducing assumptions based on the ontological peculiarities of the very being whose existence he is trying to prove.

We can get further light on how this argument goes astray by returning to an earlier point in the argument. Having established that there is a nature than which no nature is greater, Anselm asks whether there is one such nature or more than one. Given that up to that point 'nature' has meant "kind," the most natural reading of that question would be that Anselm is asking whether there can be a plurality of equally great but qualitatively different *kinds* at the top of the hierarchy. As we have seen, the remainder of the argument shows clearly that this is not the question Anselm is in fact asking. But why does he not consider this question? That is, why does it not so much as occur to him that there might be a tie for greatness between two or more kinds than which no kind is greater? Any answer to this question would have to be pure speculation, but it seems likely to us that Anselm assumes that in general there is only one kind on any rung on the ladder of greatness. For God is a perfectly rational Creator, and it would be irrational to create two distinct natures of equal greatness; that would be disorderly overkill of a sort that would be unfitting for God and therefore impossible for him. And given that in general there is only one kind at each level of the hierarchy, the only plurality that Anselm thinks to ask about when he comes to the top level is a plurality of individuals, not a plurality of kinds.

Anselm's Instructive Failures

Our examination of Anselm's theistic proofs in the *Monologion* has shown them to be failures. But their failure is illuminating. They founder on Anselm's inadequately worked out metaphysics, and it is clear that Anselm fails to work out the relevant metaphysical details because he is thinking too much about the nature of the being he is trying to prove. For example, he will argue later that God is neither a universal substance nor an individual substance:

> This substance is not included in any common classification of substances, since every other nature is excluded from having an essence in common with him. Indeed, every substance is classified as either universal or individual. A universal substance is essentially common to several substances, as being-a-man is common to individual men; an individual substance has a universal essence in common with others, as individual men have in common with other individual men the fact that

they are men. So how would someone understand the supreme nature as being included in this classification of other substances, since he is neither divided into several substances nor conjoined with any other through a common essence?[27]

Since what Anselm is really interested in is God, to whom the distinction between universal and individual substance does not apply, he simply doesn't bother working out a consistent metaphysics of universals, essences, properties, and individuation. That failure dooms any argument from creatures to God; Anselm's metaphysics of creatures is too inchoate to support the inferences he wishes to make.

In a roundabout way, then, Anselm's proofs in the *Monologion* are all question-begging. They gloss over difficulties in formulating the premises and in justifying certain inferences because Anselm is not really interested in the nature of the creatures on the basis of which he is purportedly arguing. Instead, he illicitly takes for granted the metaphysically peculiar nature of the being whose existence he is trying to prove. The only way for Anselm to avoid this problem would be for him to formulate an argument that legitimately and overtly depends on working out a conception of God first and then deriving from that conception the claim that such a being exists. As we shall show in the next chapter, that is exactly the method Anselm will adopt in the argument of the *Proslogion.*

THE *PROSLOGION* ARGUMENT
FOR THE EXISTENCE OF GOD

In her discussion of Anselm's influence on subsequent thinkers, Gillian Evans notes that "it is beyond dispute that—apart from his popular devotional writings—his works did not become and remain influential at once, although they were copied and circulated. The most probable explanation is that they were of a type which did not fit the practical teaching needs of the working schools which were going to evolve in the next generation or two into the first universities. Because of the way the arguments unfolded, and their profundity, the books were not easy to lecture on or to divide up satisfactorily for quotation or extract in *florilegium* or commentary."[1] Evans's suggestion gains even more plausibility when we note the perennial fascination with the one thing in Anselm's work that has "that desirable easy availability for those who wished to make extracts and compile scrapbooks of quotations":[2] the argument of *Proslogion* 2. In the *Proslogion,* Anselm tells us, he presents a single argument, as opposed to the complicated chain of multiple arguments found in the *Monologion.* And since chapter 2 of the *Proslogion* is entitled "That God truly exists," most readers have understandably assumed that the single argument is found in that chapter. So we find the argument of *Proslogion* 2 treated as a stand-alone proof: extracted and anthologized, criticized or defended, and even baptized with the curiously unhelpful name "ontological argument."

Unfortunately, Anselm did not really have it in him to produce an argument that can stand on its own as a brief excerpt to be anthologized and circulated independently. The only way he managed even the appearance of such a thing was to express his reasoning in language so compressed as to be elliptical and indeed misleading. For that matter, his desire for stylistic grace and rhetorical effectiveness—which are on display in the *Proslogion* to a markedly greater degree than in any of his other systematic works—sometimes obscures his train of thought or misdirects the unwary reader. For example, Anselm famously contrasts "existing in the understanding" with "existing in reality," as though he had some metaphysical doctrine about two modes of existence. As we shall see, he has no such doctrine; such a thing never entered his mind. He clearly just thought the phrasing sounded nice and made the argument memorable. And he was right on that score; he was just wrong to suppose that memorable phrasing did the argument any good.

Even the title of the work is arguably a bad rhetorical choice. "Proslogion"—a speech made to another—is pithy and provides a nice contrast with "Monologion"—a speech made to oneself. But the original titles of the two works were much better descriptions of their content. The *Monologion* really is "A pattern for meditating on the reason of faith," and the *Proslogion* is much more aptly described as exemplifying "Faith seeking understanding."[3] The fact that the latter work is called "A speech made to another" has encouraged some readers to lean too heavily on the nature of the *Proslogion* as speech addressed to God; but actually the *Proslogion*'s being addressed to God is of no more consequence for our understanding of its arguments than the *Monologion*'s being addressed to oneself is of consequence for our understanding of its arguments.

Thus, Anselm's language in *Proslogion* 2 is so compressed, and his rhetorical choices throw up so many red herrings, that anyone who looks to that chapter alone for Anselm's statement of the "single argument" is almost certain to misunderstand the argument of the *Proslogion*. Even those who read chapter 2 in conjunction with chapters 3 and 4 (as is sometimes done) or the *Proslogion* as a whole (as is done all too rarely) are likely to fall into quite mistaken ideas about both the argument of chapter 2 and its relation to the rest of the work. Yet in order to make our case for a quite different approach to the argument of *Proslogion* 2, we will first sketch a standard exposition of the argument that relies exclusively on chapter 2.

As we will show, that standard treatment leads to serious difficulties in understanding Anselm's exchange with Gaunilo, the first critic of the *Proslogion*. In order to resolve those difficulties, we examine Anselm's reply to Gaunilo. His reply is not so much a rejoinder to Gaunilo's objections as it is a diagnosis of Gaunilo's misreading. In setting Gaunilo straight Anselm decompresses his language, distinguishes his rhetorical frills from the philosophical substance, and offers us a clear and consistent restatement of the "one argument" of the *Proslogion*.

A Conventional Reading of *Proslogion* 2

At the beginning of chapter 2, Anselm addresses God as "you who grant understanding to faith" and asks God to grant him the understanding that "you are, as we believe you are, and that you are what we believe you to be."[4] In this way Anselm indicates that his argument will begin from faith. Accordingly, his first premise is a claim about God that he accepts on faith. "We believe," Anselm says, "that you are something than which nothing greater can be thought," and this characterization of God can serve as the first premise of the argument:

(1) God is something than which nothing greater can be thought.

Now the question is, does God, that is, something than which nothing greater can be thought, exist? After all, as the Psalmist says, "The fool has said in his heart, 'There is no God.' " So it is *possible* to deny that God exists. We somehow have to *prove,* given this description, that God exists. So, Anselm says, consider this fool. When he hears this phrase, "something than which nothing greater can be thought," he surely understands what he hears. In other words, he forms a concept of something than which nothing greater can be thought. He just doesn't believe that the concept is instantiated, that it corresponds to anything in reality.

But now Anselm points out an interesting fact. Since the fool understands "something than which nothing greater can be thought," we can say that something than which nothing greater can be thought exists in his understanding.

(2) Something than which nothing greater can be thought exists in the understanding.

The analogy here is that of the painter and his work. Before the painting exists in reality, it exists in his understanding as a merely possible painting; once the painter has completed the work, it exists both in his understanding and in reality as well. Anselm will now argue, by *reductio,* that God cannot be like the merely possible painting. If he exists in the understanding (as he clearly does), he must exist in reality as well. So assume, for *reductio,* that

(3) Something than which nothing greater can be thought exists in the understanding alone.

Now even if something than which nothing greater can be thought does not exist in reality, it can be *thought* to exist in reality (just as the merely possible painting can be thought to exist in reality). And when we think of something than which nothing greater can be thought existing in reality, we think of something greater than when we think of something than which nothing greater can be thought existing in the understanding alone. Thus,

(4) Something than which nothing greater can be thought "can be thought to exist in reality as well, which is greater."[5]

(4) entails

(5) Something than which nothing greater can be thought is something than which a greater *can* be thought,

which is clearly contradictory. So the *reductio* has succeeded, and we are entitled to deny (3). Therefore,

(6) Something than which nothing greater can be thought exists in reality.

And although Anselm does not bother saying so explicitly in *Proslogion* 2, from (1) and (6) we can conclude that

(7) God exists in reality.

The best-known criticism of Anselm's argument—the Lost Island argument first propounded by Anselm's contemporary, Gaunilo of Marmoutiers—depends on reading *Proslogion* 2 in the way we have just laid out. We know nothing of Gaunilo apart from his "Reply on Behalf of the Fool," but his Lost Island argument has given him undying fame as a sort of Edmund Gettier of the eleventh-century theological scene. Gaunilo wrote:

There are those who say that somewhere in the ocean is an island, which, because of the difficulty—or rather, impossibility—of finding what does not exist, some call "the Lost Island." This island (so the story goes) is more plentifully endowed than even the Isles of the Blessed with an indescribable abundance of all sorts of riches and delights. And because it has neither owner nor inhabitant, it is everywhere superior in its abundant riches to all the other lands that human beings inhabit.

Suppose someone tells me all this. The story is easily told and involves no difficulty, and so I understand it. But if this person went on to draw a conclusion, and say, "You cannot any longer doubt that this island, more excellent than all others on earth, truly exists somewhere in reality. For you do not doubt that this island exists in your understanding; and since it is more excellent to exist not merely in the understanding, but also in reality, this island must also exist in reality. For if it did not, any land that exists in reality would be greater than it. And so this more excellent thing that you have understood would not in fact be more excellent."—If, I say, he should try to convince me by this argument that I should no longer doubt whether the island truly exists, either I would think he was joking, or I would not know whom I ought to think more foolish: myself, if I grant him his conclusion, or him, if he thinks he has established the existence of that island with any degree of certainty, without first showing that its excellence exists in my understanding as a thing that truly and undoubtedly exists and not in any way like something false or uncertain.[6]

If we tidy up Gaunilo's formulation, it seems we have an argument exactly parallel to Anselm's. So if Anselm's argument proves the existence of a being than which a greater cannot be thought, Gaunilo's argument proves the existence of an island than which no greater can be thought. And there is nothing special about islands, of course: we could equally well prove the existence of a live oak than which a greater cannot be thought, a cockroach than which a greater cannot be thought, you name it.

Because the Lost Island argument is so vivid and memorable—and because it seems to provide an exact parallel to Anselm's argument—it is not surprising that philosophers have read Anselm's response to Gaunilo primarily in order to discover his response to the Lost Island argument. But this is where the standard approach tends to go astray. For if one reads Anselm's response in light of this problematic, it looks remarkably non-responsive. Some interpreters sympathetic to the ontological argument simply state their own defense against Gaunilo's objection and ascribe it to

Anselm. Others, less sympathetic, note Anselm's failure to respond to the Lost Island objection and argue that Anselm knew Gaunilo's objection was devastating but could not bring himself to acknowledge it in print.

Nicholas Wolterstorff has made a powerful case for this less favorable construal of Anselm's response.[7] As Wolterstorff notes, Anselm makes only two references to the Lost Island in his long reply to Gaunilo. In neither place does he give any reason to think that Gaunilo's argument is not a good analogue to the argument of *Proslogion* 2. There seem to be only two reasons, Wolterstorff says, why Anselm would have failed to point out the disanalogy. One is that Gaunilo's argument was so obviously disanalogous that it would been unkind of Anselm to point out the mistake. But in that case, "why the bluster? Why the sarcasm? If charity to the befuddled Gaunilo inspired Anselm's silence concerning the point of disanalogy, what inspired his sharp bluster?" Moreover, in the rest of his reply Anselm does not hesitate to identify Gaunilo's mistakes, however obvious they may have been: even the ones of which he says "anyone with much sense at all can easily see through them."[8]

The second possible explanation for Anselm's failure to point out the disanalogy is "that Anselm realized that there was no disanalogy to point out."[9] After an admirably careful analysis of Gaunilo's reply and Anselm's rejoinder to Gaunilo, Wolterstorff concludes that this is in fact what happened. He offers evidence that Anselm understood clearly what Gaunilo thought was wrong with the *Proslogion* argument. Having nothing to offer in support of the principles to which Gaunilo objected, Anselm simply reaffirmed those principles, adding that they were self-evident. He left the Lost Island argument unanswered, because he realized he had no answer to give; but he spoke about it, somewhat disingenuously, as though he had shown how it failed. In short, "he concealed when he should have conceded."[10]

Wolterstorff gives a forceful defense of this reading of Anselm's reply to Gaunilo. Indeed, one of us found his interpretation so persuasive that he has cited it with approval in more than one place.[11] But Wolterstorff's view seems very hard to square with a crucial piece of evidence that comes to us from outside Anselm's writing. In his life of Anselm, Eadmer tells us that Anselm himself ordered that his exchange with Gaunilo be appended to the *Proslogion:*

[The *Proslogion*] came into the hands of someone who objected vigorously to some of its reasoning; he was convinced that this reasoning was unconvincing. In an effort to refute it he composed a rejoinder and appended it to the end of Anselm's work. One of Anselm's friends sent this rejoinder to him, and he found great delight in thinking through it. He thanked his critic and wrote a reply of his own, which he attached to the treatise that had been sent to him. He returned it to the friend from whom it had come, requesting that the friend and others who might see fit to have his work should copy the criticism of his argument, and his response to the criticism, at the end of the original work.[12]

It would be an act of admirable humility to draw attention to a devastating refutation of one's own work, but it would be sheer lunacy to write a lame, blustery, and transparently nonresponsive reply to the refutation and insist on drawing attention to *that*.

So it seems more reasonable to us to conclude that Anselm thought his reply to Gaunilo was successful; and since he does not concede any of Gaunilo's criticisms, he must also have thought that the original argument of the *Proslogion* was correct as it stood. Yet he must also have thought that some purpose was served by acquainting readers of the *Proslogion* with the exchange with Gaunilo. Gaunilo's objections offered Anselm some sort of opportunity: to expand on what he had stated in too compressed a way, to forestall misunderstandings that he had not originally anticipated, to state presuppositions that he had left implicit. If we read Anselm's reply to Gaunilo in this way, rather than primarily in order to locate a response to the Lost Island argument, we find a patient, careful, and admirably clear exposition of the single line of reasoning—the "one argument"—that Anselm had exploited in a variety of ways not only in the second chapter but throughout the *Proslogion*.

The Evidence from the Reply
to Gaunilo

At the beginning of his reply Anselm identifies the two issues that he thinks are most crucial in responding to Gaunilo: "You say—whoever you are who say that the fool could say these things—that something than which a greater cannot be thought is in the understanding no differently from that which cannot even be thought according to the true nature of anything at all. You also say that it does not follow (as I say it does) that that than which a greater cannot be thought exists in reality as well simply because it exists in the understanding, any more than it follows that the Lost Island most certainly exists simply because someone who hears it described in words has no doubt that it exists in his understanding."[13] That is, Anselm sees Gaunilo as having raised two main objections:

(G1) That than which nothing greater can be thought cannot be thought (or not in any meaningful way); and

(G2) It does not follow that if that than which nothing greater can be thought can be thought, it exists in reality.

Anselm's reply therefore focuses on defending two claims:

(A1) That than which nothing greater can be thought can be thought, and

(A2) If that than which nothing greater can be thought can be thought, it exists in reality.

He does reply to other objections Gaunilo raises, but always by showing how a defense of either (A1) or (A2) neutralizes Gaunilo's objections. And since by *modus ponens* (A1) and (A2) entail

(A3) That than which nothing greater can be thought exists in reality,

a successful defense of (A1) and (A2) leaves Anselm with a sound argument for the existence of God.

We begin with (A1): That than which nothing greater can be thought can be thought. In the *Proslogion* Anselm had not realized that (A1) needed much of a defense, but several of Gaunilo's objections prompt Anselm to clarify what he means by thinking or understanding in general, and by thinking or understanding that than which nothing greater can be thought in particular. What he says in the reply to Gaunilo rests on the theory of thought that he had put forward in the *Monologion*. Since we explored Anselm's theory of thought in detail in Chapter 2, we will here state just the essentials that are necessary for understanding the argument of *Proslogion* 2.

The kind of thinking that is at issue in the argument of *Proslogion* 2 is what Anselm calls "mental conception" (*mentis conceptio*). For example, I have a mental conception of a human being when "my mind sees the man himself... through reason (as when it thinks his universal essence, which is rational, mortal animal)."[14] In a case of mental conception, "things themselves, whether they already exist or are yet to exist, are examined within the mind by the gaze of thought."[15] Note that we can "examine" things that do not yet exist; in fact, we can have mental conceptions of things that are completely imaginary.[16] We cannot, however, think something that is impossible. This last qualification is crucial for understanding the argument of *Proslogion* 2, since it shows that (contrary to some interpreters[17]) Anselm must either assume or prove that that than which nothing greater can be thought is possible in order for the argument to succeed.

Anselm's theory of thought allows for the possibility that thought can, in a sense, misfire. I can suppose myself to be thinking something when in fact I am not, because I have not succeeded in getting before my mind the thing I intend to "examine with the gaze of thought." In the *Proslogion* Anselm argues that the Psalmist's fool, "who has said in his heart, 'There is no God,'" is in such a state. Anyone who really has that than which nothing greater can be thought before his mind sees that that being not only does but must exist; for that reason, then, that than which nothing greater can be thought "cannot be thought not to exist."[18] Yet, on Anselm's own view, to "think" and to "say in one's heart" are exactly the same thing. So if the fool has said in his heart that God does not exist, he has thought that God does not exist. Do we not then have an obvious counterexample to the claim that God cannot be thought not to exist? Not at all. For as Anselm carefully explains in *Proslogion* 4, "there must be more than one way in which something is 'said in one's heart' or 'thought.' A thing is thought in one way when the word that signifies the thing is thought, but in another way when what-the-thing-is[19] is understood. God can be thought not to exist in the first sense, but not at all in the second sense. No one who understands what God is can think that God does not exist, although he may say these words in his heart with no signification at all, or with some peculiar signification."[20] Either the fool's words mean nothing at all, or they mean something other than "there is no being than which a greater cannot be thought." For whoever genuinely thinks that than which nothing greater can be thought "understands that this being exists in such a way that he cannot, even in thought, fail to exist."[21]

Thus, when Anselm speaks of "thinking that than which nothing greater can be thought," he has in mind a fairly rich or robust mental activity, rich enough that it rules out entertaining the possibility of God's nonexistence. In the believer, this rich mental activity will be (or at any rate *can* be) a spiritual exercise of the sort Anselm demonstrates in the first chapter of the *Proslogion*. In the fool, it will be a purely rational, philosophical activity—but a philosophical activity that, if carried out fully, will

(Anselm thinks) ineluctably lead to the understanding that God exists. When Gaunilo denies, on behalf of the fool, that God can be thought at all, he is suggesting that the fool does not, and cannot, have any such robust notion of God. Ordinarily, Gaunilo argues, if we do not have firsthand knowledge of something, we can at least "form an idea of it on the basis of something like it." But we cannot do that in the case of God, "since you yourself claim that it is so great that nothing else could be like it." And God belongs to no genus or species, so I cannot form an idea of God by using my knowledge of a genus or species, as I can form an idea of an unknown human being by using my knowledge of the species *human being*. So, Gaunilo concludes, "in the case of God, I can think of him only on the basis of the word. And one can seldom or never think of any truth solely on the basis of a word." Perhaps the fool "thinks only of the impression made on his mind by hearing the word and tries to imagine its meaning," but this sort of thinking is clearly not robust enough to yield any insight that God really exists, let alone that he cannot fail to exist.[22]

According to Anselm, Gaunilo has gone astray in supposing that there is nothing sufficiently like God for us to be able to form an idea of God. "That is clearly wrong," he says, because any lesser good is like a greater good, insofar as both are good. Hence,

> it is clear to every reasonable mind that by raising our thoughts from lesser goods to greater goods, we are quite capable of forming an idea of that than which a greater cannot be thought on the basis of that than which a greater can be thought. Who, for example, is unable to think ... that if something that has a beginning and end is good, then something that has a beginning but never ceases to exist is much better? And that just as the latter is better than the former, so something that has neither beginning nor end is better still, even if it is always moving from the past through the present into the future? And that something that in no way needs or is compelled to change or move is far better even than that, whether any such thing exists in reality or not? Can such a thing not be thought? Can anything greater than this be thought? Or rather, is not this an example of forming an idea of that than which a greater cannot be thought on the basis of those things than which a greater can be thought? So there is in fact a way to form an idea of that than which a greater cannot be thought.[23]

What is crucial about Anselm's reply is not merely that he defends the claim that God can be thought, but that he shows just how much is involved in thinking God. We cannot even think God—that is, we cannot have God before our minds—without engaging in serious and sustained thinking about what would have to be true of a thing in order for it to count as an unsurpassable good.[24]

In other words—and this is the key point that nearly every interpretation misses, but which becomes unmistakable on a careful reading of Anselm's reply to Gaunilo—when Anselm says in *Proslogion* 2 that that than which nothing greater can be thought exists in the understanding, he is not talking about someone's understanding the verbal formula "that than which a greater cannot be thought" and being able to do logical moves with it. He is talking about someone's actually having that than which nothing greater can be thought before his mind: having a thought that does not, as it were, misfire, but is actually about that than which nothing greater can be thought. And such a thought is not the easiest thing in the world to achieve. Anselm's reader, or the Psalmist's fool, must "form the idea" on the basis of the kind of rational reflection that Anselm lays out in the *Monologion* and then later in the reply to Gaunilo.

Once we have succeeded in forming the idea of that than which nothing greater can be thought, careful examination of that idea makes it very clear that it is the idea of a really existing being and not of what Gaunilo had called "a false thing." In other words, Anselm's defense of

(A1) That than which nothing greater can be thought can be thought

is supposed to provide us with everything we need for a defense of

(A2) If that than which nothing greater can be thought can be thought, it exists in reality.

The basic form of argument, which Anselm repeats in a variety of ways throughout his reply to Gaunilo,[25] is to identify some feature of that than which nothing greater can be thought that cannot belong to a possible but nonexistent being. The first version of the argument, for example, takes the impossibility of having a beginning as the salient feature:

> You think that from the fact that something than which a greater cannot be thought is understood, it does not follow that it exists in the understanding; nor does it follow that if it exists in the understanding, it therefore exists in reality. But I say with certainty that if it can be so much as thought to exist, it must necessarily exist.[26] For that than which a greater cannot be thought cannot be thought to begin to exist. By

contrast, whatever can be thought to exist, but does not in fact exist, can be thought to begin to exist. Therefore, it is not the case that that than which a greater cannot be thought can be thought to exist, but does not in fact exist. If, therefore, it can be thought to exist, it does necessarily exist.[27]

Other versions of the argument focus on omnipresence (both temporal and spatial) and necessary existence.

What is perhaps most striking to those of us who are accustomed to the standard approach sketched above is that nothing in Anselm's defense of (A1) and (A2) requires him to claim that one and the same thing is greater if it exists in reality than if it exists in the understanding alone, or (to use the usual language) that existence is a perfection. Has Anselm abandoned the argument of *Proslogion* 2 in his reply to Gaunilo, without acknowledging the fact? The textual evidence suggests very strongly that Anselm takes himself to be offering the same argument in the reply that he had made in *Proslogion* 2. As we said above, the fact that Anselm wanted his exchange with Gaunilo copied along with the *Proslogion* indicates that he thought his reply was successful; the fact that he concedes nothing to Gaunilo indicates that he thought the original *Proslogion* 2 argument was correct as it stood. But the strongest evidence is that right in the middle of his defenses of (A2) Anselm offers what is very clearly a point-by-point restatement of the argument of *Proslogion* 2, with explanatory glosses.[28] Thus, it seems clear that for Anselm, the *Proslogion* 2 argument is another version of the same argumentative strategy, that of showing that there are features of that than which nothing greater can be thought that cannot belong to a possible but nonexistent being. Our conclusion, then, is that despite appearances, it had never so much as crossed Anselm's mind that one could treat existence as a perfection. That the *Proslogion* 2 argument seems to treat existence as a perfection is a consequence of the compression of Anselm's language. The more expansive treatment of the argument in the reply to Gaunilo thus has two functions: to acknowledge the serious amount of preliminary reflection that goes into thinking that than which nothing greater can be thought, and to spell out the features of that than which nothing greater can be thought that are incompatible with its being a possible but nonexistent object.

Indeed, the notion of existence as a perfection was so far from Anselm's mind that he simply failed to understand Gaunilo's reply at a crucial point. On Gaunilo's reading, the *Proslogion* 2 argument treats existence as a perfection; the Lost Island argument exploits the absurd consequences that can be derived from such an assumption. But Anselm never catches on that this is what Gaunilo finds so problematic. Compare the way Gaunilo articulates the reasoning of the Lost Island argument with the way Anselm presents it. First Gaunilo:

> You cannot any longer doubt that this island, more excellent than all others on earth, truly exists somewhere in reality. For you do not doubt that this island exists in your understanding, and since it is more excellent to exist not merely in the understanding, but also in reality, this island must also exist in reality. For if it did not, any land that exists in reality would be greater than it. And so this more excellent thing that you have understood would not in fact be more excellent.[29]

Now Anselm:

> But, you say, this is just the same as if someone were to claim that it cannot be doubted that a certain island in the ocean...truly exists in reality, because someone can easily understand it when it is described in words.[30]

For Gaunilo, the premise that does the mischief is "it is more excellent to exist not merely in the understanding, but also in reality." Anselm, by contrast, thinks Gaunilo is objecting to the inference, "If it exists in the understanding, it exists in reality."[31]

Once we realize that this is how Anselm understood Gaunilo's objection, we can see that his dismissal of the Lost Island example, which follows immediately after the words just quoted, is not a mere brush-off. Anselm continues: "I say quite confidently that if anyone can find for me something existing either in reality or only in thought to which he can apply this inference in my argument, besides that than which a greater cannot be thought, I will find and give to him that Lost Island, never to be lost again. In fact, however, it has already become quite clear that that than which a greater cannot be thought cannot be thought not to exist, since its existence is a matter of such certain truth. For otherwise it would not exist at all."[32] "This inference in my argument" refers, not to anything having to do with existence as a perfection, but to "If it exists in the understanding, it exists in reality." Anselm challenges Gaunilo to come up with any other object of thought whose intrinsic character is incompatible with its being a possible but nonexistent object. That *God's* intrinsic character is incompatible with his being a possible but nonexistent object "has already become clear" in the four defenses of (A2) that Anselm has already stated by this point in his reply to Gaunilo.

At only one point in his reply does Anselm come close to seeing what Gaunilo had really made of the *Proslogion* 2 argument. Without quite noticing that the argument Gaunilo attributes to him depends on taking existence as a perfection, he does at least notice that Gaunilo attributes the argument to him, and Anselm disclaims ever having offered it: "You repeatedly say that I argue that that which is greater than everything else exists in the understanding; and that if it exists in the understanding, it also exists in reality, for otherwise that which is greater than everything else would not be greater than everything else. Nowhere in anything I said can such an argument be found."[33]

Unfortunately, Anselm goes on to complain that "that which is greater than everything else" does not have the same argumentative power as "that than which nothing greater can be thought." So it looks as if Anselm is raking Gaunilo over the coals for an infelicitous formulation rather than addressing the substance of the objection. But in fact the way in which Anselm shows that Gaunilo's formulation fails where his own succeeds offers further confirmation that Anselm understood his argument quite differently from Gaunilo (without ever quite realizing how Gaunilo had gone wrong). What distinguishes the two formulations, according to Anselm, is that it is clear that that than which nothing greater can be thought cannot be thought not to exist, whereas it is not clear that "that which is greater than everything else" cannot be thought not to exist:

> For if someone says that that than which a greater cannot be thought is not something existing in reality, or is capable of not existing, or can be thought not to exist, he is easily refuted. For whatever does not exist is capable of not existing, and whatever is capable of not existing can be thought not to exist. Now whatever can be thought not to exist, if it does exist, is not that than which a greater cannot be thought; and if it does not exist, it would not be that than which a greater cannot be thought, even if it were to exist. But it makes no sense to say that that than which a greater cannot be thought, if it exists, is not that than which a greater cannot be thought, and that if it [does not exist but] were to exist, it would not be that than which a greater cannot be thought. This does not seem to be so easily proved with regard to what is said to be greater than everything else.[34]

As Anselm reads him, Gaunilo has correctly seen that the argument of *Proslogion* 2 is a *reductio*; it is meant to show that the assumption of God's nonexistence generates a contradiction. But Gaunilo is mistaken about what the contradiction actually is. Gaunilo thinks the kernel of the *reductio* is this:

> That which is greater than everything else exists in the understanding. Suppose it exists *only* in the understanding. Then it is not in fact greater than everything else, because a thing is greater if it exists in reality. Therefore, that which is greater than everything else exists in reality as well.

Now if indeed Anselm were thinking that one and the same thing is greater if it exists in reality than it is if it exists only in thought, Gaunilo's change of formulation would not affect the success of the *reductio*. That which is greater than everything else would not in fact be greater than everything else if it failed to exist in reality, just as that than which nothing greater can be thought would not in fact be that than which nothing greater can be thought if it failed to exist in reality.

But Anselm insists that the change in formulation does make a difference, and his reason for thinking so shows just how different his understanding of the *Proslogion* 2 argument is from Gaunilo's. After stating Gaunilo's *reductio,* Anselm complains, "Nowhere in anything I said can such an argument be found." And no wonder, since the *reductio* Gaunilo has attributed to Anselm is a nonstarter:

> For what if someone were to say that something exists that is greater than everything else that exists, and yet that this very thing can be thought not to exist, and that something greater than it can be thought, although this greater thing does not actually exist? Can it be just as easily inferred in this case that it is not greater than everything else that exists, as it was perfectly certain in the previous case that it was not that than which a greater cannot be thought? In the second case we would need another argument, besides the mere fact that this being is said to be "greater than everything else," whereas in the first case there was no need for anything more than the expression "that than which a greater cannot be thought."[35]

Gaunilo's change in formulation has ruined the argument because there is nothing in the notion of "that which is greater than everything else" that is incompatible with its being an existent but possibly nonexistent being, or with its being surpassable by some other being.[36] The right way to run the *reductio,* Anselm says, is like this:

> A non-existent being is such that, if it were to exist, it would not be that than which nothing greater can be thought; and an existent but possibly non-existent being is not that than which nothing greater can be thought. Suppose, then, that that than which nothing greater can be thought does not exist. Then that than which nothing greater can be thought, if it were to exist, would not be that than which nothing greater can be thought: which is absurd. Or suppose that it exists but is capable of not existing. Then it is not that than which nothing greater can be thought: which, again, is absurd. Therefore, that than which nothing greater can be thought exists, and it exists necessarily.

According to Anselm, then, it is this argument, and not Gaunilo's, that accurately restates the reasoning of *Proslogion* 2.

Proslogion 2: Read in Light of the Evidence from Anselm's Reply

In light of Anselm's reply to Gaunilo, we can now return to the argument of *Proslogion* 2 and show how Anselm meant it to be understood. So far as possible, we will follow our earlier reconstruction, showing how the various premises must be understood in ways that are far from obvious if we read *Proslogion* 2 independently. Anselm begins by offering a description or conception of God:

> (1) God is that than which nothing greater can be thought.

Now whatever is understood, Anselm says, exists in the understanding; and the fool understands that than which nothing greater can be thought. So

> (2) That than which nothing greater can be thought exists in the understanding.

Premise (2) is a good deal more complicated than it appears. There are at least three distinct points that Anselm is making in his uncharacteristically compressed language:

> (2a) That than which nothing greater can be thought can be thought: that is, it is a possible being.

(2b) Someone who thinks that than which nothing greater can be thought understands what a thing would have to be in order to count as that than which nothing greater can be thought.

(2c) Not every possible object (not everything that can be thought) is actual.

By now (2a) needs no further comment; we have discussed the close association in Anselm's philosophy between "it can be thought" and "it is possible" in chapter 2, and the previous section of this chapter considers Anselm's attempt to prove, in reply to Gaunilo, that that than which nothing greater can be thought can be thought.

(2b) is intended to make explicit that (2) refers to a far more robust intellectual achievement than Anselm lets on in *Proslogion* 2. In that chapter Anselm writes, "even the fool must admit that something than which nothing greater can be thought exists at least in his understanding, since he understands this when he hears it, and whatever is understood exists in the understanding."[37] This makes it sound as though premise (2) means merely that someone (the fool, or anyone) understands the *words* "that than which nothing greater can be thought" and attaches some sort of meaning to them. But as we have seen, one has that than which nothing greater can be thought in the understanding only when that than which nothing greater can be thought is "examined within the mind by the gaze of thought."

(2c) expresses the upshot of the painting example to which Anselm appeals in his explanation of premise (2). Anselm's rhetorical choice to contrast "exists in the understanding" with "exists in reality" leaves the impression that he has in mind some metaphysical doctrine according to which things can exist in two different modes, with premise (4) informing us about which mode has more metaphysical "oomph" to it. Anselm's use of the painting example merely strengthens that impression: he seems to envision one and the same object, the painting, as having first merely intentional being and then real being. It is this impression that gives rise to all the learned discussion of Meinongianism in connection with Anselm's argument; Gaunilo plays Frege to Anselm's Meinong, we are told.[38] But the impression is completely mistaken. Here again, Anselm's reply tells us what we need to know. Gaunilo had objected that the painting analogy—which he obviously read in much the same way as many contemporary interpreters—was beside the point. The painter's conception of the work he is planning, Gaunilo insisted, is not literally the painting itself, existing in a metaphysically odd way, but rather "a part of his intelligence." (Think of Gaunilo as an adverbialist of sorts: for the painter to "have the painting in his understanding" is just for his mind to be configured in a paintingish way.) Anselm replies that Gaunilo has entirely missed the point of the analogy: "You go to some trouble to show that that than which a greater cannot be thought is not the same sort of thing as a picture, not yet painted, in the understanding of the painter, but your argument is not to the point. I did not bring up the picture that is thought out beforehand in order to claim that it was the same sort of thing as the being I was discussing, but merely so I could show that something exists in the understanding that would not be understood to exist [in reality]."[39] So the chief point of the painting example is to establish that we can think about or understand something without being committed to believing that it exists; in effect, it is to secure Anselm against charges of begging the question. We can perhaps agree that the analogy is not an especially apt choice to make this point; but if one rereads *Proslogion* 2 after learning how Anselm intended the analogy to be understood, one finds that, sure enough, that was indeed the main point he was making.[40]

The painting example makes a further, and subtler, point as well. Anselm notes that once the painter has executed his work, "he both has it in his understanding and understands that it exists because he has now painted it."[41] The point is that there is nothing in the painting as "examined by the gaze of thought" that would enable the one who understands it to know whether the painting actually exists. It is only because he has actually executed the work that the painter, or anyone else, can understand that the painting exists in reality. The contrast, of course, will be with that than which nothing greater can be thought, since Anselm will proceed to argue that anyone who thinks that than which nothing greater can be thought (in the sense explained in [2b]) can know simply from the nature of that possible being (as in [2a]) that it exists in reality.

So we have that than which nothing greater can be thought before our minds, Anselm is saying, but merely having something before our minds is no guarantee that the thing in fact exists. Can we coherently suppose that that than which nothing greater can be thought does not exist? In other words, is there in the thought of that than which nothing greater can be thought, unlike in the thought of the painting, something that entails the existence of the object of our thought? In order to show that there is, Anselm will proceed by *reductio*. Suppose, for *reductio*:

(3) That than which nothing greater can be thought exists only in the understanding.

What happens when we try to conceive the nonexistence of that than which nothing greater can be thought? We find that we cannot. For the being that we have before our minds would, if it existed, be greater than any being that is capable of nonexistence. Anselm expresses this claim in a quite misleading way:

(4) That than which nothing greater can be thought "can be thought to exist in reality as well, which is greater."[42]

The most natural reading of (4) is the standard one, which is also Gaunilo's reading: namely, that Anselm is claiming that existence is a perfection, a great-making property. But by now we have seen that whatever Anselm means, it cannot be that. So what does he mean?

Instead of saying that existence is a great-making property, Anselm is saying that certain great-making properties entail existence. What are those properties? He does not identify any in chapter 2 of the *Proslogion,* but his reply to Gaunilo is full of examples, as we have seen. That than which nothing greater can be thought is incapable of having a beginning or end of existence; it is spatially and temporally omnipresent; it is a necessary being.[43] For example, a being that cannot fail to exist is greater than a being that can fail to exist, and a being that has no beginning or end to its existence is greater than a being that comes into being or passes out of being; so a being than which a greater cannot be thought must be necessary and eternal. The reasoning behind premise (4) is that when we are thinking that than which nothing greater can be thought as nonexistent, we are obviously thinking of it as a being that can fail to exist. Moreover, it could come to exist only by beginning to exist. Hence, even if it did exist, it would have a beginning of existence and would be a contingent being; therefore, even if it did exist, it would be less great than that than which nothing greater can be thought. So when we think of that than which nothing greater can be thought existing in reality, we are thinking something greater than this being whose nonexistence we were imagining a moment ago.

Anselm expresses this conclusion as follows:

(5) That than which nothing greater can be thought is something than which a greater *can* be thought.

In order words, the being that in premise (3) we were thinking of as nonexistent was not in fact that than which nothing greater can be thought at all. Since (3) entails (5), which is an absurdity, we are entitled to deny (3). Therefore, it is not the case that that than which nothing greater can be thought exists only in the understanding. In other words, it is not the case that that than which nothing greater can be thought is a possible but nonexistent being. From that claim, together with (2a), Anselm can derive

(6) That than which nothing greater can be thought exists in reality.

And from (1) and (6) it follows that

(7) God exists in reality.

Conclusion

Our reconstruction of the argument of *Proslogion* 2 makes it clear that Anselm's reasoning is a version of what has come to be called a *modal* ontological argument. That is, its essential structure is as follows:

(MOA1) A necessary being is possible.
(MOA2) If a necessary being is possible, it exists.
(MOA3) Therefore, a necessary being exists.

Anselm expresses this argument very clearly in his reply to Gaunilo, using his own distinctive vocabulary:

(A1) That than which nothing greater can be thought can be thought.
(A2) If that than which nothing greater can be thought can be thought, it exists in reality.
(A3) Therefore, that than which nothing greater can be thought exists in reality.

And our contention is that the argument Anselm makes again and again in the reply to Gaunilo is the very same argument that he makes, rather elliptically, in *Proslogion* 2.

Accordingly, Anselm's argument is vulnerable at precisely the point at which the modal ontological argument is vulnerable: he does not have an adequate argument for the claim that God is a possible being. In replying to Gaunilo's contention that that than which nothing greater can be thought cannot be thought, Anselm explains how we can form a concept of God by reflecting on the limited and partial perfections that we know in creatures. In the *Proslogion* he also addresses several contradictions that someone might attempt to derive from the concept of that than which nothing greater can be thought. But even if Anselm is completely successful in showing that the putative contradictions are merely illusory, that falls short of showing that the concept of that than which nothing greater can be thought is the concept of a possible being; it merely shows that the reasons offered so far for thinking that it is *not* the concept of a possible being have all failed. So although anyone who is willing to grant the first premise of the modal ontological argument will have to concede its conclusion, Anselm has not shown that there is any absurdity in refusing to grant it.

THE DIVINE ATTRIBUTES

Many contemporary philosophers of religion devote a great deal of attention to what are usually called "the divine attributes," qualities such as omnipotence, omniscience, and perfect goodness that God is often said to possess. The expression 'divine attributes' is not an altogether felicitous one for an exposition of Anselm's account of the divine nature, for two reasons. First, 'attribute' might be taken to suggest a property or feature possessed by God that is distinct from God himself; and second, the plural 'attributes' suggests that God has a plurality of such features. Anselm, as we shall see, denies that God has any features distinct from himself, let alone that he has a plurality of them. Yet in keeping with the standard contemporary vocabulary, and in order to avoid awkward locutions along the lines of "things that are true of God," we shall continue to speak of "divine attributes."

In both the *Monologion* and the *Proslogion,* Anselm devotes considerable attention to arguing for and analyzing a number of divine attributes. The two works differ in their argumentative strategies and in the emphasis laid on particular attributes, but Anselm reaches the same conclusions in both works, and we will draw on both in our exposition of Anselm's account of the divine attributes.[1]

Divine Aseity and Its Corollaries

The arguments of the first four chapters of the *Monologion* are intended to establish that there is a single nature or being that is supremely good, supremely great, and supremely existent. Though Anselm postpones calling this being "God" until the final chapter of the *Monologion,* we will go ahead and speak of it as God.[2] Anselm has not merely argued that God is supremely good and great and existent. He has argued that God is all these things *through himself;* we will call this feature of God *divine aseity.* Furthermore, whatever is good (or is great, or exists) is good (or is great, or exists) through God; we will call this feature of God *divine ultimacy.*

Divine aseity and divine ultimacy play important roles in Anselm's arguments for further divine attributes. It follows from divine ultimacy that God made all things other than himself—that is, they do not merely depend on his existing or having certain features, but on his exercising causal power. There are, Anselm says, only three ways in which things other than God can exist through God: he made them, he provided matter for them, or he in some way helped them to exist. We cannot say that he merely helped them to exist, because that would give some other agent or matter the principal responsibility for their existence, in violation of divine ultimacy. Nor can we say that he provided the matter for them, because if something less than God can come to exist from the matter of God, God is corruptible and mutable and therefore not the supreme good. So we have to conclude that God made all things other than himself, including the ultimate "matter of the mass of the world," whatever that might turn out to be. Hence, God made all things from nothing: that is, not from anything.[3]

Moreover, God is responsible not only for the initial existence of things, but for their continued existence. This conclusion again depends on divine ultimacy:

> Now only an irrational mind could doubt that all created things remain and continue in existence, as long as they do exist, because they are sustained by the very same being who made them from nothing, so that they exist in the first place. For by an exactly similar argument to the one that shows that all existing things exist through some one thing, and so he alone exists through himself and all other things exist through another—by a similar argument, I say, it can be proved that everything that remains in existence does so through some one thing, and so he

alone remains in existence through himself and all other things remain in existence through another.[4]

It follows that "where God does not exist, nothing exists."[5]

What Can Be Said Substantially of God

The supremacy, aseity, and ultimacy of God mark him out as irreducibly different from creatures. Our language, however, is suited for creatures. So, Anselm says, "I would be amazed if, among the nouns or verbs that we apply to things made from nothing, any can be found that are appropriately said of the substance that creates all things."[6] In chapter 15 of the *Monologion* Anselm asks what, if anything, can be said "substantially" of God. By this he means to ask what predications concerning God "reveal what he is," as opposed to revealing merely "what sort of thing he is or how great he is."[7] No relative term reveals what a thing is, so we can immediately eliminate any predication that describes how God is related to creatures. Though some such predications are certainly true—for example, that God is the highest of all things and that God is greater than all the things he made—they do not reveal what God is in himself. For if there were nothing but God, he could not be correctly described as "highest" or "greater," but he would still be exactly what he is.[8]

So let *F* range over nonrelative predicates. Anselm says that for all *F*, either (i) *F* is in every respect better than not-*F*, or (ii) not-*F* is in some respect better than *F*. *Wise* falls in category (i) and *gold* in category (ii). It is, Anselm says, better in every respect to be wise than not-wise. This does not mean that every wise thing is better than every nonwise thing, since "a just person who is not wise seems to be better than a wise person who is not just." Rather, it means that "whatever is not-wise in an unqualified sense, insofar as it is not-wise, is less than what is wise, since everything that is not-wise would be better if it were wise."[9] This suggests that we could state category (i) more perspicuously as follows:

(a) what is *F* is, *qua F*, better than what is not-*F*, *qua* not-*F*,

or perhaps as follows:

(b) what is not-*F* would be better if it were *F*.

Formulation (b) looks easier to apply, and it seems to be at work in Anselm's explanation of why *gold* falls in category (ii): "It is better for a human being to be not-gold than gold, even though perhaps it would be better for something—say, for lead—to be gold than not-gold. For although both a human being and lead are not-gold, a human being is better than gold in proportion as he would be of an inferior nature if he were gold, and lead is baser in proportion as it would be more precious if it were gold." The argument here seems to be that *gold* does not fall into category (i) because a human being, who is not-gold, would not be better if he were gold. That argument suggests formulation (b). Yet we cannot take Anselm quite so flat-footedly here. Anselm understands essential properties as well as anyone else, and he clearly does not think it's actually possible for human beings to be gold. The point has to be that even though some gold things are superior to some nongold things, it is not the case that all gold things are, *qua* gold, superior to any nongold thing, *qua* nongold. So we should take formulation (a) of category (i). Everything that does not fall into category (i) falls into category (ii).[10]

The rule is that every predicate in category (i) must be said substantially of God, and no predicate in category (ii) may be said of God in any way. We should not, however, treat this rule as a decision procedure for generating a list of divine attributes, for Anselm does not actually use the rule in this way. Instead, we should think of the rule as a theoretical abstraction that captures what is common to all the items that appear on the list of divine attributes. The list itself is generated by other means. It is no accident that Anselm states the rule only *after* he has already established God's supremacy, aseity, and ultimacy, and shown that God is the Creator and Sustainer of all things. The rule stated in *Monologion* 15 gets its warrant from some of those conclusions, particularly those of chapters 1 through 4; they do not get their warrant from it. And as we shall show, even after the rule is stated, those earlier conclusions continue to play an independent role in Anselm's arguments concerning several of the attributes that he considers. Indeed, once Anselm has stated the rule, he never explicitly invokes it again and seldom appeals to it even implicitly.

Divine Simplicity, Eternity, and
Omnipresence

Anselm originally introduced the rule of *Monologion* 15 to help us determine what can be said substantially of God. Yet among the predicates that fall into category (i), and can therefore be said of God, are 'living', 'wise', 'all-powerful', 'just', and 'happy': all of which, it seems, do not "reveal what he is, but rather what sort of thing he is or how great he is."[11] Appearances in this case are misleading. Aseity entails that God is *identical* with life, wisdom, power, justice, and so forth.

So God is justice, God is life, God is wisdom, and so forth. If justice, life, wisdom, and the rest are distinct things, then God is a composite. But divine aseity rules out God's being a composite. A composite depends on the things of which it is composed: "every composite needs the things of which it is composed if it is to subsist, and it owes its existence to them, since whatever it is, it is through them."[12] Therefore, God is simple. Justice, life, wisdom, and the rest are all one and the same thing; they are God.

The *Proslogion* offers a different argument for divine simplicity: "Whatever is composed of parts is not completely one. It is in some sense a plurality and not identical with itself, and it can be broken up either in fact or at least in the understanding. But such characteristics are foreign to you, than whom nothing better can be thought. Therefore there are no parts in you, Lord, and you are not a plurality. Instead, you are so much a unity, so much identical with yourself, that you are in no respect dissimilar to yourself. You are in fact unity itself; you cannot be divided by any understanding."[13] This argument seems less compelling than the argument from aseity in the *Monologion,* and for reasons that make it puzzling that Anselm should have offered it in the first place. As we have seen, it is crucial to the argument of *Proslogion* 2 that impossibilities cannot be thought. Now suppose that God is a composite in the sense that he has a plurality of attributes, each distinct from the others and from God himself. Suppose further that God has each of these attributes *necessarily.* There seems to be nothing intrinsically impossible in supposing both these things at once. (Indeed, it seems to us that most analytic philosophers who are theists do suppose both those things at once. Their error, if it is an error, is not on the order of their supposing that one and the same thing is both round and square.) It would then follow, on Anselm's own theory of thought, that God cannot "be broken up...in the understanding," even though on these suppositions he is a composite.

In both the *Proslogion* and the *Monologion* Anselm appeals to simplicity in his discussion of God's relation to place and time. In the *Proslogion* Anselm argues directly from simplicity to the claim that God is outside both time and place: "Since you have no parts, and neither does your eternity, which you yourself are, it follows that no part of you or of your eternity exists at a certain place or time. Instead, you exist as a whole in every place, and your eternity exists as a whole always."[14] The arguments of the *Monologion* are considerably more complicated, and the role of simplicity is much more limited. Anselm invokes simplicity to rule out some hypotheses about how God might be related to space and time. For example, since God has no parts, it cannot be the case that God is present to individual places and times in such a way that one part of him is present to one individual place or time and another part of him is present to another.[15] But simplicity is not the only, or even the primary, doctrine on which Anselm relies in the *Monologion* in analyzing God's relation to place and time. Divine ultimacy and aseity play a much more important role.

Anselm invokes divine ultimacy and aseity most crucially to resolve a dialectical impasse. In chapter 20 Anselm argues, primarily on the basis of divine ultimacy, that God exists in every time and place. In chapter 21 he argues, primarily on the basis of divine simplicity, that God exists in *no* time or place. In chapter 22 he explains what brought us to this impasse. The problem, Anselm explains, is that we have been treating God as if he had the same relationship to space and time that we have: a relationship that Anselm describes as being "subject to the laws of place or time."[16] If something is subject to the laws of place and time, it is constrained by or confined in that place and time. If it is to be in more than one place or time, it must have parts—spatial parts or temporal parts—and it cannot be present as a whole in more than one place. But God is free from the laws of place and time, because he is the Creator of place and time. He holds them in being; they are totally dependent on him. So naturally he is totally independent of them, and none of the characteristics of place and time affect him in any way.

From this we can conclude, Anselm says, that God is both timeless and immaterial. He has neither spatial parts nor temporal parts. So when we say that God exists in a given place or time, we don't mean that he is *contained by* that place or time; we mean only that he is *present in* that place or time. What do we mean by present, though, if we don't mean it in the usual sense, which involves spatial or temporal location? Once again, Anselm appeals to divine ultimacy: "And yet God can be said in his own way to exist in every place or time, since whatever else exists is sustained by his presence so that it does not fall into nothingness."[17] It is even better to say that God exists everywhere, since 'everywhere', unlike 'in all places', can be used idiomatically to include nonspatial "locations."[18] Similarly, it is better to say that God exists always, since 'always' can signify eternity, whereas 'at every time' can't.[19]

As this discussion shows, Anselm regularly explains God's relation to place and time by contrast with creatures. The proper understanding of this contrast, however, has recently been the subject of debate.[20] In particular, is Anselm a presentist or an eternalist with respect to time? Presentism is the view that only the present time is real; the past and the future do not exist. Eternalism is the view that past and future things exist, just as present things do. The easiest way to get a handle on the difference between these views is by means of an analogy with place. On the eternalist view, distant places (places distant from *here*) are like distant times (times distant from *now*). Just as Canterbury and Tampa are equally real, though spatially distant from each other, so too 2008 and 1108 are equally real, though temporally distant from each other. There is, on the eternalist view, no privileged "now," just as there is no privileged "here." On the presentist view, however, there *is* a privileged "now"; things in distant times, unlike things in distant places, do not exist.

Anselm is clearly and unequivocally a presentist. He denies that past and future are real. For example, "all things other [than God] exist changeably in some respect, so that at some time they were or will be something that they are not now, or they are now something that at some time they were not or will not be. What they once were no longer exists, and what they will be does not yet exist, and what they are in the fleeting, utterly brief, and barely-existing present barely exists."[21] Anselm here expresses the view that only what creatures are in the "barely-existing present" is actually real; that is precisely how we differ from God, who "is whatever he is, once and for all, all at once, and illimitably."[22] As Anselm says, "The fact that God existed or exists or will exist does not mean that something of his eternity has vanished from the present time with the past, which no longer exists; or passes away with the present, which barely exists; or is yet to come with the future, which does not yet exist."[23] These passages point to a real and irreducible difference between present times and past times. Only the present time and the things that exist in the present time exist. Past things used to exist, but exist no longer; future things will exist, but do not exist yet. Thus, to recur to our earlier language, Anselm holds that distant times, unlike distant places, do not exist.[24]

Presentists tend to hold that objects that persist through time do so by "enduring": that is, by existing as a whole at different times. Eternalists tend to hold instead that objects "perdure": that is, they have distinct temporal parts that exist at distinct times. If we are correct that Anselm is a presentist, one should expect him also to be an endurantist.[25] And so he is. "A human being," he says, "exists as a whole yesterday, today, and to-morrow."[26] Indeed, the fact that objects endure is the very reason that Anselm gives in chapter 21 of the *Monologion* for treating God's relation to place differently from God's relation to time. (Recall that insisting on a sharp disanalogy between place and time is a typical presentist move.) Anselm holds that a thing cannot exist as a whole in different places at once, but a thing can exist "as a whole separately and distinctly at individual times,"[27] as human beings do. For that reason his argument for the claim that God has no spatial location has to proceed differently from his argument that God has no temporal location.

Yet although Anselm is clearly an endurantist about human beings, it does appear that he holds that some objects perdure. In *De incarnatione Verbi* 11 Anselm uses the example of the Nile as an image of the Trinity: the spring from which it arises, the river that flows forth from the spring, and the lake into which the river empties are three things, in such a way that no one of them is either of the others, and yet they are one, in that all three of them are the Nile. Anselm imagines that someone might object to his analogy on the grounds that the spring, the river, and the lake are not in fact the Nile, but merely parts of the Nile. So he suggests tweaking his original analogy in order to avoid this objection: "Let him conceive that whole Nile [i.e. the spring plus the river plus the lake] as existing for its entire lifetime, so to speak, from the time it begins to exist until it ceases to exist. After all, that whole does not exist all at once in either a place or a time, but only part by part; and it will not be complete until it ceases to exist. In this respect it is like an utterance, which is incomplete as long as it is still springing forth from the mouth, and no longer exists once it has been completed."[28] The suggestion that distinct temporal parts of the Nile exist at distinct times, just as its different spatial parts exist in distinct places, implies that the Nile persists by perduring rather than enduring. Yet note that Anselm is introducing this revised understanding of what "the whole Nile" consists in as a dialectical maneuver to answer the objection of an imagined interlocutor; nothing in the text actually commits Anselm to accepting the revised understanding as an element of his own ontology.

On the other hand, Anselm's comparison of the whole Nile to an utterance speaks less equivocally in favor of the claim that Anselm recognizes some objects that perdure: that is, temporally extended objects that persist by having distinct temporal parts at distinct times. For Anselm describes an utterance in exactly this way; an utterance "is incomplete as long as it is still springing forth from the mouth, and no longer exists once it has been completed."[29] This suggests that the utterance consists in the sum of its temporal parts; it goes out of existence just as its last temporal part goes out of existence. If indeed Anselm is a presentist but also allows some perduring entities (such as utterances and, possibly, the temporally extended Nile) in his ontology, he has a metaphysics of temporal objects much like that of the many contemporary presentists who allow that events and processes perdure.

Yet one might well argue that this combination of views is problematic. If an utterance perdures, one might object, it has parts that do not exist at the present time; and according to presentism, there are no such parts, since what does not exist at the present time does not exist, period.[30] The texts of Anselm give us no reason to suppose that Anselm is worried about this problem. In giving the example of an utterance, Anselm seems perfectly happy with the idea of an entity composed of parts, some of which do not exist. So the most reasonable interpretation is that he is a presentist who allows for perduring entities like utterances in addition to enduring entities like human beings. Anselm does not think that recognizing perduring entities forces him into eternalism.[31]

In short, Anselm's presentism is unmistakable. There are, however, other aspects of his views that one might expect to push him to eternalism. Most notably, a strong doctrine of divine foreknowledge (or, strictly speaking, of God's knowledge of what to us is future) is often associated with eternalism. Anselm certainly has a strong doctrine of divine foreknowledge. And one might wonder how God can know the future unless—contrary to presentism—the future is in some way as real as the present. Granted, if causal determinism were true, God could read the entire future off the present. But as we will see in chapter 11, Anselm rejects causal determinism. So if the future is neither real nor determinately grounded in the present, how can God know it? These considerations suggest that presentism with respect to created time is incompatible with divine fore-knowledge, at least given the denial of determinism.

Nonetheless, it is clear that Anselm believes presentism is compatible with divine foreknowledge. He expresses the combination of the two positions most clearly in this striking passage from *De concordia:*

> In eternity it is not the case that something was or will be, but only that it is; nonetheless—and without any inconsistency—in time something was or will be. And in just the same way, something that in eternity cannot be changed is proved, without any inconsistency, to be change-able in time until it exists, thanks to free will. Now although in eternity there is only a present, it is not a temporal present like ours, but an eternal present that encompasses all times. Just as every place, and those things that are in any place, are contained in the present time, so too every time, and those things that are at any time, are enclosed all at once in the eternal present.[32]

Because all times are "enclosed all at once in the eternal present," God can know them, even though *in time* only the "fleeting present"[33] is actually real.

The only reason we find this difficult to conceive, Anselm thinks—that is, the only reason we feel drawn to eternalism in order to account for God's foreknowledge—is that we insist on a single frame of reference from which to evaluate the question, "Which times are real and therefore knowable?" But there is no such privileged frame of reference; once again, Anselm makes use of the contextualism that we first encountered in his theory of truth in chapter 3. From the vantage point of the eternal present, all times are real, and everything that exists in those times is immutable. From the vantage point of a being with temporal location, however, only the present time is real, and things that do not yet exist are mutable. Neither perspective is reducible to the other, and neither is privileged over the other.

An analogy from our understanding of place might be helpful here. All places are present to God, in the sense that all places are causally and cognitively accessible to him. From the perspective of a spatially located being, some places are here and some are there; some places are near and some are distant. But from God's perspective, no place is here, for God has no spatial location; and no place is any more or less distant from God. We do not ask how God can know places where he is not. Similarly, from the perspective of a temporally located being, some times are past, some are present, and some are future; some times are near and some are distant. But from God's perspective, no time is now, for God has no temporal location; and no time is any more or less distant from God. So just as we can see that it would be senseless to ask how God can know Canterbury when we are in Tampa, we ought to see that it would be equally senseless to ask how God can know 1108 when it is 2008.

Granted, the analogy with place is somewhat misleading here, since as a presentist Anselm has to treat times other than now differently from the way in which he treats places other than here. On his view, Tampa and Canterbury are equally real, but 1108 and 2008 are not; 1108 does not exist. So isn't it sensible after all to ask how God can know 1108? It is not, Anselm thinks, because we are in effect asking how God can know times that are not real *now*. But God's now is not a temporal now; it is an eternal now that "encompasses all times."[34] Times that are not real with respect to the temporal now can still be real with respect to the eternal now. To insist otherwise would be tantamount to denying the irreducibly distinct character of time and eternity. For Anselm there can be no single frame of reference that encompasses both.

Divine Immutability and God as Substance

Immediately following his discussion in the *Monologion* of God's relation to place and time, Anselm asks whether God has accidents. The placement of this question might seem odd; we would expect Anselm to connect his discussion of accidents in God with the doctrine of divine simplicity. But for Anselm the worry about accidents is not that they would compromise simplicity, but that they seem to threaten divine immutability; and God's immutability is a consequence of the fact that God "enjoys illimitable life as a whole, perfectly, and all at once."[35] Moreover, the accidents about which Anselm is concerned are *relative* accidents. The discussion that led to the doctrine of divine simplicity had excluded relatives, leaving us only with what looked like qualitative accidents (wisdom, goodness, and the like) that proved, on examination, not to be accidents at all. Thus, simplicity by itself does not settle the question whether God has relative accidents. Recall, too, Anselm's principle that no relative term "reveals what a thing is." Simplicity is a doctrine about what God is. As Anselm construes the doctrine of divine simplicity, therefore, it is at least prima facie possible that a simple God is subject to relative accidents even though he has no qualitative accidents.

It certainly appears that God is subject to relations, and such relations are not essential to him: "how is he not subject to accidents, when the very fact that he is greater than all other natures, and that he is unlike them, seems to be accidental to him?"[36] Yet if God can take on accidents, he is "sometimes different from himself, at least accidentally"; and that possibility implies that God is subject to change. Anselm's solution is to distinguish accidents that imply mutability from those that do not, a discussion that parallels the familiar (if slippery) distinction between "real change" and "mere Cambridge change." Some accidents cannot begin or cease to characterize a thing without there being some real change in the thing itself. If a thing ceases to be white and begins to be black, it undergoes a real change. Other accidents, however, bring about no change at all in a thing by beginning or ceasing to characterize it: "For example, it is evident that I am not taller than, shorter than, equal to, or similar to a human being who will be born after this year. But once he has been born, I will be able—without any change on my part—to have and to lose all these relations with respect to him as he grows or is changed by various qualities."[37] The relations that characterize God are accidents of this second sort, which strictly speaking should not even be called "accidents." And although Anselm does not deal with the matter explicitly at this stage, he will argue later that in addition to these relations to creatures, there are relations within the Godhead. The principle that relations are not predicated substantially, and that they do not imply change, will play an important role in Anselm's Trinitarian theology.

Because God does not have accidents in the strict sense, we cannot properly call God a "substance" as distinguished from accidents, though we can call God a substance in the sense that he is a being—such a unique being, because of his aseity, that any word applied to him in common with other beings has a very different meaning.[38] Even calling God a substance in this sense is tricky. We classify substances as either individual or universal: individual substances have a universal essence in common with other individual substances (as one human being has the essence *human being* in common with other human beings), and universal substances are essentially common to a plurality of individual substances (as the universal substance *human being* is essentially common to all human beings). God cannot be a universal substance, since he is not "divided into a plurality of substances"; but neither can he be an individual substance, since he is not "conjoined with any other through a common essence."[39] Nonetheless, "since he not only most assuredly exists but also exists in the highest way of all things, and the essence of any given thing is generally called a substance, surely, if he can be worthily called anything at all, there is nothing to prevent us from calling him a substance."[40] Spirit is the highest kind of substance, so God is a spirit, but a necessarily individual spirit, since he is in no way divisible.

Because of his eternity and immutability, God alone exists in an unqualified sense. For "whatever he is, he is once and for all, all at once, and illimitably."[41] Everything else, by comparison, barely exists: "By contrast, all other things exist changeably in some respect, so that at some time they were or will be something that they are not now, or they are now something that at some time they were not or will not be. What they once were no longer exists, and what they will be does not yet exist, and what they are in the fleeting, utterly brief, and barely-existing present barely exists. Therefore, since they exist so changeably, it is not unreasonable to deny that they exist in an unqualified sense and perfectly and absolutely, and to assert that they nearly do not exist, and barely do exist."[42] We could even say, hyperbolically, that God is the only thing that exists—though in fact other things do exist, precisely because "they have been made from nothing by him who alone exists absolutely."[43]

Justice and Mercy

In the *Proslogion* Anselm examines several apparently contradictory pairs of putative divine attributes. He gives by far the most attention to the apparent conflict between God's justice and mercy. It seems that if God is supremely just, he will give both the good and the wicked their due by rewarding the good and punishing the wicked. Yet it seems that if God is supremely merciful, he will spare at least some of the wicked. And "what sort of justice is it to give everlasting life to someone who deserves eternal death?"[44]

Anselm first suggests that God can spare the wicked because he is supremely good, and it is better to be good to both the good and the wicked than to be good only to the good. So God is merciful because he is good. But God is good because he is just, so it follows that God is also *merciful* because he is just. It is not God's justice to creatures, however, that explains God's mercy; it is, in effect, God's justice to himself. It is just for God to be so good, and to act so powerfully, that he cannot be understood to be better or thought to act more powerfully; "and this would certainly not be the case if you were good only in punishing and not in sparing, and if you made only those not yet good to be good and did not do this also for the wicked."[45]

Anselm accepts this solution, as far as it goes; but it does not answer all the questions. For even though it is in this way just for God to spare the wicked, it is also (and more obviously) just for God to punish the wicked. How can both punishment and mercy be just? In sparing the wicked, Anselm says, God is just in relation to himself; he is giving his own goodness its due. In punishing the wicked he is just in relation to creatures; he is giving them their due.[46] Yet even this solution does not get to the heart of the matter, since when God punishes the wicked he is also being just in relation to himself: it is "just for you to be so just that you cannot be thought to be more just. And you would by no means be so just if you only repaid the good with good and did not repay the wicked with evil. For one who treats both the good and the wicked as they deserve is more just than one who does so only for the good."[47] In this way we can, if only barely, comprehend the ways in which God is both just and merciful in his treatment of creatures. What we cannot comprehend is why God spares one wicked person and punishes another, even though they are "alike in wickedness."[48]

Although Anselm does not return to this exact question in his later work, the fact that he leaves his discussion of divine justice and mercy uncharacteristically open-ended should prompt one to wonder whether the *Proslogion* expresses his deepest and most considered thoughts on the matter. In our view, Anselm's last word on divine justice and mercy is to be found in his account of God's plan of redemption in *Cur Deus Homo*—a suggestion that is by no means original with us.[49] Only there does he show how God's justice in upholding his own creative purpose works together with the mercy demonstrated by the Incarnate Son's willingness to lay down his life for the sake of the wicked.

Is Anselm Engaged in "Perfect-Being Theology"?

Philosophers of religion and commentators on Anselm typically agree in labeling Anselm's approach to understanding the divine nature "perfect-being theology."[50] Our brief survey of Anselm's account of the divine attributes ought to make one wonder how informative, or even accurate, that label really is. We have seen that Anselm employs a variety of argumentative strategies in drawing his conclusions about God. Even in the *Proslogion,* where the "perfect-being" concept of God as "that than which nothing greater can be thought" is explicitly employed and developed, Anselm's arguments do not typically take the form "being X is a perfection; therefore, God is X"—or even lend themselves to being restated in that form, at least without some loss of cogency. Granted, in the *Monologion* Anselm articulates the principle that "God must be said to be whatever it is in every respect better to be than not to be," which looks like a "perfect-being rule"[51] for generating a list of divine attributes. Yet as we noted above, Anselm does not in practice treat the principle as a decision procedure for generating an acceptable list of theological predications; and the principle depends for its warrant on a number of divine attributes that Anselm establishes before announcing the rule. So the label "perfect-being theology" suggests a uniformity in Anselm's argumentative method, and a limitation on the kinds of considerations to which Anselm appeals, that one does not actually find in either the *Monologion* or the *Proslogion.*

Nevertheless, though "perfect-being theology" is not an apt description of Anselm's *method,* it can remain a useful label for the *conception* of God that Anselm develops by means of his more fine-grained and variable arguments. Though few descriptions of God follow directly and unproblematically from the claim that God is a perfect being, Anselm would never permit any description of God to be taken literally or strictly if it implied that God is less than perfect. Moreover, God's perfection is what gives unity and intelligibility to the list of divine attributes; it explains why all and only those attributes are on the list. If understood in this more limited way, the label "perfect-being theology" can be retained.

THINKING AND SPEAKING
ABOUT GOD

For much of the *Monologion* Anselm speaks with apparent confidence
about the existence and nature of God, as though our language about God
were utterly unproblematic. He even sets forth a detailed theory explaining how our language can, despite appearances, reveal the very essence of God: not merely what God is like, but what God is. But his
account of the language we use in talking about God takes an unexpected
turn when he reflects on the utter uniqueness of God and remarks, "If he
ever shares a name with any other things, undoubtedly a very different
signification must be understood."[1] Unfortunately, this observation threatens to undermine his entire project in natural theology. After all, the
numerous arguments in which he establishes positive conclusions about
the divine nature all seem to depend on taking words in their usual
senses—a point that is not lost on Anselm himself: "What meaning did
I understand in all the words I thought, if not their ordinary and customary meaning? So if the customary meaning of words is inapplicable to
God, none of my conclusions about him are correct."[2]

Anselm thus recognizes that he needs to provide an account of our
language about God that respects God's transcendence and uniqueness but
does not preclude our coming to know truths about God on the basis of
rational argument. He presents his account in three stages. In the first
stage, which occupies chapters 15 and 16 of the *Monologion,* he sets forth a

test by which to determine what can be said of God, and he explains how our language signifies God's essence. In the second stage, which occupies chapters 26 and 27, he shows how ordinary words can be properly applied to God despite his metaphysical uniqueness. In the third stage, which occupies chapters 64 and 65, he reconciles divine ineffability with the possibility of rational theology by setting forth an account of the way in which our words, and the thoughts that give them their meaning, express God.

The First Stage: How We Can Express the Substance of God

At the beginning of chapter 15, Anselm steps back from his discussion of the existence and activity of God to raise a question in theological semantics: "At this point I am, quite justifiably, strongly moved to inquire, as diligently as I can, which of all the things that can be said of something can be applied substantially to this quite astounding nature. For I would be amazed if, among the nouns or verbs that we apply to things made from nothing, any can be found that is fittingly said of the substance that creates all things. Nonetheless, we must try to see what conclusion reason will lead us to in our investigation."[3] Note that Anselm's question is not more generally "What can we say about God?" but specifically "What, if anything, can we say about God that applies to him substantially?"—that is, do we have words that signify God's substance?[4] He has already said quite a lot about God in the first fourteen chapters, and he is not now expressing any tentativeness about those earlier discussions. But he notices that his conclusions thus far have all involved comparing or relating God to other things. For example, he has described God as best, greatest, and highest; he has spoken of God's activity in creating and sustaining all other things. So he now wonders whether he has yet managed to say anything about the substance of God, and indeed, whether it is even possible to signify the divine substance using words drawn from our experience of creatures, which are the only words we have.

In the previous chapter we saw that Anselm eliminates relative terms from consideration on the grounds that no relative term is predicated substantially. He divides all the predicates that remain into two classes. For all *F,* either

(i)   what is F is, *qua* F, better than what is not-F, *qua* not-F, or

(ii) it is not the case that what is F is, *qua* F, better than what is not-F, *qua* not-F.

Adopting a term from later medieval thinkers, let us call the features that fall in class (i) "unqualified perfections."[5]

Anselm concludes with breathtaking speed that all terms signifying unqualified perfections are said of God substantially. For "just as it is impious to think that the substance of the supreme nature is something that it is in some way better not to be, so he must be whatever it is in every respect better to be than not to be. For he alone is that than which absolutely nothing else is better, and he alone is better than all things that are not what he is."[6] Notice that we determine which features are unqualified perfections by applying a test that essentially involves a relation ("better than"), but those features themselves are not relational features. (Remember, Anselm had already excluded relatives from the scope of his test.) This is how Anselm gets us from the purely relative predications that dominated the earlier chapters, in which we discovered that God is best, greatest, and highest, to nonrelational predication that "designates the substance" of God.

Among the predicates that signify unqualified perfections, and can therefore be said of God's substance, are 'living', 'wise', 'powerful', 'true', and 'just'. But Anselm immediately sees a difficulty. If I say, "James is just," I do not designate James's substance but a quality that he possesses; in more Anselmian language, this predication does not reveal what James is, but what he is like (*quale est*).[7] The surface grammar of "God is just" looks like another case of qualitative rather than substantial predication. So, Anselm says, "perhaps when [the supreme nature] is said to be just or great or something like that, this does not reveal what it is, but rather what sort of thing it is or how great it is. For it certainly seems that each of these is said through quality or quantity. After all, everything that is just is just through justice, and so on in similar cases. Hence, the supreme nature is just precisely through justice. So it seems that the supremely good substance is called 'just' in virtue of its participation in a quality, namely, justice."[8] But the structural similarity between "James is just" and "The supreme nature is just" turns out to be quite misleading. For Anselm has already argued that whatever God is, he is through himself, not through anything distinct from himself. So if God is just through justice, God must himself *be* justice, because God is just through himself. Thus, justice is not a quality God has; it is what God is. 'Just' therefore "reveals the substance" of God, as does 'justice'. It really makes no difference whether we say "God is just" or "God is justice," because in either case we are saying not merely what God is like, but what God is.

The Second Stage: Semantic
Continuity without Ontological
Overlap

The view of theological language that Anselm puts forward in *Monologion* 15 and 16 is remarkably confident about the power of human language to fix our thoughts on the substance of God: that is, to get before the mind not merely how God is related to other things but what God is in his very essence. He gives no indication that there is any change in sense when a word is taken from its mundane use in describing creatures and employed in speaking about God. Indeed, he seems to accept implicitly the doctrine of univocity, according to which at least some of the predicates that can be truly predicated of both God and creatures (such as 'just' and 'good') have exactly the same meaning when predicated of God that they have when predicated of creatures.[9] Moreover, Anselm's approach seems unabashedly kataphatic. That is, the arguments of the opening chapters of the *Monologion* appear to reach genuinely positive or affirmative conclusions about God, and the semantics of chapters 15 and 16 shows us how those conclusions support positive, nonrelational predications in which we signify God's substance.

So it comes as a surprise when the *Monologion*'s second venture into theological semantics, which comes in chapter 26, concludes with a much grimmer assessment of our language about God: "If he ever shares a name with any other things, undoubtedly a very different signification must be understood."[10] Taken as a free-standing observation, this looks like as clear a repudiation of univocity as one could ever expect to see. But in fact, as we shall argue, the context in which Anselm makes this remark shows that he is not withdrawing or even qualifying the epistemological and semantic optimism that prevailed earlier in the *Monologion*.

The arguments that lead up to chapter 26 detail God's relation to place and time. God has neither a beginning nor an end in time (chapter 18). Nothing existed before God, and nothing will exist after him (19). God exists in every place and time, because nothing exists without God (20); yet in another sense God exists in no place or time, because he is not contained by any place or time or parceled out among different places or times (21–22). It is better, in fact, to say that God exists everywhere than to say that he exists in every place (23); it is better to say that he exists always than to say that he exists in every time (24).

In these chapters Anselm grows increasingly attentive to ways in which words we use of both God and creatures must be taken to have different meanings when applied to God. For example, we say of both God and creatures that they exist in a time or a place, but we cannot mean quite the same thing in both cases: "For if that supreme essence is said to exist in a place or a time, even though the very same expression is used both of him and of localized or temporal natures because of our customary way of speaking, there is a different meaning (*intellectus*) because of the dissimilarity of the things themselves. When it comes to localized or temporal natures, this one expression signifies two things: that they are *present at* the times and places in which they are said to exist, and that they are *contained by* those times and places. But in the case of the supreme essence, only one of them applies, namely, that he is present, not that he is contained by them."[11] So Anselm acknowledges here that an expression applied to both God and creatures has a different signification in these disparate uses. Yet this does not mean that we do not know quite what we are saying when we say that God is in a time or a place. On the contrary, Anselm is confident that we can say exactly what the expression means in both cases; we can even explain the ontological basis for the different meanings. God cannot be contained by any place or time because he is simple, eternal, and unchangeable; but he is nonetheless "present to all circumscribed and changeable things just as if he were himself circumscribed by those same places and changed by those same times."[12] In this way Anselm resolves the nonunivocal predication of 'is in a place/time' into the univocal predication of 'is present at a place/time'.

Anselm then turns to the question of whether God has accidents (25). On the one hand, he does have features such as *being greater than all other natures,* which (as we have already seen) do not belong to his substance and are therefore presumably accidental. On the other hand, something that is susceptible of accidents is capable of change, whereas God is immutable. Anselm resolves the problem by reaffirming divine immutability and noting that the presumably accidental features of God do not imply change;

for that reason, they are not properly called "accidents" at all. But this conclusion raises a further problem, which Anselm addresses in chapter 26. Since we understand substances by contrast with accidents, and God cannot take on any accidents, what sense can we make of calling God a substance? The solution is simple: when we call God a substance, 'substance' is used to mean 'essence' or 'being' (*essentia*). Thus, we see that not only is God above every substance, in the sense that he is greater, better, and higher than every other substance, he is also beyond (*extra*) every substance, in the sense that he has nothing in common with any other substance:[13]

> For however great the difference is between the being that is through himself whatever he is and makes every other being from nothing, and a being that through another is made from nothing to be whatever it is, the difference is every bit as great between the supreme substance and those [substances] that are not the same thing that he is. And since he alone among all natures has from himself, without the help of any other nature, whatever being he has, how is he not uniquely whatever he is, having nothing in common with his creatures? Accordingly, if he ever shares any name with other things, undoubtedly a very different signification must be understood.[14]

Now given the context we have carefully laid out—Anselm's confidence in drawing positive conclusions about the divine nature, his resolution of nonunivocal predications into univocal—it is clear that we cannot charitably read the last sentence as a sudden lurch into apophaticism (the view that we can at best say of God what he is not) or into a general skepticism about the success of theological language. So how are we to read it?

Note first that although the conclusion Anselm draws is perfectly general ("*any* name"), the immediate context concerns the proper use of the word 'substance'. We cannot call God a substance in the sense in which substances are contrasted with accidents, but we can call God a substance if we use 'substance' to mean an essence or being. So when we call God a substance we are drawing attention to his being. But God's being is utterly unique, because he alone has all his being from himself, whereas all other beings have their being from another. So when Anselm says that the signification of the word 'substance' is "very different" in "God is a substance" from what it is in "Socrates is a substance," he is not talking about the concept that the speaker associates with the term; he is talking about the *significate* of the term.[15] That is, in both sentences the word 'substance' makes us think of being; but since the being of God is utterly different from the being of Socrates, the significate of 'substance' is utterly different in those two different uses. Moreover, this conclusion applies to "any name," not just to 'essence' or 'substance', because, as Anselm argued in chapter 16, *any* nonrelative name that can be legitimately predicated of God signifies God's substance. Thus, Anselm is neither repudiating univocity nor endorsing apophaticism at the end of chapter 26. Indeed, his main point is neither semantic nor epistemological, but metaphysical: there is no ontological overlap between God and creatures—there is no genus to which both God and creatures belong, no property that both God and creatures possess—and the fact that there are predicates that apply to both should not tempt us to suppose otherwise. The next two chapters confirm this reading, since Anselm goes on to note additional ways in which the divine substance is metaphysically unique, all the while permitting us to describe God using words in their everyday senses.

The Third Stage: How to Say an Ineffable God

After this discussion of God's metaphysical uniqueness, Anselm turns to Trinitarian theology, which occupies him in chapters 29 through 63 of the *Monologion*. Reflecting on this discussion, he remarks at the beginning of chapter 64:

> The mystery of so sublime a thing seems to me to transcend every gaze of human understanding, and for that reason I think the attempt to explain how this is the case should be held in check. For I think someone investigating an incomprehensible thing ought to be satisfied if his reasoning arrives at the knowledge that the thing most certainly exists, even if his understanding cannot fathom how it is so. Nor should we withhold any of the certainty of faith from beliefs that are asserted on the basis of necessary proofs and are contradicted by no other argument, simply because, owing to the incomprehensibility of their natural sublimity, they do not yield to explanation.[16]

These observations set the agenda for Anselm's third venture into theological semantics, which occupies chapters 64 and 65. Anselm wants to find a way to acknowledge that God is beyond our power to understand without casting doubt on the success of his own arguments, which he describes as "necessary proofs" and as possessing "the solidity of certainty."[17]

Anselm recognizes that it is not obvious one can have it both ways: if his conclusions about God's triune nature "have been explained by a sound argument, how is [God] ineffable? Or if he is ineffable, how can our conclusions be correct?"[18] One might say that the divine nature can be explained to some extent, thus allowing us to maintain the correctness of the conclusions reached thus far, while consistently acknowledging that God is ineffable, in the sense that we can never fully comprehend God. Yet Anselm thinks this solution is too pat, because it does not take account of the semantic problem raised in chapter 26:

> But then what can be said in response to the point that became evident earlier in this very discussion: that the supreme essence is so much above and beyond every other nature that if anything is ever said of him in words that are common to other natures, their meaning is in no way common? After all, what meaning did I understand in all those words I thought, if not their common and customary meaning? So if the customary meaning of words is foreign to the supreme essence, none of my conclusions applies to him. How, then, was anything true discovered concerning the supreme essence, if in fact everything that has been discovered is very different from him?[19]

Although Anselm speaks as if the semantic doctrine that threatens to evacuate all his arguments is the same as the semantic doctrine first propounded in chapter 26—"what reply can be made to the point that became evident earlier?"—he changes the wording in quite significant ways. In chapter 26 he had said that when words are applied to both God and creatures, their *significatio* is very different; now he says that their *sensus* is in no way common. Clearly "in no way common" is stronger than "very different," and *sensus* is not the same as *significatio*. As we have already noted, Anselm can use *significatio* for the significate of a term; but the *sensus* of a term is always its meaning, that is, the informational content that the term brings to mind.[20]

Anselm says in *De grammatico* that we do not have the common term necessary for a valid syllogism "if the term is common in sound and not in *sensus*"[21]—in other words, if there is equivocation. So we might phrase Anselm's challenge in *Monologion* 65 like this: "God has nothing in common with creatures. But if he has nothing in common with creatures, then there is nothing common to the meanings of words that are predicated of both God and creatures. Where the meanings of words are not common, there is equivocation; and where there is equivocation, there is no successful argumentation. Therefore, there are no successful arguments from what we know about creatures to any conclusion about God." Anselm quite clearly rejects this final conclusion, yet he continues to uphold the first premise, that God has nothing in common with creatures. He must therefore find a way to safeguard divine uniqueness and ineffability while providing an account of the language we use about God that permits successful argumentation.

Anselm distinguishes two ways of saying a thing as well as two ways of seeing (presumably, of understanding) a thing. We can say (or signify, or express) a thing "through its own *proprietas*" or "through something else"; we can see a thing "through its own *proprietas*" or "through some likeness or image." A good deal hinges on what Anselm means by *proprietas*, and unfortunately he is not forthcoming about how he is using the word in this context. One frequent meaning of *proprietas* in Anselm is the proper use of a word or phrase; in this usage it is the abstract noun corresponding to *proprie*, properly.[22] When we use an expression properly, we use it in accordance with its *proprietas*. But that can't be what Anselm has in mind here. *Proprietas* in that sense is a feature of an expression or of the way in which it is used, whereas in the distinction between saying something "through its own *proprietas*" and saying it "through something else," the *proprietas* belongs to the thing our words are describing, rather than to the words themselves.

The other main use of *proprietas* in Anselm is for a distinguishing or individuating characteristic. An individual is a species plus a collection of *proprietates*.[23] And, more frequently, the feature that is unique to each of the Persons of the Trinity, as opposed to the divine nature they have in common, is called a *proprietas*.[24] It is reasonable, therefore, to take *proprietas* here to refer to what sets a thing apart, what distinguishes it from other things. Now Anselm continues to insist that God has nothing in common with creatures. God is, as it were, all *proprietas*. Yet both our descriptions of God and our knowledge of God are derived from creatures—or in Anselm's terminology, we both say God and see God through creatures. Accordingly, we neither say God nor see God through his *proprietas*.

Yet this does not mean that we do not say God or see God at all. When we cannot say or see something through its *proprietas*—and Anselm suggests that this happens frequently, and not only in the case of God[25]—we can still say or see it. For example, we say a thing through something else when we speak *per aenigmata:* through figurative or enigmatic language; we see a thing through a likeness or image when we examine someone's face in a mirror. In this way, Anselm says, "we both say and do not say, we both see and do not see, one and the same thing. We say and see through something else; we do not say, and we do not see, through the thing's own *proprietas.*"[26]

Let's first explore what it is to say a thing *per aliud.* The example of speaking *per aenigmata* is not obviously helpful, since it is hard to see how figurative or enigmatic language about God could ever serve as the basis for rational conclusions about God; and it is the possibility of such conclusions that Anselm is trying to defend here. Moreover, Anselm gives 'wisdom' and 'essence' as examples of words that we say of God *per aliud,* and those words certainly do not appear to be figurative or enigmatic. Fortunately, as we have seen, Anselm develops a theory of signification *per aliud* in *De grammatico,* and we can apply that theory here. A word brings to mind what it signifies. When it signifies something *per se,* it brings that thing to mind directly or straightforwardly; when it signifies something *per aliud,* it brings that thing to mind only in virtue of some additional knowledge or some other feature of the context of utterance.

We say God *per aliud* because all the words we use in speaking about God bring him to mind only indirectly, in light of knowledge about God derived either from natural theology or from Scripture. What 'wisdom' brings straightforwardly to mind is the perfection that we discern in human beings who order their affairs well or have a grasp of philosophical truth. Yet 'wisdom' does bring God to mind, if only obliquely, because both Scripture and reason tell us that good order and truthful thinking reflect the all-encompassing governance of divine truth, in which they find their ultimate source. In this way the word 'wisdom' "hints at" (*innuit*) divine wisdom "through a certain likeness." Thus, Anselm says, "when I think the significations of these words" that can be said of God, "I more readily conceive in the mind what I observe in created things than that which I understand to transcend all human understanding. For by their signification they establish something much less than, indeed something far different from, that which my mind is trying to progress toward understanding through this tenuous signification."[27] The signification is tenuous, not because the connection with ordinary usage is thin,[28] but because the connection between mind and world that is established through signification is more than usually oblique and unsatisfactory.

In short, we say God *per aliud* because the words we use in speaking about God bring God to mind only obliquely and because of additional knowledge that is not ordinarily implicated in our use of those words. This account of *per aliud* saying even makes sense of Anselm's example of speaking *per aenigmata,* since figurative or enigmatic language can work in precisely this way, by provoking us to draw on a wider base of knowledge to interpret language that does not bear its meaning on its face. It also enables us to understand what it is to *see* something *per aliud* or "through some likeness or image." Now as we saw in chapter 2, Anselm holds that *all* human cognition involves likenesses or images. But when we think a human being through the concept *rational, mortal animal,* our mental likeness captures the *proprietas* of human beings in a way that is never possible when we think God. Moreover, the likeness through which we think human beings is derived from our experience of human beings, whereas the likeness through which we think God is derived from our experience of things other than God. Thus, we see God *per aliud* in two senses: we think God through likenesses that do not reveal God's *proprietas,* and those likenesses get their content from our experience of things other than God.

For Anselm, then, to call God "ineffable" is not to make a vague gesture toward apophaticism, but to say something very specific about the limitations of our thought and language about God. God is ineffable in the sense that we see him or say him *per aliud,* but we do succeed in seeing him and saying him. Something that is ineffable in this sense can still be successfully investigated through reasoning: "it is perfectly possible for our conclusions thus far about the supreme nature to be true and yet for that nature itself to remain ineffable, if we suppose that it was in no way expressed through the *proprietas* of its essence but in some way or other designated *per aliud.*"[29] And since there is no successful argumentation where the senses of words are not common, Anselm does not in the end accept the claim that the words used of both God and creatures have a different sense in those two uses. In fact, his account of divine ineffability rests on the assumption that such words are used in their customary senses even when we are talking about God: for it is precisely *because* the senses of our words are derived from, and straightforwardly applicable to, creatures that we can see and say God only *per aliud*.[30] Those words, used in those senses, can establish only a tenuous connection between the human mind and an utterly unique God; but a tenuous connection is still a connection, enough to banish the specter of equivocation and permit a robust, if always cautious, rational theology.

8

CREATION AND THE WORD

Anselm allows two interpretations of the claim that God made all things from nothing. First, they were not made from anything, that is, from any preexistent matter. And second, "those things that formerly were nothing are now something."[1] But there is a sense in which created things were not nothing before God made them. They existed—or rather, some likeness or pattern of them existed—in the mind of their Creator: "There is no way that anything can be made rationally by anyone unless some sort of exemplar (or perhaps it would be more aptly called a form or likeness or pattern) of the thing to be made already exists in the reason of the maker. And so it is evident that before all things were made, what-they-were-going-to-be or what-they-were-going-to-be-like or in-what-way-they-were-going-to-be existed in the reason of the supreme nature."[2] Anselm goes on to say that this preexisting form in the divine reason is an utterance (*locutio*) of things that will be made, "as when a craftsman who is going to make some product of his craft first says it within himself by a mental conception."[3]

The craftsman analogy is, as Anselm is quick to say, merely a first pass at understanding the way in which created things first exist in the mind of their Maker. He notes two disanalogies right away.[4] First, a craftsman gets the content of his conception from experience, and hence from outside himself. Even if he "creates" something he has never seen before, as an illustrator might draw an imaginary animal, he is merely reassembling mental contents that first came to him piecemeal from other, real things. God, by contrast, does not draw on anything external to himself in order to form the conception by which he utters creation. And second, a craftsman is not the "sole or sufficient" cause of his finished product. At the very least, he requires material on which to work. God, however, needs nothing other than himself in order to create the things he first conceives. Thus, the craftsman's products "would not exist at all if they were not already something" independently of the craftsman's conception, whereas the things God creates owe everything they are to God's conception.[5]

If the disanalogies stopped here, we could understand Anselm's doctrine of God's utterance of creation as a version of the doctrine of divine ideas associated with Augustine. The divine ideas are like Platonic Forms except that instead of subsisting independently, they have a dependent existence as thoughts in the divine mind. Augustine describes the ideas as "certain fixed and immutable fundamental forms or essences (*rationes*) of things, forms that are not themselves formed and are therefore eternal and always disposed in the same way, that are contained within the divine intellect."[6] Those reasons or ideas serve as blueprints for God's act of creation; without them God would be creating irrationally. Anselm, too, bases his argument for the divine utterance of creation on the claim that God must create rationally, in accordance with a pattern or exemplar. So it seems natural at first to suppose that what Anselm calls God's utterance of creation is more or less the same as what Augustine calls divine ideas.

But when Anselm returns to his discussion of God's utterance of creation, he develops the account in ways that modify the standard doctrine of divine ideas beyond recognition.[7] First, Anselm argues that this utterance must be the very same thing as God himself: "for if he made nothing otherwise than through himself, and whatever was made by him was made through his utterance, in what way is his utterance anything other than what he is himself?"[8] Moreover, it is not possible for anything to exist other than the Creator and what he creates. God's utterance of creation cannot itself be a creature, since all creatures are made through God's utterance and nothing is made through itself. "And so," Anselm concludes, "since the supreme spirit's utterance cannot be a creature, the only remaining possibility is that its utterance must be nothing other than the supreme spirit."[9] But since the supreme spirit is a single, individual spirit, it follows that the supreme spirit and its utterance are not two spirits, but one spirit. Using the language of the Nicene Creed, Anselm also expresses this conclusion by saying that the utterance is "consubstantial with" the supreme spirit. Accordingly, whatever is true of the substance of the supreme spirit is true also of its utterance. And one thing that is true of the supreme spirit is that it is "supremely simple." Therefore, the supreme spirit's utterance is also supremely simple, which means that it does not consist of a plurality of words, but rather is a single Word through which all things were made.[10]

Anselm's conclusion is thus very different from the conclusion that Augustine draws in the same context. Augustine, having argued that a rational Creator must create according to a reason, continues, "Nor were a human being and a horse created according to one and the same reason. It would be absurd to think *that*. Individual things, therefore, were created according to their own individual reasons."[11] For Anselm, by contrast, God utters all creatures through a single Word, and that Word is itself God. Anselm recognizes that this Word has turned out to be something very different from the kind of word suggested by his original craftsman analogy. He brings out the difficulty by invoking the notions of truth and likeness:

> All such words by which we say certain things in the mind—that is, think them—are likenesses and images of the things whose words they are. And every likeness or image is more or less true to the extent that it imitates more or less the thing of which it is a likeness. So what are we to hold concerning the Word by which all things are said and through which all things were made? Is it, or is it not, a likeness of the things that have been made through it? If it is a true likeness of mutable things, it is not consubstantial with the supreme immutability, which is false. On the other hand, if it is not an altogether true likeness of mutable things, but merely a qualified likeness, the Word of the supreme truth is not altogether true, which is absurd. And if it has no likeness to mutable things, in what way have they been patterned after it?[12]

The difficulty, then, is that the Word of the supreme truth ought to be supremely true, and a true word is one that bears a true likeness to the things of which it is a word. But the Word of the supreme truth cannot bear a true likeness to creatures, since it must be immutable and they are mutable.

Anselm begins to address the problem by offering a new example of the relationship between truth and likeness. "The truth of [the common nature] human being is said to be in a living human being," whereas in a painting there is only "a likeness or image of that truth." That is, the living human being is the standard by which we judge the adequacy of the likeness in the painting; the truth or reality of human nature exists in the original of which the painting is an image. In the same way, we should recognize that "the truth of existing is in the Word, whose essence exists so supremely that in a certain way it alone exists; by contrast, in those things that by comparison with it in a certain way do not exist and yet have been made something through it and in accordance with it, there is discerned a certain imitation of that supreme essence."[13] To return to the comparison between a living human being and a painted one, the Word has "the truth of existing," like the living human being; and creatures, like the painting, are "a likeness or image of that truth." In this way we can rank creatures in terms of their likeness to the Word, rather than evaluating the Word in terms of its likeness to creatures—as the original craftsman analogy might have been taken to suggest. What we ought to say, then, is not that the Word is more or less true depending on how similar it is to creatures, but rather that creatures "exist more greatly and are more excellent to the extent that they are more like that which supremely exists and is supremely great."[14]

The likeness of creatures to the Word, however, is not a matter of pictorial resemblance, but of possessing a range of features that the Word also possesses. Likeness to the supreme nature is measured according to three features: "For since the supreme nature in a certain singular[15] way of its own not only exists but also lives, has awareness (*sentit*), and is rational, it is clear that among all the things there are, that which in some way lives is more like the supreme nature than that which does not live in any way; and that which cognizes in any way—even by means of a bodily sense—is more like it than that which has no awareness at all; and that which is rational is more like it than that which does not have the capacity for reason."[16] Though Anselm does not say so explicitly here, it is clear that we cannot understand these features as properties exemplified by both God and creatures.[17] For example, it is not as though God exemplifies the property *being rational* to an infinite degree and we exemplify the same property to a finite degree. For Anselm, rationality is not a quality distinct from the divine nature that God exemplifies or in which God participates; God's rationality *just is* the divine nature. And clearly creatures do not exemplify or instantiate the divine nature. This, no doubt, is why Anselm says that in creatures there is "scarcely some imitation of that true essence":[18] the properties in virtue of which creatures "approach" God are not in any literal sense shared with God, but merely mimic, in a fragmentary way, the unitary perfection of the divine nature.

This picture of the relation between the Word and creation explains why so many commentators have come to grief in their attempts to pin down Anselm's view of properties and universals.[19] The most Anselm can say is that creation imitates God. Imitation is not participation or exemplification; it is a kind of likeness. And there is very little that is informative that can be said about the sort of likeness that can obtain between the perfect, eternal, and simple Word and the imperfect, mutable, and metaphysically complex creatures that imitate the Word. Anselm's analogy to the likeness between a person and a portrait of that person is instructive. Though it seems obvious that we know how a portrait resembles the person portrayed, a moment's reflection will reveal that it is actually rather difficult to say clearly how the picture is like the living original. But now imagine trying to convey the idea to someone who had never seen a portrait or a photograph: "There is this thing that is like Joe over here—although of course it isn't alive, can't think, is two-dimensional, and in fact has hardly any of the same properties that Joe has." We are in a somewhat similar position when it comes to imagining the likeness of creatures to the Word, except that in our case it is the original rather than the copy that we know only by description.[20]

Now the words by which we say things in our mind are likenesses of those things, but (according to Anselm) the Word by which the supreme spirit utters creation is not a likeness of creation; rather, creation is, in a sense difficult to pin down, a likeness of the Word. So the Word is not the word *of* creation. Yet every word is the word *of* something. In what sense, then, is the Word a word?

Before Anselm answers this question, he offers a second reason for denying that the Word is a word of creation: "Furthermore, if no creature ever existed, there would be no word of a creature. What, then? Are we to conclude that if no creature existed in any way, that Word, which is the supreme essence and needs nothing, would by no means exist? Or perhaps that the supreme essence that is the Word would indeed be eternal but would not be a Word if nothing were ever made through it? For there can be no word of that which neither was nor is nor will be."[21] This argument reveals an assumption that was not explicit in, or even entailed by, the craftsman analogy as originally presented. It is easy to imagine a craftsman conceiving of or "uttering" not only his actual products but also products that he will never in fact make. Similarly, it is natural for us to think of God as uttering not only his actual creatures but also other possible creatures—*all* other possible creatures, in fact, since God's utterance will presumably be as complete as an utterance could possibly be. Yet for Anselm God's utterance of creation is limited to actual creatures: "there can be no word of that which neither was nor is nor will be." If God were never to create, he would never utter any creature.

According to this argument, Anselm points out, if there were never any being other than God, there would be no Word in God. But if there were no Word in God, he would not "say anything within himself." Now God's saying something is equivalent to his understanding it. So if God said nothing, God would understand nothing—an absurd conclusion, since God is necessarily the supreme wisdom. We must therefore say that God would necessarily say, or understand, something, even if he were the only thing that existed. And what would God understand, if he alone existed? He would, at any rate, understand himself:

> How can one so much as entertain the thought that the supreme wisdom ever fails to understand itself, given that the rational mind can remember and understand not only itself but also the supreme wisdom? For if the human mind could never have any memory or understanding of the supreme wisdom or of itself, it would never distinguish itself from irrational creatures, or distinguish the supreme wisdom from every creature, by reasoning silently within itself and by itself, as I am doing now. Therefore, just as that supreme spirit is eternal, so too does it eternally remember and understand itself after the likeness of the rational mind—or rather, not after the likeness of anything; instead, the supreme spirit does so paradigmatically, and the rational mind does so after its likeness.[22]

In this way there is eternally and necessarily a Word in God because God eternally and necessarily understands, and thus utters, himself.

We can understand the divine Word better by exploring further the analogy with human understanding. Anselm writes that "when the mind desires to think a given thing in a truthful way, whether through the imagination of a body or through reason, it tries to form a likeness of that thing in its thought, so far as it can. The more truly it does this, the more truly it thinks the thing itself."[23] For example, suppose one decides to think a man whom one knows but who is not present at the moment. In that case one forms an image of the man that is like the image one would receive through the senses if he were present. This image is a word of the man, and one says or utters the man by thinking him. Now suppose instead that the mind thinks itself. In this case as well the mind forms an image, though this time it is an image of itself. This image of the mind is the word by which the mind says or utters itself. The mind is, as it were, stamped on the mind in such a way that the mind and its image are inseparable, although reason can distinguish the two.

In this way, Anselm argues, when the supreme wisdom understands itself, it generates its own likeness, which is consubstantial with itself. This likeness is the Word by which the supreme wisdom utters itself. But is there, in addition, a Word by which God utters creation as well? There is not. For as we have already seen, every word is the word—that is, the likeness—*of* something; and there is no word of creation in God. Moreover, the Word is consubstantial with the Father, who is one and simple; so the Word must also be one simple Word. So there is only one Word in God, and God utters not only himself but also creation through that one Word.

Anselm realizes that it is difficult to understand how "such different things—the creating essence and created essence—can be said by means of one Word, especially given that the Word itself is coeternal with the One who utters it, whereas creation is not coeternal with him."[24] The account he offers of the way in which God utters both himself and creation through a single word does help minimize the difficulty, though, as we shall see, it does so at the cost of leaving Anselm with nothing to say about some crucial further questions. Anselm explains that God utters creation in uttering himself because God is himself "the supreme wisdom and supreme reason in which all the things that have been made exist."[25] Thus, in uttering himself, God utters the creatures that exist in him. The sort of being that creatures have in God is comparable to the being that the product of a craft has in the craft: "not only when it is made, but also before it is made and after it has fallen to pieces (*dissolvitur*), it always exists in the craft itself as nothing other than what the craft itself is."[26] It is this last point that is most important: the product-in-the-mind is not an additional item in the mental furniture of the craftsman; it is nothing other than the craft itself. Analogously, creatures-in-the-Word are nothing other than the Word.

Now this account of the existence of creatures in the Word does, in a way, eliminate the puzzle about how God can utter both himself and creatures by means of a single Word. Since creatures-in-the-Word simply *are* the Word, God's self-utterance and his utterance of creatures are one and the same thing. Unfortunately, by solving the puzzle in this way, Anselm deprives himself of the conceptual apparatus needed to say much that is informative about creation in its specificity and particularity. For example, we know that both dogs and cats in some way imitate the Word. Like the Word, they have not only life but also awareness (though they lack reason). But it does not seem that Anselm can say anything at all specific about the way in which cats imitate the Word differently from dogs, even though it is only by imitating the Word in different ways that they can be different kinds of things. The apparatus of divine ideas, however problematic it might be in other respects, at least offers a clear metaphysical grounding for the differentiation among creatures that all occupy the same level of imitating the Word. According to the doctrine of divine ideas, the Word contains both the idea of Cat and the idea of Dog; some creatures imitate the one idea and others imitate the other. No such explanation is available to Anselm.

Thus, Anselm can say very little about the metaphysical basis for the variety of actual creatures. *A fortiori* he can say even less about the metaphysical status of unrealized possibilities. Someone who accepts a straightforward doctrine of divine ideas can posit ideas of unrealized possibilities—whether of uninstantiated kinds or of merely possible individuals of kinds that do have instances—in the Word.[27] In this way the doctrine of divine ideas can serve a function analogous to that of possible worlds in contemporary philosophy. Anselm can only ask whether there are ways of imitating the Word that are never actually exemplified, and since we can say so little that is informative even about the different ways in which *actual* creatures imitate the Word, it is not at all clear that we know enough to go about answering that question. For this reason it is also difficult for Anselm to say unambiguously whether God could have created otherwise than he actually did. The mere fact (if it is a fact) that there are unrealized possibilities does not entail that God could have created otherwise than he did, since there might be additional facts about the divine nature or the content of those unrealized possibilities that would entail that God created exactly as he did. But the fact that there are unrealized possibilities at least opens up the conceptual space necessary to pose the question in the first place. If we cannot say for certain that there are unrealized possibilities, we certainly cannot say determinately whether God could have actualized some of them.

A further difficulty for Anselm, and the only one on which he comments explicitly in the *Monologion,* is how to understand God's knowledge of creatures. God utters creatures—that is, God expresses his knowledge of creatures—by uttering himself, since creatures are "in the Word" by being identical with the Word. The Word is thus the expression of God's self-knowledge but thereby also an expression of God's knowledge of creatures. But again, this seems to account for God's knowledge of creatures only in the most general way. Yet Anselm never doubts that God knows creatures in all their particularity. He frankly admits that this knowledge is "incomprehensible":

> From this it can be most clearly comprehended that no human knowledge can comprehend how that spirit utters or knows the things that were made. For no one doubts that created substances exist in themselves quite differently from how they exist in our knowledge. After all, in themselves they exist through their own essence, whereas in our knowledge it is not their essences but their likenesses that exist. So it follows that they exist more truly in themselves than in our knowledge to the extent that they exist more truly somewhere through their essence than through their likeness. And it is also clear that every created substance exists more truly in the Word, that is, in the understanding of the Creator, than in itself, to the extent that the creating essence exists more truly than a created essence. So if our knowledge is as much surpassed by created substances as their likeness falls short of their essence, how will the human mind understand what that utterance and that knowledge are like, since they are far higher and truer than created substances?[28]

From these remarks in his first systematic work through the end of his life, Anselm remained content with this confessedly aporetic discussion of God's knowledge of creatures. He never went on to offer an ontological or epistemological theory about that knowledge; he never even tried to provide a model or image for the way in which God knows created things in all their particularity. God's knowledge remained, in this respect at least, a greater mystery even than the Trinity.

The doctrine of divine ideas, as it appears in Augustine and others, had both an ontological and an epistemological use. Ontologically, it served as a theory of universals; it provided a recognizably Platonic account of creatures as participating in or imitating certain unchangeable forms or essences. Epistemologically, it accounted for the Creator's knowledge of creation. When Anselm first introduces the divine utterance or Word, it appears that he intends the doctrine of the Word to have both uses: "It therefore quite rightly seems that such an utterance of things not only existed in the supreme substance before the things existed, in order that through it they might be made, but also exists in him now that they have been made, in order that through it they might be known."[29] But the unitary, simple Word that emerges from Anselm's discussion is ill-suited for such a role. In the end, Anselm's doctrine of the Word is not, and was not intended to be, an element in an account of the metaphysical or epistemological relations between God and creatures. It is, rather, the first element in Anselm's account of the divine Trinity.

THE TRINITY

Anselm's Trinitarian speculations in the *Monologion* are obviously reminiscent of Augustine's in *De trinitate,* and Anselm himself invites us to evaluate his teaching on the Trinity by comparing it with Augustine's.[1] In particular, Anselm follows Augustine's lead in attempting to understand the Trinitarian nature of God by exploring analogies drawn from the structure and activity of the human mind. Yet the two are engaged in somewhat different enterprises. As we noted in chapter 1, Augustine is quite explicit that one must first appeal to Scripture in order to establish that God is a Trinity. The various psychological triads that Augustine explores in Books 8 through 15 of *De trinitate* are not meant to function as arguments for the claim that God is a Trinity, but as models for the trinity-in-unity that is known to us only by faith in Scripture. They help believers conceptualize the doctrines that they hold by faith. In this way the psychological analogies offer a rebuttal to attacks on the coherence or intelligibility of Trinitarian doctrine; they also (and this is of crucial importance to Augustine) offer believers a way of coming to deeper knowledge of God and thereby of coming to love God more fervently. But they do not provide independent positive warrant for Trinitarian doctrine itself.

Like Augustine, Anselm does not appeal to psychological analogies in order to establish the truth of Trinitarian doctrine, but to illustrate claims that are established by other means. But Anselm's use of such analogies is much less extensive than Augustine's—they punctuate, rather than propel, his exposition—and only one of Augustine's many psychological triads from *De trinitate* appears in the *Monologion*.[2] The most important contrast between the two authors, however, has nothing to do with their use of psychological analogies, but with how they establish the claims that those analogies are meant to illustrate. Anselm does not appeal to Scripture to establish that God is a Trinity. Instead he professes to offer arguments that show, by reason alone, that God is "one essence and three persons or three substances."[3]

The Metaphysics of the Trinity

There are two works in which Anselm engages philosophically with Trinitarian doctrine. In the *Monologion* he makes his constructive case for the doctrine, and in *De incarnatione Verbi* he clarifies the metaphysics of the Trinity in order to meet a challenge posed by Roscelin of Compiègne.[4] Although Anselm made his constructive case for the Trinity first, it will be helpful if we begin instead with *De incarnatione Verbi*. Anselm's response to Roscelin did not require him to revise the claims of the *Monologion* in any way, but it did force him to treat explicitly and systematically the key metaphysical problems that the *Monologion* had engaged with in a more piecemeal fashion. By looking at *De incarnatione Verbi* first, we can gain a better understanding not only of the conclusions for which Anselm was trying to provide arguments in the *Monologion*, but also of how to construe those arguments.

Anselm did not have access to anything Roscelin had written on the subject; he knew of Roscelin's heresy only by report. According to Anselm's correspondent, Roscelin had argued that "If in God the three persons are just one thing and not three things (each person a thing in himself taken separately, like three angels or three souls, but such that they are altogether the same in will and power), then the Father and the Holy Spirit were incarnate along with the Son."[5] Because Roscelin wished to uphold the traditional view that only the Son was incarnate, he believed he had no choice but to conclude that God is three things in the same way that three angels are three things.

But this, Anselm insists, is either blatant tritheism or complete nonsense: "Surely he either intends to acknowledge three gods or else does not understand what he is saying."[6] A proper understanding of the meta-physics of the Trinity easily overcomes Roscelin's dilemma. The key distinction, to which Anselm returns again and again in *De incarnatione Verbi,* is between common features (*communia*) and distinguishing or proper features (*propria*). (Latin grammar allows Anselm to use neuter adjectives and avoid nouns altogether; since English does not, we will use the word 'feature' to avoid the misleading connotations of words like 'property'.) The divine nature or essence—Anselm uses the two words interchangeably in *De incarnatione Verbi*—is common to all three persons of the Trinity, but over and above the divine nature there are the proper features that distinguish the Father, the Son, and the Holy Spirit from each other.

In general, Anselm holds that concrete individuals possess a nature and a set of distinguishing features. In the case of created beings, a nature or essence is a set of features that makes a thing the sort of thing it is, and distinguishing features are accidental features. For example, two human beings have the same essence—not numerically the same essence, as an extreme realist would say, but a qualitatively indistinguishable set of species-defining features, such as rationality and animality; they are distinguished by such accidental features as hair color, height, and so on. Two cautions are necessary here. First, we should not think of either the nature or the distinguishing characteristics as properties that inhere in an otherwise propertyless substratum. The core object in Anselm's metaphysics is not a substratum but a concrete particular of an identifiable kind, that is, one that as such possesses the features that are collectively called its essence or nature. And second, we have to avoid the common contemporary equation of essential features with necessary ones and accidental features with contingent ones. Any feature that is not kind-defining is accidental, but some accidents belong necessarily to the individual that possesses them. Anselm does not explicitly discuss examples of necessary but nonessential features in created beings, but nothing in his metaphysics rules them out.

God, too, Anselm argues, has both a nature and distinguishing features, just as created beings do. In the case of God, however, there is only one nature. The three persons do not have the same essence merely in the sense in which three human beings have the same essence (that is, a qualitatively indistinguishable set of kind-defining features), but in the strictest sense: there is numerically one nature that the three persons have in common. And unlike any created nature, the divine nature is not a collection or set of features, but a simple concrete individual. The three persons are distinguished by relations: the Father begets, the Son is begotten, and the Holy Spirit proceeds. These distinguishing features are possessed by each person necessarily, but (by definition, since they are distinguishing features) they do not belong to the divine nature that the three persons have in common.[7] Much of the *Monologion* is dedicated to arguing that given what we know of the simple divine nature, we can prove that this nature begets, is begotten, and proceeds. In other words, Anselm argues that God is necessarily Father, Son, and Holy Spirit, even though the relations of paternity, filiation, and spiration are not part of the divine essence—an essence that, in fact, has no parts.[8]

Armed with these distinctions, Anselm argues that Roscelin has fallen into error because he has conflated questions about God's nature with questions about the three persons and their distinguishing features. God is indeed three things if we are talking about the relations that distinguish the three persons; he is one thing if we are talking about the divine nature. Although Anselm does not have the technical vocabulary to make the move explicitly, it is clear that his replies invite us to give up thinking in terms of absolute or classical identity and to think instead in terms of relative identity. For example, we cannot say unambiguously that the Father is the same as the Son or that the Father is not the same as the Son. The Father is the same *God* as the Son, for there is only one simple divine nature that is common to the Father and the Son; but the Father is not the same *person* as the Son, because the distinguishing relation of begetting belongs solely to the Father and that of being begotten belongs solely to the Son.

For this reason, both our language and our inferences about God will inevitably go astray if we are careless about whether we are talking about God in terms of the proper characteristics in virtue of which God is three or instead in terms of the simple divine nature in virtue of which God is one. For example, the relation of begetting is the distinguishing feature of the Father; it does not belong to the common divine nature. So although we can say that God begets (for the Father begets, and the Father is God), we cannot infer that the Son begets (even though the Son, too, is God); begetting characterizes the Father *qua* Father and not *qua* God. But from the fact that the Father is omnipotent we *can* infer that the Son is omnipotent, since omnipotence belongs to (and indeed is identical with) the divine nature that is common to the Father and the Son.

This kind of nonidentity (*separatio*) or plurality within the Godhead is all we need, Anselm says, in order for the Son to be incarnate by himself.

Anselm—speaking, for ease of exposition, only of the Father and the Son—imagines Roscelin as reasoning thus:

> If God is numerically one and the same thing, and that very thing is the Father and is also the Son, how can it be that the Father is not incarnate as well, given that the Son is incarnate? Clearly an affirmation and its negation are not both true of one and the same thing at one and the same time. But it is perfectly fine to affirm something of one thing and deny it of another thing at one and the same time ... So if the Father and the Son are numerically one thing and not two distinct things, it is not true that something ought to be affirmed of the Son and denied of the Father or affirmed of the Father and denied of the Son. Therefore, whatever the Father is, the Son is too; and what is said of the Son should not be denied of the Father. But the Son was incarnate, so the Father too was incarnate.[9]

We can now see why Roscelin's inference fails. The very reason that we can speak of two persons in the first place is that there are distinguishing features: "For if there is not in God someone distinct from the Father whose Father he is, God cannot be a Father. And similarly, if there is not in God someone distinct from the Son whose Son he is, God cannot be a Son."[10] So there is some sense in which the Father and the Son are two things, not one; and there is nothing untoward about affirming of one thing what one denies of a distinct thing.

In *De incarnatione Verbi* Anselm simply assumes the truth of Trinitarian doctrine and tries to show that, properly understood, it has the resources to meet Roscelin's challenge. The fact that Roscelin's arguments entail heresy is enough to show that Roscelin is wrong: "if this reasoning is sound, the heresy of Sabellius is true."[11] His image of the Nile—in which a spring, a river, and a lake are all one body of water—is meant to illustrate the coherence of Trinitarian doctrine but not to persuade anyone of its truth.[12] Yet, as we have seen, Anselm does think that he can provide rational arguments for Trinitarian doctrine that ought to persuade any fair-minded inquirer of its truth. For those arguments Anselm refers us to the *Monologion,* to which we will now turn.

The Word Was God

As we saw in the previous chapter, the first stage of Anselm's constructive arguments for the claim that the supreme essence must be three persons is his introduction of the divine Word, by which God utters both himself and creation. When Anselm first introduces the Word in the *Monologion,* it is not obviously a second divine person. Just as the artisan's internal utterance of his work is simply a feature of his thought, the divine utterance might be taken at first to be no more than a divine thought or speech act. In order to show that the Word is a second divine person, Anselm will argue first that the Word is *divine* and only then that the Word is a *person.* That is, Anselm argues first that the Word is fully divine—not merely an act or aspect of God, but actually God in the fullest sense—and then shows how the divine Word is distinct from the One who utters the Word. In Johannine terms, Anselm must show first that "the Word *was* God" and then that "the Word was *with* God."

Anselm's first argument for the claim that "the utterance of the supreme essence is nothing other than the supreme essence"[13] is perfunctory and clearly unsatisfactory. Because it has already been shown that God made everything through himself, and we have now discovered that God made everything through his utterance, it follows that God and his utterance are one and the same. The problem with this argument is that even if the divine utterance of creation were simply a feature or aspect of God, after the manner of a thought or speech act, it would still be true that in making creatures through that utterance, God would be making them through himself. There would be no violation of divine ultimacy in such a case. Anselm's conclusion will follow only if there is no feature or aspect of God that is distinct from God—in other words, only if the divine nature is simple—and Anselm has not yet established divine simplicity at this point in the *Monologion.* So it is not surprising that he immediately drops not only this argument but all discussion of the divine utterance until after he has investigated divine simplicity and its implications.[14]

When Anselm returns to the divine utterance seventeen chapters later, he repeats the argument (which now has divine simplicity to give it force) and adds two others. We can represent the first of these as follows:

(1) Everything that is made is posterior to that through which it was made.

(2) Nothing is posterior to itself.

Therefore, (3) nothing is made through itself.   from (1) and (2)

Therefore, (4) the divine utterance was not made
through itself.   from (3)

(5) All created things were made through the divine utterance.

Therefore, (6) the divine utterance is not a created thing.　　from (4) and (5)

(7) "Nothing at all ever could or can subsist other than the creating spirit and what he creates."[15]

Therefore, (8) the divine utterance is the creating spirit.　　from (6) and (7)

Anselm's inferences in this argument are all valid, and he seems entitled to all his premises. By "posterior to" Anselm means something like "metaphysically dependent on," and on that understanding of the *posterior to* relation, (1) and (2) seem reasonable enough; and he takes himself to have established (5) and (7) earlier. So in its context, the argument is compelling. Note, however, that (8) doesn't look prima facie as if it's talking about an additional divine person. Instead it looks like the same sort of identity statement as "The supreme essence is existent justice"—merely another example of the doctrine of divine simplicity. But this is no objection to the argument, since Anselm's only concern at this stage is to show that the Word is consubstantial with the Father.[16] The distinctness of the Word from the Father will be established later.

The final argument in chapter 29 for the claim that the divine utterance is identical with the supreme essence is similarly limited in scope. Anselm writes, "Finally, this utterance cannot be understood as anything other than the understanding of that spirit, by which he understands all things...Therefore, if that supremely simple nature is nothing other than what his understanding is, just as he is the same as what his wisdom is, then it must be that in the same way he is nothing other than what his utterance is. But since it is already evident that the supreme spirit is only one, and in every way individual, his utterance must be consubstantial with him, so that they are not two spirits, but one."[17] Here again, the conclusion of Anselm's argument suggests no more than an identity statement of the sort associated with divine simplicity.

As we saw in the last chapter, Anselm appeals to the human mind's self-understanding in order to help us conceptualize the divine self-utterance. By the time he introduces this analogy, he has already proved to his own satisfaction that the supreme spirit utters himself by a Word that is coeternal and consubstantial with himself. So his appeal to the human mind's self-understanding is not intended as part of his constructive case for the claim that God must be a Trinity. Instead, it is meant to illuminate the claims that he has already proven—to give us a way of conceptualizing them and thereby understanding them more deeply.[18] Anselm writes, "When the rational mind understands itself by thinking itself, it has within itself its own image, born from itself—in other words, its thought of itself, formed to its own likeness as by its own impress—although the mind can distinguish itself from this image of itself only by reason. This image of the mind is its word. And so who could deny that in this way, when the supreme wisdom understands himself by uttering himself, he begets a likeness of himself that is consubstantial with himself: that is, his Word?"[19]

In perfect self-understanding, the mind and its image are fully conformed to each other. That is a helpful illustration of the claim that the divine Word is consubstantial with the One who utters it. But Anselm also seems to indicate that in the case of the human mind, there is only a conceptual distinction between the mind that has perfect self-understanding and the image that is born from it: "the mind can distinguish itself from this image of itself only by reason" (*ipsa se a sui imagine non nisi ratione sola separare possit*). Since there needs to be more than a conceptual distinction between the divine mind and its perfect image, the Word, the analogy seems to pose a problem. We might think Anselm needs to identify the relevant point of disanalogy in order to justify the claim that the Father and the Word, unlike the mind and its self-understanding, are more than conceptually distinct.

It is not surprising, however, that Anselm saw no need to identify the relevant disanalogy between human and divine self-understanding. The analogy was meant only to illuminate, not to prove, the Word's consubstantiality with the Father. If the analogy illuminates the oneness but casts a shadow on the twoness, that is no objection either to the analogy or to Anselm's constructive Trinitarian project as a whole. Just as the oneness of the divine utterer and his Word is established by independent argument, without help from the analogy, so also is their twoness established by independent argument, without hindrance from the analogy.

The Word Was with God

Anselm makes his case for the distinctiveness of the Word gradually—indeed, almost casually—in the course of discussing the issues concerning the relationship between the Word and creation that we treated in the preceding chapter. We will not follow Anselm's circuitous route, but instead present two connected arguments that represent the cumulative case for the distinctiveness of the Word as it emerges over the course of *Monologion* 33–39. We can call these *the argument from the nonidentity of discernibles* and *the irreflexive relations argument.*

The argument from the nonidentity of discernibles goes like this:

(1) If what is true of *x* is not true of *y, x* and *y* are not identical.

Now as we have learned from *De incarnatione Verbi,* one has to be careful in interpreting the consequent. Identity and difference are not all-or-nothing, since we are working in terms of relative identity rather than classical identity. So "*x* and *y* are not identical" does not mean that *x* and *y* are in every respect distinct, or that there is no count noun *N* such that *x* and *y* are the same *N*. It means simply that there is some respect in which *x* and *y* are not the same, some sortal under which they do not both fall.

(2) The Father is an utterer and not a word.[20]
(3) The Word is a word and not an utterer.
Therefore, (4) the Father is not identical with the Word.

This conclusion does not of course mean that there is *no* respect in which the Father and the Word are the same—in other words, that there is no *N* such that one can truly say that the supreme spirit and the Word are one *N*. For Anselm has already established that the Father's "utterance must be consubstantial with him, so that they are not two spirits, but one" spirit.[21] Instead, (4) is making a weaker claim; it means that there is *some* respect in which the supreme spirit and his Word are two, not one.[22]

The argument from the nonidentity of discernibles is at best implicit in the *Monologion.* By contrast, Anselm states his second argument for the distinctiveness of the Word, the irreflexive relations argument, fairly explicitly. The relation *being the Word of* is irreflexive; a thing cannot bear it to itself. Thus, "the one of whom there is a Word cannot be his own Word, and the Word cannot be the one of whom he is the Word." The irreflexivity of this relation seems self-evident: "After all, the Word's being a Word or image implies a relationship to another: he must be the Word or image *of something.*" Moreover, the Word exists from the Father, but the Father does not exist from the Word. Consequently, "in virtue of the fact that the supreme spirit does not exist from the Word, whereas the Word exists from him, they admit an ineffable plurality."[23]

On the basis of these arguments, Anselm affirms both the oneness of God and the distinctness of the Father from the Son. Summarizing his earlier conclusions, he writes, "For behold, it is impossible for him who begets to be the same as him who is begotten, and for the parent to be the same as the offspring—so much so that it is necessary that the begetter be one thing and the begotten something else, and that the Father be one thing and the Son something else. Nevertheless, it is necessary that he who begets be the same as him who is begotten, and that the parent be the same as the offspring—so much so that it is impossible for the begetter to be other than what the begotten is, and for the Father to be other than what the Son is."[24] On this basis Anselm then develops the principles that figure so prominently in *De incarnatione Verbi*. Because the Father and Son are one in virtue of their common nature or essence but distinct in virtue of their relations, we cannot speak in the plural of anything that is common to them. The Father and the Son are one spirit,[25] one essence,[26] one God.[27] Nor can we predicate of one the relation that is the distinguishing feature of the other. The Father is not begotten or a Son or a Word; the Son is not a begetter or a Father. It is only when we speak of the Father and the Son together, as distinguished by their mutual relations, that we can speak in the plural. And even then we are stymied for lack of an appropriate noun. The Father and the Son are two: but two *what*? As Anselm says— carefully avoiding count nouns to make his point—"Now the Father and the Son are distinct in such a way that when I speak of both of them, I see that I have spoken of two; and yet what-the-Father-is and what-the-Son-is is so much one and the same that I do not understand what two I have spoken of."[28] Not until the next-to-last chapter of the *Monologion* does Anselm finally settle on 'person' or 'substance' as legitimate, "in the absence of a strictly appropriate word."[29]

Note that Anselm has established all the metaphysical apparatus that he thinks is necessary for a coherent statement of Trinitarian doctrine before there is any mention of the third person of the Trinity. From the sheerly metaphysical or logical point of view, the difficulties of Trinitarian doctrine come from any sort of plurality in unity; God's being three persons is no more challenging than his being two. Moreover, the names 'Father' and 'Son' are clearly relative terms and therefore hint at a key element of what Anselm takes to be the proper account of the Trinity: the claim that the distinguishing features of the persons are relations. The name 'Holy Spirit' is not clearly relative, and indeed does not clearly belong to the third person alone. As Anselm says, "the name 'Holy Spirit' is not foreign to the Father and the Son, since both of them are spirit and both are holy."[30] So there is good reason for Anselm to settle the metaphysical issues before he treats the Holy Spirit in the *Monologion*.

The Procession of the Holy Spirit

The first clear echo in the *Monologion* of an Augustinian psychological triad comes only after Anselm has established, to his own satisfaction, that the supreme essence "utters itself" and thereby gives birth to, or "begets," a Word, who is himself the supreme essence, a Son consubstantial with the Father who begot him. Having reached these conclusions, Anselm explains that since we can call the Word "understanding," we can aptly call the Father "memory":

> since it cannot be denied that the supreme spirit remembers himself, nothing could be more appropriate than to use 'memory' to signify the Father, just as we use 'Word' to signify the Son; for it seems that a word is born from the memory, as is more clearly seen in the case of our own mind. For since the human mind is not always thinking of itself, as it always remembers itself, it is clear that when it does think of itself, its word is born from its memory. Hence it is evident that if it were always thinking of itself, its word would always be born from its memory. For to think of a thing we remember is to utter it in our mind; the word of that thing, then, is that very thought, formed out of our memory after the likeness of the thing. And so from this we can quite clearly understand that his coeternal Word is born from the eternal memory of the supreme substance, who always utters himself, just as he always remembers himself. Therefore, just as the Word is fittingly understood to be an offspring, so the memory is quite appropriately called a parent.[31]

Notice that in keeping with Anselm's consistent method, the psychological analogy does not justify the constructive arguments; the constructive arguments justify the psychological analogy.

The sense that 'memory' has here is distinctively Augustinian. Augustine explains his usage in *De trinitate*: "Therefore, just as in things past we give the name 'memory' to that in virtue of which they can be recalled and remembered, so too in things present—and the mind is, with respect to itself, something present—it is quite legitimate to give the name 'memory' to that by which the mind is present (*praesto*) to itself in such a way that it can be understood by its own thought."[32] So we can think of memory as, roughly, the mind itself, regarded as a capacity for awareness. When the mind is turned upon itself, it actualizes that capacity and thereby produces perfect self-knowledge: a Word or understanding (*intelligentia*) consubstantial with the mind (*memoria*) that produced it.[33] Readers of *De trinitate* will know what comes next: the triad is memory, understanding, and *love*. But once again, for Anselm the psychological analogy cannot be a premise in the constructive arguments; the constructive arguments must justify the analogy. There needs to be a positive reason to introduce love, given that we already have memory and understanding, beyond simply the need to find structural isomorphism between the three-personal character of God and some aspect of human psychology.

Anselm finds this positive reason in a claim about teleology.[34] Perfect mind eternally turned upon itself, producing perfect self-knowledge, is teleologically stunted; it is not *for* anything. Anselm writes:

> But behold! As I consider with delight the distinguishing characteristics and the common features of the Father and the Son, I find nothing that brings me greater delight to consider than their affection of mutual love (*mutui amoris affectum*). For how absurd it would be to deny that the supreme spirit loves himself, just as he remembers and understands himself, when even the rational mind can be shown to love itself and him in virtue of the fact that it can remember and understand itself and him! After all, the memory and understanding of a thing is idle and completely useless (*otiosa et penitus inutilis*) unless the thing itself is either loved or repudiated as reason requires.[35]

This love, by which the self-contained and static divine wisdom is made dynamic and purposive, proceeds equally from memory and understanding—in other words, from the Father and the Son. It must also be equal to the Father and the Son, since "God's love of himself is as great as his memory and understanding of himself, and his memory and understanding of himself is as great as his essence."[36] Though this love proceeds from both the Father and the Son, it is one love, not two. For this love "does not proceed from that in virtue of which the Father and the Son are more than one, but from that in virtue of which they are one."[37] It is in virtue of their relations that the Father and the Son are more than one, and their love does not proceed from them in virtue of the relations *being a Father* and *being a Son* (or *begetting* and *being begotten*). Instead, their love proceeds from them in virtue of their nature, which is one.

John Milbank has suggested that Anselm's emphasis on the unity of the Holy Spirit, as proceeding from that in virtue of which the Father and the Son are one, undermines the distinctiveness of the three persons: "It is he who deepens the Augustinian tendency to subordinate the persons to the substance, and who makes the Spirit proceed *a Patre Filioque tamquam ab uno principio* [from the Father and the Son as from one principle]. For the *per Filium* [through the Son] is substituted the notion of a procession from Father and Son in virtue of their substantial identity as God. This move is on the road to modalism."[38] Modalism is the heresy that denies the threeness of God. On a modalist view, the three persons are merely distinct roles played by a single, undifferentiated God—different "modes" in which an utterly unitary God relates to creation at different times or for different purposes.

Now it is hard to see why the doctrine that the Holy Spirit proceeds from the Father *and* the Son in virtue of the divine nature rather than in virtue of their distinguishing relations would be any more likely to lead to modalism than the view that the Holy Spirit proceeds from the Father *through* the Son. Indeed, both views entail the denial of modalism, since both views make the three-personal character of God a matter of God's internal constitution (so to speak) rather than merely his external manifestation, as modalism would have it. Nevertheless, Milbank's challenge invites us to consider more carefully the ways in which Anselm attempts to do justice both to the threeness and to the oneness of God.

It is a venerable principle of Trinitarian theology, at least in the West, that the three persons always act together in everything God does outside himself. For example, it is the whole Trinity that creates, not merely the Father; it is the whole Trinity that redeems, not merely the Son; it is the whole Trinity that sanctifies, not merely the Spirit. Moreover, the three persons have a common divine nature, so whatever is true of one person is true of the others, except insofar as their distinguishing characteristics are concerned. Even so, it has been considered legitimate to associate certain activities or characteristics with one person in particular. This association is called "appropriation." By appropriation we speak of the Father as

Creator, the Son as Redeemer, and the Holy Spirit as Sanctifier, or of the Father as Power, the Son as Wisdom, and the Holy Spirit as Love.[39]

How exactly to understand and justify the practice of appropriation in light of the principle that the three persons equally possess all the divine attributes and act inseparably in all actions *ad extra* is a difficult theological question—one that fortunately we need not address. Our concern is with Anselm's use of appropriated names. For him, especially in the *Monologion,* the most salient names are memory, understanding (or Word), and love. Their use is underwritten by the constructive arguments that reveal God first as self-understanding mind—memory begetting understanding or uttering a Word—and then as dynamic and purposive—love proceeding from memory and understanding together. These arguments, and the psychological analogies that illuminate them, require that each person be understood in relation to the other two. A Word must be the Word *of* something; love is inseparable from the wisdom that love makes dynamic. There can accordingly be no question of a single, undifferentiated unity that is successively memory, understanding, and love. God is at once memory and understanding and love, and each of those can be what it is only in virtue of its relation to the others.

It is worth noting as well that Anselm sees no tension between the doctrine of appropriation and an orthodox understanding of perichoresis, the mutual indwelling of each person of the Trinity in the others. Though the appropriated names emphasize the distinctiveness of the persons and their mutual relations, Anselm uses those names as an essential part of an argument for the perichoretic unity of the Godhead: "For indeed the supreme spirit understands and loves his whole memory, remembers and loves his whole understanding, and remembers and understands his whole love. Now by 'memory' we mean the Father, by 'understanding' the Son, and by 'love' the Spirit-of-both. Therefore, the Father, the Son, and the Spirit-of-both embrace one another and exist in one another with such equality that none of them is found to exceed another or exist apart from another."[40] This is a particularly deft move, by which Anselm makes the threeness of God into an argument for divine unity while insisting that the unity is constituted by the dynamic interrelations of the three persons. No one who had taken even the first step on the road to modalism could have argued in this way.

Part III

THE ECONOMY OF REDEMPTION

MODALITY

Many of the philosophical and theological statements that Anselm finds most interesting include modal terms:

God *cannot* lie.

Necessarily, what God foreknows will come to pass.

Free choice is the *power* to preserve rectitude of will for its own sake.

Fallen human beings are *unable* to recover rectitude by their own efforts.

Anselm accordingly devotes considerable attention not only to the semantics of modal terms but also to the ontology of modality. He does so in a somewhat ad hoc way, telling us just enough at a given point to enable us to solve the particular problem that is capturing his attention. Yet underlying these scattered, episodic forays into modal theory is a consistent and fairly complete account of the nature of necessity and possibility, an account that has applications in several areas of Anselm's thought. We will begin by examining Anselm's conception of necessity. For Anselm, all necessity is a matter of causal compulsion. But Anselm uses terms like 'cause', 'bring about', and 'compel' so broadly that two quite disparate sorts of things can stand in the causal relation that constitutes necessity. Hence, he identifies two different kinds of necessity: antecedent necessity, which obtains when the causal relation holds between concrete individuals, and subsequent necessity, which obtains when the causal relation holds between concepts. After laying out Anselm's account of both kinds of necessity, we show how he uses his modal theory in his discussion of the problem of freedom and foreknowledge. We will then clarify some of the distinctive features of Anselm's modal theory by examining it in light of contemporary discussions of modality.

Necessity

Anselm's core notion of necessity is that of causal compulsion: "All necessity is either compulsion or constraint. These two necessities are related to each other as contraries, just like necessary and impossible. For whatever is compelled to be is constrained from not being, and what is compelled not to be is constrained from being, just as what is necessary to be is impossible not to be, and what is necessary not to be is impossible to be, and vice versa."[1] Since compulsion and constraint are interdefinable in this way, we can understand Anselm's notion of necessity entirely in terms of compulsion. What necessarily is, is what is compelled to be; what necessarily is not, is what is compelled not to be.

But precisely because Anselm understands necessity in terms of compulsion, it is crucially important not to misunderstand what Anselm means by "compulsion" in this context. 'Compulsion' translates the Latin *coactio,* which is rarely used in classical Latin (and never with the meaning "compulsion"), but which by the time of Aquinas had come to mean "compulsion" in the sense of coercion. In that later sense, an action that is a product of *coactio* is involuntary: "Compulsion in us excludes an act of will, since what we do under compulsion is the opposite of what we will."[2] *Coactio* is to the will what *violentia,* violence, is to any object; it involves moving something in a way contrary to its natural inclination.

That this is not Anselm's understanding of *coactio* is clear when we look at his use of the verb *cogere* (of which *coactio* is the noun form) in the passages in which necessity and possibility are at issue.[3] In such contexts Anselm uses *cogere* (compel) interchangeably with *facere* (make the case, bring about) and *efficere* (bring about). For example, in *De concordia* 1.3 Anselm contrasts one kind of necessity, "which brings it about [*facit*] that a thing exists," with another kind of necessity, "which does not compel [*cogit*] anything to be."[4] The contrast would be lost if *facit* and *cogit* did not mean at least roughly the same thing. The same point applies to *Cur Deus Homo* 2.17: "For the violence of their natural creation compels [*cogit*] the heavens to revolve, whereas no necessity brings it about [*facit*] that you speak."[5]

Not only does Anselm not differentiate between *cogere* and *facere*, but he also uses *facere* quite broadly. Consider the following excerpt from the Lambeth Fragments:

> If we say, "A human being is an animal," the human being is a cause of his being an animal and being called an animal. I do not mean that the human being is a cause that an animal exists, but that the human being is a cause that he himself is an animal and is called an animal. For by means of the name 'human being' the whole human being is signified and conceived, and animal is a part of that whole. And so in this case the part follows from the whole in this way, because where the whole is, the part must also be. So because the whole human being is conceived in the name 'human being', the whole human being is himself a cause that he is an animal and is called an animal, since the conception of the whole is a cause that the part is conceived in it and is said of it.[6]

In this passage Anselm extends the use of causal language—both "is a cause" (*causa est*) and "brings about" (*facit*)—to include what we would think of as relations of entailment. A human being is a cause that he is an animal. This is not to say that the human being produces an animal, but that the human being, just by being a human being, makes it the case both that he is an animal and that 'animal' is predicated of him. This sort of "making it the case" is in turn explained by an appeal to concepts—or, more properly, to the contents of concepts. That is, we can say that the human being brings it about that he is an animal because the concept *human being* includes the concept *animal*: "The conception of the whole is a cause that the part is conceived in it."

So the relation of causation or compulsion, which Anselm identifies with necessity, holds between two quite different sorts of things. It holds between particular concrete objects, as when fire causes water to grow hot; but it also holds between concepts, as when *human being* causes *animal*. When the relation holds between particular concrete objects, we have a case of what Anselm calls "antecedent necessity." When it holds between concepts, we have what Anselm calls "subsequent necessity." On Anselm's view, a great deal of philosophical confusion comes from the failure to keep these two sorts of necessity clearly distinct. Accordingly, we shall examine both in some detail.

Natures and Antecedent Necessity

We will begin with antecedent necessity, for two reasons. First, it is the kind of necessity that we would more naturally associate with causal compulsion. Second, it is the kind that is more obviously relevant to the questions about free action in which Anselm is particularly interested.

As we have already seen, Anselm does not think of *coactio* in the stronger sense that would come to predominate in later thought, namely, as moving something in opposition to its natural inclination. Yet there is an intelligible connection between Anselm's usage of the term and that later usage. Both have at their root the idea of an external agency. In the later usage, such external agency is contrasted with a thing's own internal principles of change. In Anselm's usage, however, the Creator who implanted those internal principles of change in the first place is also thought of as an external agency. In other words, Anselm can think of the natural activity of creatures as exhibiting compulsion, and thus antecedent necessity, because that natural activity is a consequence of the nature of those creatures—and that nature was received from God. This is the sort of thinking that underlies Anselm's startling-sounding claim that "the violence of their natural creation compels the heavens to revolve."[7] To say that the revolution of the heavens is a result of violence or compulsion is of course not to say that the heavens are inclined not to revolve and are somehow dragged along against their natural bent. The "violence" that compels them to revolve is a feature of their "natural creation." It is what they are inclined to do—what they must do, given how God made them. Yet because the nature that so inclines them was received from God, we can think of them as compelled to do what they do when acting in accordance with their nature.

Perhaps the best way to see that Anselm understands 'compulsion' in such a way as to apply to the natural action of creatures is to attend to the variety of terminology he uses in contrasting natural action with the kind of action characteristic of wills. In *De veritate* 5, natural action is said to be necessary, whereas voluntary or rational action is not:

> T: You see, there is rational action, such as giving to charity, and irrational action, such as the action of a fire that causes heat. So think about whether it would be appropriate for us to say that the fire is doing the truth.

S: If the fire received the power to heat from the one from whom it has being, then when it heats, it is doing what it ought to. So I don't see what is inappropriate about saying that the fire does the truth and acts correctly when it does what it ought to.

T: That's exactly how it seems to me. Hence we can note that there is one rectitude or truth in action that is necessary, and another that is not. When the fire heats, it does the truth and acts correctly out of necessity; but when human beings do good, it is not out of necessity that they do the truth and act correctly.[8]

This sort of natural or necessary action is also regularly contrasted with "spontaneous" action:

S: What then? Shall we say that a stone is just when it seeks to go from higher to lower, since it is doing what it ought to, in the same way that we say human beings are just when they do what they ought to?

T: We don't generally call something "just" on the basis of that sort of justice.

S: Then why is a human being any more just than a stone is, if both act justly?

T: Don't you think what the human being does differs in some way from what the stone does?

S: I know that the human being acts spontaneously, whereas the stone acts naturally and not spontaneously.

T: That is why the stone is not called just: something that does what it ought to is not just unless it wills what it does.[9]

A: Thereby, what will does spontaneously in a rational nature is also done naturally, through God's ordering, by creatures that are not capable of experiencing God.[10]

Thus far we have seen that natural action is antecedently necessary; action that is not natural in this way is said to be spontaneous. But Anselm also contrasts spontaneous action with action that is compelled, with action that is necessary, and even with both. For example, in *De casu diaboli* he contrasts spontaneity with compulsion:

T: And there is something else that I think shows convincingly that the angel did not in any way conceive his future sin beforehand.

> Certainly he would have conceived it as either compelled or spontaneous.[11]

Later in that same work he contrasts spontaneity with necessity:

> T: Then isn't the angel's perseverance more resplendently satisfactory when only one cause of that perseverance is seen in him, a cause that is both useful and honorable because it is spontaneous, than if at the same time another cause were to present itself, one that is useless and dishonorable because it is understood to be necessary?[12]

And we see that same contrast between spontaneity and necessity in *De libertate arbitrii*:

> T: It was through the power of sinning, and spontaneously, and through free choice, and not out of necessity that our nature, and that of the angels, first sinned.[13]

Just a few lines down, Anselm opposes spontaneity to both compulsion and necessity:

> T: And so [the apostate angel and the first human being] are justly reproached, since, having this freedom of choice, they sinned: not because any other thing compelled them, and not out of any necessity, but spontaneously.[14]

When these passages (and others like them[15]) are taken together, we can see that for Anselm the modal landscape as it relates to the causal powers of concrete particulars is divided into two main regions. In one region falls everything that is spontaneous. What falls in the other region is called, indifferently, "natural," "necessary," or "compelled." What is natural, necessary, or compelled is what is brought about by a thing whose activity is wholly determined by the nature God gave it. What is spontaneous is, as we shall see at much greater length when we come to discuss freedom, what has its ultimate causal origin in the agent.

Proper and Improper Ascriptions of Possibility and Necessity

The fundamental constituents of Anselm's theory of antecedent necessity are therefore particular concrete objects that possess and exercise causal powers. Accordingly, the truthmakers for all such modal judgments are concrete particulars and their powers, not abstract objects like possible worlds or states of affairs. For this reason, Anselm holds that any meaningful talk about possibility and necessity in this domain will be either expressed as, or reducible to, ascriptions of powers to particular individuals. As he realizes, such strictures seem to require a wholesale revision of the traditional and commonsensical equivalences and entailments. For example, according to the received wisdom among philosophers of both Anselm's day and ours, "x cannot exist" entails "Necessarily, x does not exist." But the entailment does not hold for Anselm. For the first statement properly means that x has no causal power to bring itself into existence, and the second means that there is some causal power that prevents x from existing. Now the first statement holds of anything that does not yet exist, so if the first statement entailed the second, nothing that does not now exist could ever be brought into existence. Clearly, then, on a proper Anselmian understanding of modal statements, "x cannot exist" does not entail "Necessarily, x does not exist."

Anselm explicitly poses such difficulties for himself in the Lambeth Fragments. In one fragment, the student says:

> I will say again: that which in no way exists has no power. Accordingly, it does not have a power for being or for not being. And so it follows that what does not exist both cannot exist and cannot not exist. And what goes along with the negative statement, "what does not exist cannot exist," is that what does not exist is such that (a) it is not possible for it to exist, (b) it is impossible for it to exist, and (c) it is necessary that it does not exist. Or, if we take the other negation, "what does not exist cannot not exist," we find that what does not exist is such that (a) it is not possible for it not to exist, (b) it is impossible for it not to exist, and (c) it is necessary that it exists. Therefore, because that which in no way exists cannot exist, it is impossible for it to exist and necessary that it does not exist; but from the fact that it cannot not exist, it follows that it is impossible for it not to exist and necessary that it exists...
>
> But all these conclusions are perfectly ridiculous. For "impossible to exist" and "impossible not to exist," or "necessary to exist" and "necessary not to exist," or "power and inability" either to exist or not to exist, never hold [of the same thing] at the same time. So, given that these things are impossible, that from which they follow is also impossible: namely, that "what in no way exists both cannot exist and cannot not exist, since it has no power." But I cannot at all figure out how this is false.[16]

Unfortunately, we receive no answer to this challenge in the Fragments. Anselm says that his reply requires a good bit of preliminary material, and the fragment breaks off before he returns to the student's original questions. But it is clear from other passages what Anselm would have said. In *De casu diaboli* 12, for example, Anselm and his student are considering whether, before it wills, an angel has the power to will. The student quite sensibly invokes the principle that actuality implies possibility: "given that he wills, he can will; therefore, it must be the case that before he willed, he could will." Anselm, however, rejects that principle:

T: Do you think that what is nothing has nothing at all and therefore has no power, and that without power there is absolutely nothing it can do or be?

S: I can't deny that.

T: I believe that before the world was made, it was nothing.

S: You're right.

T: Therefore, before it existed, there was nothing it could do or be.

S: That follows.

T: Therefore, before it existed, it could not exist.

S: And I say that if it could not exist, it was impossible for it ever to exist.

T: That was both possible and impossible before it existed. It was impossible for the world, since the world did not have the power to exist; but it was possible for God, who had the power to make the world. Therefore, the world exists because before it was made, God could make it, not because before it existed the world itself could exist.

The student concedes the force of Anselm's argument, but he complains that "our normal way of speaking is against you." Anselm replies,

T: That's not surprising. Many things are said improperly in ordinary speech; but when it is incumbent upon us to search out the heart of the truth, we must remove the misleading impropriety to the greatest extent possible and as much as the subject-matter demands. Because of such impropriety in speaking we quite often apply the word 'can' to a thing, not because it can do anything, but because something else can; and we apply the word 'cannot' to a thing that can do something, simply because some other thing cannot. For example, if I say "a book can be written by me," the book certainly can't do anything, but I can write the book. And when we say "This man cannot be defeated by that man," we understand this to mean simply, "That man cannot defeat this man."[17]

Anselm's discussion in *De casu diaboli* shows that the problems raised in the Fragments are merely apparent. Despite the student's claim in that passage, such apparent contradictories as "possible to exist" and "impossible to exist" do in fact hold of the same thing at the same time. Before the world was made, it could be characterized as possible, because God had the power to make the world, or impossible, because the world did not itself have any power. Admittedly, Anselm does not develop his modal semantics to such an extent that we can show formally exactly how the student's arguments in the Fragments go wrong. The student began by observing that what does not exist has no power; it follows, therefore, both that (1) what does not exist cannot exist (because it has no power for existing) and that (2) what does not exist cannot not exist (because it has no power for not existing). The further absurdities and contradictions that the student derives are all inferred from (1) and (2). It may be that Anselm would regard both (1) and (2) as improper, on the grounds that there can be no proper ascriptions of possibility or impossibility to nonexistent things; after all, only what exists can have or lack a power. But Anselm might allow both (1) and (2) as proper and then show that, properly understood, they do not lead to any absurd or contradictory conclusions. The argument of *De casu diaboli* 12 suggests that Anselm would take the second approach, but he does not feel the need to work out the details.

Anselm is particularly concerned with modal language that is applied to God. In *Cur Deus Homo* 2.17, Anselm writes, "it is improper to say that God cannot do something or that God does something by necessity." God is all-powerful, and he is subject to no constraint. Yet when we say that God cannot do something, we seem to imply a lack of power in God; and when we say that God does something by necessity, we seem to imply some constraint on God. Such expressions are improper, for the lack of power or the constraint to which they point exists not in God but in creatures: "When we say that something necessarily exists or does not exist in God, it is not understood that there is any compelling or constraining necessity in him, but it is signified that in all other things there is a necessity constraining them from acting and compelling them not to act contrary to what is said of God. For when we say that it is necessary that God always speaks the truth, and that it is necessary that he never lies, what is being said is nothing other than that there is in God such steadfastness of preserving the truth that it is necessary that no thing can make it the case that he does not speak the truth or that he lies."[18] In a philosophically perspicuous language, therefore, we would not say "God cannot lie" but rather "Nothing can bring it about that God lies."

Subsequent Necessity

As we have said, antecedent necessity holds when there is a relation of causal compulsion between particular concrete objects. We now turn to subsequent necessity, which holds when there is a relation of causal compulsion between concepts. It appears that Anselm recognizes three kinds of conceptual relation that involve this sort of compulsion: identity, inclusion, and entailment. In his explicit discussions of subsequent necessity, all of Anselm's examples are cases of identity; but we will see that the same sort of necessity is operative where the relation is that of inclusion or entailment.

There are only two passages in which Anselm explicitly identifies subsequent necessity and contrasts it with antecedent necessity: *Cur Deus Homo* 2.17 and *De concordia* 1.2–3. In both places Anselm provides statements like the following as examples of subsequent necessity:

A white board is white.

Every human being is a human being.

Tomorrow's future rebellion is future.

Everything that was, was.[19]

In what way are these necessary? Here is how Anselm explains the necessity of "A white board is white": "a board is not always necessarily white, since before it was made white, it was able not to be made white; and once it is white, it can be made not white. And yet a white board is necessarily always white, since neither before it is white nor after it is white can it be made to be both white and not white at the same time."[20] In other words, although "This board is white" is not necessary—I need not have painted it white, and I could paint it red this very moment—"This white board is white" is necessary, since nothing can make it the case that a *white* board is *not white*. Anselm gives a similar account of the necessity of the past, present, and future:

> Similarly, a thing is not by necessity present, since before it was present, it was possible that it not become present; and once it is present, it can become not present. Yet it is necessary that a present thing always be present, since neither before it is present nor once it is present can it be both present and not present at the same time. In the same way, a given thing (say, an action) is not by necessity something future, since before it is, things can turn out in such a way that it is not going to be in the future. Yet it is necessary that what will be in the future will be in the future, since what is future cannot at the same time not be future. And similar things are true about what is past. A given thing is not by necessity past, since before it was, it could have turned out not to be; but it is necessary that what is past is always past, since what is past cannot at the same time not be past.[21]

In these paradigmatic instances of subsequent necessity, the relation that holds between the subject-concept and the predicate-concept is simply identity. That is, these statements are all of the form "x is x"—a fact that Anselm notes explicitly: "And so when a future thing is said to be future, what is said is necessary, since a future thing is never not future—as happens whenever we say the same of the same. For when we say 'Every human being is a human being' or 'If he is a human being, he is a human being' or 'Every white thing is white' or 'If it is white, it is white,' what is said is necessary, because something cannot be and not be at the same time."[22]

So Anselm clearly regards all such statements as instances of the law of noncontradiction, and the necessity that attaches to them is the garden-variety logical necessity that in contemporary philosophy is represented in such formulas as these:

Necessarily, if p, then p.

Necessarily, if x is F, x is F.

Not all cases of subsequent necessity fit this model, however. In the example already cited from the Lambeth Fragments, the relation is not identity but *inclusion:* "For by means of the name 'human being' the whole human being is signified and conceived, and animal is a part of that whole.

And so in this case the part follows from the whole in this way, because where the whole is, the part must also be."[23] And elsewhere Anselm speaks of necessity where there is neither identity nor inclusion but *entailment*. For example, in *De casu diaboli* 3, Anselm says, "burning is not the cause of fire; rather, fire is the cause of burning. And yet if we posit that there is burning, this always causes it to follow that there is fire. For if there is burning, there must be fire."[24] In fact, *De casu diaboli* 2 and 3 are particularly helpful to our case that Anselm uses causal language indifferently for both physical necessity and logical entailment. He distinguishes the two by saying that in the case of physical necessity, a thing is the cause of another thing; whereas in the case of logical entailment, the positing of the thing is the cause that another thing follows. And in *De processione Spiritus Sancti* Anselm frequently speaks of necessity in cases of logical entailment. In the first chapter, for example, he says, "From the unity of the Godhead it follows by necessity that the Father is eternal, the Son is eternal, and the Holy Spirit is eternal."[25] Similar expressions occur in chapters 11 and 14. In each case, Anselm's formulation, *(ex) necessitate sequitur,* simply looks like the verbal equivalent of his usual name for subsequent necessity, *necessitas sequens.*

Cases of logical entailment are therefore clearly cases of subsequent necessity. And since identity and inclusion are simply special cases of entailment, we can say that all cases of subsequent necessity are cases of logical entailment. Subsequent necessity is therefore logical necessity. Simo Knuuttila, the leading contemporary writer on medieval theories of modality, has disputed the interpretation of Anselm's subsequent necessity as a kind of logical necessity: "Some authors have characterized Anselm's distinction between antecedent and subsequent necessity as a distinction between physical and logical necessity. This is misleading, since no kind of logical necessity is dealt with in the statements [quoted from *Cur Deus Homo* 2.17]. They are clearly based on the traditional doctrine of the necessity of the present and its application to past and future things, which are also immutable in so far as they are past or future facts."[26] But Knuuttila merely asserts that the quoted passages do not involve logical necessity; he offers no argument. As we have seen, an examination of the full range of texts strongly supports reading subsequent necessity as logical necessity. Moreover, it is hard to see what "Every human being is a human being" has to do with the necessity of the present. Its necessity does not depend on any temporal characterization of the things signified by the subject term, but rather on their essence.

The Problem of Foreknowledge

We have noted that for Anselm the modal landscape as it relates to the causal powers of concrete particulars is divided into two main regions. One region contains everything that is free or spontaneous, the other everything that is necessary. There can be no overlap between these two regions, since necessity and spontaneity are incompatible. But this way of dividing up the modal territory seems to imperil the possibility of human free action. For Anselm acknowledges that, necessarily, whatever God foreknows will come to pass. God's foreknowledge is all-encompassing; nothing has happened, is happening, or will happen without God's fore-knowing it. If whatever God foreknows is necessary, and God foreknows absolutely everything, it seems to follow that absolutely everything is necessary. In other words, it seems that if God has complete and infallible foreknowledge, the region of spontaneity is completely empty.

Anselm poses the familiar problem of divine foreknowledge and freedom in precisely these terms, as a question about whether the necessity associated with God's foreknowledge eliminates the spontaneity that is supposed to be characteristic of free actions: "Certainly God's fore-knowledge seems to be incompatible with free choice, since it is necessary that the things God foreknows are going to be, whereas things done by free choice do not result from any necessity."[27] Anselm first gives what will seem to most readers like a quick, preliminary solution to the prob-lem, although there is no sign that he is dissatisfied with it as far as it goes, or that he regards it as merely provisional. We can call this the "fore-knowledge guarantees spontaneity" response.[28] If indeed something in the future will be done spontaneously—that is, not out of antecedent necessity—then God foreknows that it will be done spontaneously, since God's foreknowledge is complete. And since God's foreknowledge is not only complete but also infallible, it follows that God's foreknowledge of a future spontaneous action guarantees that the future action will indeed take place spontaneously and not necessarily. As Anselm puts it, "it is necessary that some future thing is going to be without necessity."[29]

Therefore, the necessity associated with divine foreknowledge does not threaten, but in fact guarantees, the spontaneity associated with free action.

Although Anselm is perfectly happy with this solution to the problem, he recognizes that it will not be immediately convincing to everyone, especially those who don't understand the distinction between antecedent and subsequent necessity. Since it is precisely the incompatibility of necessity and spontaneity that generates the problem in the first place, there is an air of paradox about the assertion that it is necessary that some future actions will be done spontaneously. Anselm dissolves this paradox by applying the distinction between antecedent and subsequent necessity. As we have already seen, antecedent necessity, "which precedes a thing and brings it about,"[30] is incompatible with spontaneity. When we say that it is necessary that some future action will be done spontaneously, we do not mean that some future actions are antecedently necessary, though spontaneous—that would indeed be a blatant contradiction. Rather, we mean that some future actions are *subsequently* necessary, though spontaneous. Subsequent necessity is in no way incompatible with spontaneity, since it is causally inert, Anselm says, and so the paradox is dissolved.[31]

In fact, Anselm is quite clear that the necessity of "If God foreknows *x*, *x* will occur" is exactly the same as the admittedly trivial necessity of "If *x* will be in the future, *x* will be in the future": "Moreover, if one carefully considers the meaning of the word, merely by saying that something is foreknown, one is saying that it is going to be. For only what is going to be is foreknown, since only what is true can be known. So when I say that if God foreknows something, it is necessary that it is going to be, that is the same as saying that if it will be, it will be by necessity. And that necessity does not compel or constrain anything to be or not to be."[32] In case any doubt lingers, Anselm proposes one further way of getting us to see that the necessity attaching to what is foreknown is compatible with free action. Since we believe that God's foreknowledge is complete, he argues, we must suppose that God foreknows his own future actions. And it would simply be crazy to think that all of God's actions are antecedently necessary. So clearly what is foreknown need not be antecedently necessary.

Anselm does not present these considerations as an additional argument for the compatibility of foreknowledge and freedom, but simply as another way for someone who is only half-convinced to recognize their compatibility more clearly. One might say that Anselm is inviting a change of perspective rather than offering an argument in the strict sense. Yet his strategy seems to be a version of the argumentative technique that has come to be known as the "G. E. Moore shift." This expression originated with William Rowe, who used it to describe a feature of a Moorean argument against skepticism. As Rowe lays out the strategy, he imagines the skeptic arguing roughly as follows:

(1) If such-and-such philosophical doctrines are true, then I don't know that I am sitting here reading.
(2) Such-and-such philosophical doctrines are true.
Therefore, (3) I don't know that I am sitting here reading.

Moore's reply is to accept the first premise, but complete the argument rather differently:

(1) If such-and-such philosophical doctrines are true, then I don't know that I am sitting here reading.
(2') But clearly I do know that I am sitting here reading.
Therefore, (3') such-and-such philosophical doctrines are not true.

What legitimates this kind of move, Moore thinks, is that we have incomparably stronger support for (2') than we do for any arguments in favor of the skepticism-inducing philosophical doctrines referred to in (1). For that reason, it is much more reasonable to complete the argument in Moore's way rather than in the skeptics' way.

Similarly, we can think of Anselm as arguing as follows:

(1) If what is foreknown is antecedently necessary, none of God's actions is free.
(2) God acts freely.
Therefore, (3) what is foreknown is not antecedently necessary.

He recognizes that some people might be tempted to complete the argument like this instead:

(2') What is foreknown is antecedently necessary.
Therefore, (3') none of God's actions is free.

But Anselm is convinced that the case for (2) is incomparably stronger than the case for (2'). The whole of Anselm's natural theology supports (2), whereas (2') has no basis but confusion.

To get a clearer understanding of the character of Anselm's solution to the problem of divine foreknowledge and human free action, it is helpful to compare his treatment of the issue with more recent accounts.

Contemporary philosophers survey the modal landscape in a fashion radically different from Anselm. Rather than thinking about the causal powers of individual agents, contemporary philosophers think in terms of possible worlds, typically understood as maximal consistent states of affairs or maximal consistent propositions. The crucial question about freedom is whether, at the time of action, the agent has causal access to distinct possible worlds that have the same history up to that time but differ with respect to what the agent does at that time. The theological incompatibilist—someone who holds that divine foreknowledge is incompatible with free will—argues as follows:

> For any human action that God foreknows, God's belief about that action is temporally prior to the action itself; it is temporally prior even to the very existence of the agent. Any belief that God had before the agent was even born is not subject to change by that agent. But then, given that God is never mistaken, there is always only one available alternative open to human agents. In other words, it is never the case that an agent has causal access to distinct possible worlds that have the same history up to the time of the action but differ with respect to the action itself. So any action that a human agent performs that God foreknows is not free.

Someone might attempt to evade the force of this argument by appeal to the atemporal character of divine foreknowledge: God's foreknowledge, one might argue, is not part of the history of the world up to the time of the action, because that foreknowledge is outside time altogether. But theological incompatibilists can finesse this issue in a number of ways. For example, they can appeal to prophecy: God can reveal what he foreknows to a prophet, and the prophet's belief about the future will certainly be part of the history of the world. So as to avoid getting bogged down in elaborating these technical fixes, we will simply stipulate that the theological incompatibilist can always do something to smuggle the content of God's foreknowledge (improperly so called) into the history of the possible world. The relevant question will still be whether, at the time an agent performs an action, the agent has causal access to a possible world in which he or she chooses otherwise; and the theological incompatibilist will still have a strong case for saying no.

Anselm is unmoved by this argument. For him, the question is not one of alternative possibilities (as we will explain more fully in the next chapter) but whether the relevant action is agent-initiated: that is, whether the causal chain that culminates in the action has its ultimate origin within the agent. Here it is important to recall that Anselm thinks of necessity and possibility in terms of the powers of agents. If an action is initiated by an agent, it is spontaneous. If an action is ultimately determined by some external power, it's necessary. For Anselm, it is clear that God's foreknowledge is not an external power that determines actions; it is not part of an action's causal history and does not impose antecedent necessity.[33] So there is not even a prima facie reason to think that foreknown actions are necessary in the way that is incompatible with their being free.

Anselm's view thus involves rejecting the incompatibilist's view that an agent cannot now change the content of God's belief. For Anselm, human agents, when acting freely, have power over the past (or, if we insist that God's beliefs are not strictly speaking in the past, then human beings have power over whatever surrogate for God's beliefs the incompatibilist uses in making the argument sketched above). In other words, human beings have the power to perform actions such that if they were to perform them, God would have had different beliefs about what would be true in the future.[34] Anselm sees this consequence and does not find it troubling. He even goes so far as to say that everything contained in God's *predestination* is subject to change until it actually occurs.[35]

The distinctive character of Anselm's theory stands out even more sharply when we explore further a point raised earlier. As we have noted, contemporary accounts of free will and modality tend to proceed with reference to alternative possibilities. If the agent has causal access to possible worlds that have identical histories up to the time of the action but differ with respect to the action itself, that action is free; if not, then not. Anselm's view of free will cannot be easily translated into this picture. For Anselm, if there are alternative possibilities, sometimes the action is free, sometimes not. And again, if there are *not* alternative possibilities, sometimes the action is free, sometimes not. Alternative possibilities are not relevant; what is relevant is whether the action is spontaneously initiated by the agent in the precise sense of 'spontaneous' that we discussed earlier.

For these reasons, Anselm's solution to the problem of freedom and foreknowledge is difficult to express in contemporary vocabulary. He has to agree that, given God's foreknowledge, there is *in some sense* only one action genuinely open to any agent: the action that God foreknows. Thus there is (in contemporary language) only one possible world causally accessible to the agent. For the contemporary incompatibilist, this fact alone is enough to support the conclusion that the act is not free. But Anselm requires that we ask *why* there is only one alternative available. The answer is, obviously, because of God's foreknowledge. But such foreknowledge is causally inert. What Anselm points out is that there are multiple worlds whose pasts are *causally* identical. And that is what is relevant. If we insist on thinking in terms of possible worlds, Anselm will have us look, not at possible worlds *per se* but rather at *causally* possible worlds. Imagine an agent *S* at a time *t,* and examine all the possible worlds that are causally identical up to *t.* If in every such world, *S* performs the same action at *t,* then *S*'s action at *t* is not spontaneous; if not, then *S*'s action (or inaction) at *t* is spontaneous in each of those worlds. In fact, Anselm's response is similar to what contemporary theological compatibilists who are causal incompatibilists say in response to the divine foreknowledge problem.

Anselm would reject the contemporary picture, because what he takes to be the obvious solution to the problem is much less clear. However, contemporary philosophers will likely reject Anselm's picture, because his theory relies on a much less well developed and less systematic theory of modality, one that seems to evade formalization. His theory remains at the intuitive level. Anselm is no enemy of formal theories, but he has no place for them when they obscure what he takes to be central philosophical points. What Anselm takes to be central is not what contemporary philosophers take to be central, however, and so we come to an impasse.

We have shown that Anselm's solution to the problem of foreknowledge can be expressed in terms of contemporary modal theory, but in such a formulation it loses a good deal of its intuitive force and explanatory power. Whether one judges it worthwhile to give up our contemporary modal language in order to secure that explanatory power will ultimately depend on how one assesses the benefits of Anselm's complete picture of the world, and especially of his theory of human free action, which we consider in the next chapter.

Was Anselm a Cartesian about Modality?

In *Cur Deus Homo,* one of his central discussions of modality, Anselm makes what might appear to be a startling claim. "All necessity and impossibility," he says, "are subject to God's will."[36] Many interpreters have seized on this statement as proof that Anselm holds a Cartesian view of modality, according to which the divine will determines not merely what is true and false but what is necessary and impossible.[37] On this view the laws of logic are subject to the divine will in just the same way as the laws of nature. Since (as we have said) many questions of concern to Anselm involve modal claims, it is not surprising that interpreters have derived a wide range of striking conclusions from Anselm's purported Cartesianism. But Anselm is not a Cartesian about modality; the quoted passage does not mean what these interpreters have thought. A careful look at the context in which Anselm makes this statement will make it very clear that a Cartesian view of modality had barely so much as crossed Anselm's mind.

The issue that Anselm is addressing in *Cur Deus Homo* is whether the death of Christ was a matter of necessity. Boso has said that it follows from Anselm's arguments up to that point that Christ "was unable not to die and that it was necessary that he die."[38] Anselm develops his response over the course of a long chapter: Book 2, chapter 17. He first argues that it is improper to say that God cannot do something or that God does something of necessity. Taken strictly or properly, any expression of the form "It is impossible for God to do *X*" is false, because it implies that some external power constrains God from doing *X;* and any expression of the form "God does *X* of necessity" is false, because it implies that some external power compels God to do something. But in all such cases the compulsion or constraint is not in God; it is in other things: "when we say that something is necessarily the case or necessarily not the case in God, we do not mean that there is any compelling or constraining necessity in him; rather, we signify that in all other things there is a necessity constraining them from acting, and compelling them not to act, contrary to what is said of God."[39]

But it is not enough to say that all statements ascribing necessity or impossibility to God are improper. We need to understand how we can construe those statements in such a way that they express a truth. Anselm addresses this specifically with regard to the issue that prompted his discussion in the first place: the apparent inability of Christ to avoid death. Because Christ, "through unity of person, is the very same as God," we cannot properly ascribe necessity or impossibility to him. So when we say that Christ was unable not to die, or that he died of necessity, this does not mean that he lacked some power—the power to preserve his own life. Instead, Anselm says, such a statement "signifies the immutability of his will, by which he spontaneously made himself a human being so that, persevering in that same will, he might die, and the fact that no thing was able to change that will."[40]

This, then, is the sense in which an impossibility or a necessity was subject to the divine will. Anselm simply means that the necessity of Christ's death was a consequence of God's own free choice, not a result of any compulsion or constraint deriving from an external source. And there is nothing special about this particular case. *Any* impossibility or necessity in God will be a consequence of God's own will. For example, "if God immutably resolves to do something, then although what he resolves to do, before it is done, cannot fail to come about in the future, nonetheless there is not in God any necessity of doing it or impossibility of not doing it, since only God's will is at work in him."[41] In every example Anselm gives, the necessity or impossibility in question is not just any necessity or impossibility, as the Cartesian reading would have it, but the (improperly ascribed) necessity or impossibility of *God's* doing something. And that necessity or impossibility derives from God's will in the sense that the immutability and steadfastness of God's will guarantees he will act in a certain way, not in the sense that his will is responsible for the truth values of the laws of logic.

So there is not a hint of Cartesianism in this passage; indeed, a Cartesian theory of modality would be irrelevant to the point Anselm is trying to make here. And we find that in contexts in which a Cartesian theory would be relevant, it seldom occurs to Anselm to suggest such a thing. It is not up to God's will that whatever he foreknows must be the case, or that a board cannot be both white and nonwhite at the same time. The one passage in Anselm's writings that considers something like the Cartesian view emphatically rejects it. In *Cur Deus Homo* 1.12 it is Boso, not Anselm, who argues that because "God's will is so free that he is subject to no law," he ought to be able to forgive sin without punishment or recompense. Anselm rejects Boso's inference: "given that it is not fitting for God to do anything unjustly or inordinately, it does not pertain to his freedom ... or will that he should leave unpunished a sinner who does not repay God what he took from him."[42] God can will only what is fitting, and what is fitting is not determined by any free choice of the divine will. So it is not even up to God's will—at least, not in the Cartesian sense—that God cannot forgive sin without either punishment or recompense. This "inability" does depend on God's will in the sense Anselm has explained: it is a consequence of God's perfect and immutable will that he always provides a remedy for the disorder of sin. But God's will does not bring about the truth of the proposition "God cannot forgive sin without punishment or recompense."

Someone who rejects the Cartesian view of modality would say that the laws of logic cannot be otherwise than they in fact are, that even God cannot make $2 + 2 = 5$ or make contradictions true. Anselm would prefer to avoid such language, since taken strictly it implies external compulsion or constraint acting on God. But he accepts the claims that a contemporary philosopher would mean to convey by making these statements. If required to use our preferred modal vocabulary rather than his, Anselm would agree that the laws of logic are necessary. To say that God can make contradictions true would be to derogate from the perfection of God, who is supreme wisdom and exercises supreme reason in everything he does.

FREEDOM

According to Anselm's official definition, freedom of choice[1] is "the power to preserve rectitude of will for the sake of that rectitude itself."[2] From the point of view of contemporary metaphysics, this is one of the most unhelpful definitions imaginable. Does such freedom require alternative possibilities, for example? Is it compatible with causal determination? Is the exercise of such freedom a necessary and sufficient condition for moral responsibility? The definition sheds no light on these questions.

And so we need to move on from Anselm's definition to Anselm's *account* of freedom. Here, though, we encounter the opposite problem. Where Anselm's definition seems not to answer these questions at all, Anselm's account seems to answer them sometimes with a yes and sometimes with a no. Consider the question about alternative possibilities. In *De libertate arbitrii,* Anselm seems clearly to deny that freedom involves alternative possibilities. God, the good angels, and the blessed dead cannot do otherwise than preserve rectitude, but they are still free—freer, in fact, than those who are capable of abandoning rectitude.[3] On the other hand, in *De casu diaboli* Anselm seems to require alternative possibilities for freedom. For if an angel is to be just, Anselm says, he must have both the power to will rectitude and the power to will happiness. If only one power were given him, he would be able to will nothing but rectitude or nothing but happiness, as the case might be; being unable to will otherwise, his will would be neither just nor unjust. Now justice, according to *De veritate* 12, is rectitude of will preserved for its own sake. So an angel without alternative possibilities cannot have rectitude of will, and *a fortiori* cannot *preserve* rectitude of will; hence, an angel without alternative possibilities is not free.

In this chapter we offer a reconstruction of Anselm's account of freedom in which this apparent inconsistency and others like it are resolved. As it turns out, the linchpin of this account is the definition of freedom. Anselm argues that the power to preserve rectitude of will for its own sake requires the power to initiate an action of which the agent is the ultimate cause, but it does not always require that alternative possibilities be available to the agent. So although freedom is incompatible with external causal determination, agents can, under certain circumstances, act freely even though they cannot act otherwise than they do.

The Definition of Freedom and Its
Roots in *De Veritate*

Freedom of choice is the power to preserve rectitude of will for its own sake. In order to understand what Anselm means to convey by this definition, we must first turn to his dialogue *De veritate,* where the notion of rectitude is fleshed out in detail. Anselm's student asks for a definition of truth. Anselm replies that, so far as he remembers, he has never run across a definition of truth. Perhaps, he suggests, they can look for such a definition by examining the various things in which truth is said to exist.[4] Thus they consider what truth is in statements, opinions, the will, actions, the senses, and finally the essences of things.

In each case, Anselm argues that truth is a matter of *rectitude:* that is, something's being or doing what it was meant to be or do.[5] Thus the "rectitude of will" that figures in Anselm's definition of freedom is equivalent to truth in the will. The devil, Anselm points out, is said to have abandoned the truth. He asks the student to explain what is meant by 'truth' in that case. The student replies, "Nothing other than rectitude. For if, so long as he willed what he ought—i.e., that for which he was given a will—he was in rectitude and in truth, and if when he willed what he ought not, he abandoned rectitude and truth, truth in that case cannot be anything other than rectitude, since both truth and rectitude in his will were precisely his willing what he ought."[6] Just as the truth or rectitude of a statement is the statement's doing what statements were made to do, the truth or rectitude of a will is the will's doing what wills were made to do.[7]

In chapter 12 of *De veritate* Anselm links rectitude of will with both justice and moral evaluation. Justice in its most general sense is equivalent to rectitude in its most general sense; whatever is as it ought to be has both rectitude and justice. The student objects, "Shall we say that a stone is just when it seeks to go from higher to lower, since it is doing what it ought to, in the same way that we say human beings are just when they do what they ought to?"[8] After some further discussion, Anselm notes, "I see you are looking for a definition of the justice that deserves praise, just as its opposite, injustice, deserves reproach."[9] The justice that is the proper subject of moral evaluation is ultimately defined as "rectitude of will preserved for its own sake."[10] Such rectitude requires that someone perceive the rectitude of his action and will it for the sake of its rectitude. Anselm takes the second requirement to exclude both compulsion and "being bribed by some extraneous reward."[11]

Since freedom of choice is by definition the power to preserve rectitude of will for its own sake, the arguments of *De veritate* imply that freedom is also the capacity for justice and the capacity for moral praiseworthiness. So before turning to *De libertate arbitrii* it is useful to note how these equivalences must constrain Anselm's account of freedom, if he is to be consistent. It is both necessary and sufficient for justice, and thus for praiseworthiness, that an agent will what is right, knowing it to be right, because he knows it is right. That an agent wills what is right because he knows it is right entails that he is neither compelled nor bribed to perform the act. Freedom, then, must be neither more nor less than the power to perform acts of that sort.

Arriving at the Definition of Freedom in *De Libertate Arbitrii*

Much that is initially puzzling about Anselm's account of freedom in *De libertate arbitrii* becomes clear when one reads it—as Anselm meant for us to read it—with *De veritate* in mind.[12] The first question is whether free choice is, or at any rate involves, the power to sin. Anselm has two arguments to show that it does not. The first is as follows: God and the good angels have free choice; God and the good angels do not have the power to sin; therefore, free choice neither is nor entails the power to sin. But couldn't someone object (the student asks) that the divine and angelic free choice differs from human free choice? Irrelevant, says Anselm: however much their free choice might differ from ours, the definition of free choice is the same, and must apply equally to both.[13]

The second argument relies on the premise that a will is freer when it is incapable of sin than when it can be turned to sin. So if the power to sin is added to a will, its freedom is diminished; and if it is removed, the will's freedom is increased. Obviously, though, if something's absence increases freedom and its presence diminishes freedom, that thing cannot itself be identical with freedom, or even a part of freedom.

Both these arguments are valid, but each relies on a controversial premise. In the first argument, Anselm assumes that God and the good angels have free choice, and the student raises no objection. But why should this assumption be so obvious? Since Anselm has yet to define free choice, we can only assume at this stage that free choice is something good, the lack of which would be a defect. But when we come to chapter 3 and the definition of free choice, it will turn out (as we have already seen) that no one can be just or praiseworthy without possessing free choice.[14] It would be impious (*nefas*) to deny that God and the good angels are just and praiseworthy, so it would also be impious to deny that they have free choice. So the controversial premise will turn out, in retrospect, to have been justified.

The disputable premise in the second argument is that a will is freer when it cannot sin. Here the student raises the obvious objection: "I don't see why a will isn't freer when it is capable of both [sinning and not sinning]." Anselm replies, "Do you not see that someone who has what is fitting and expedient in such a way that he cannot lose it is freer than someone who has it in such a way that he can lose it and be seduced (*adduci*) into what is unfitting and inexpedient?" The student, perhaps unlike the contemporary reader, replies, "I don't think anyone would doubt that."[15] Anselm's interrogative argument for the questionable premise is philosophically revealing. Unlike most contemporary philosophers, he thinks of freedom as teleological. Freedom is a power *for* something, and that power is greater just insofar as it is less apt to fall short of its purpose. Specifically, beings have freedom for the purpose of having what is fitting and expedient; the more tenuous a being's grip on what is fitting and expedient, the less free that being is.

But if free choice is the power to hold on to what is fitting and expedient, and it is not the power to sin, does it make any sense to say that the first human beings and the rebel angels fell through free choice? The student formulates the problem acutely:

> I cannot rebut your arguments at all, but it strikes me quite forcefully that in the beginning both the angelic nature and our own had the power to sin—if they had not had it, they would not have sinned. But if both human beings and angels sinned through this power, which is extraneous in this way to free choice, how can we say they sinned through free choice? And if they did not sin through free choice, it seems they sinned out of necessity. After all, they sinned either spontaneously or out of necessity. And if they sinned spontaneously, how was it not through free choice? So if it was not through free choice, they apparently sinned out of necessity.[16]

Anselm insists that human beings and angels did in fact fall through free choice:

> It was through the power of sinning, and spontaneously, and through free choice, and not out of necessity that our nature, and that of the angels, first sinned ... The fallen angel and the first human being sinned through free choice, since they sinned through their own choice, which was so free that it could not be compelled to sin by any other nature ... They sinned through their choice, which was free; but they did not sin through that in virtue of which it was free, that is, through the power by which it was able not to sin and not to be a slave to sin. Instead, they sinned through that power they had for sinning.[17]

Though embedded in what looks like an unpromising bit of proto-Scholastic distinction-mongering, Anselm's point is both subtle and plausible. The argument clearly relies on taking *arbitrium* (choice) to be the power to perform what we shall call a "self-initiated" action: an action that has its ultimate causal origin in the agent, and not in any external agency; an action that is spontaneous in the sense explained in the previous chapter. So when Anselm says that the *arbitrium* of angels and human beings before the fall was *liberum* (free), he is saying that they had a power for self-initiated action that was not compelled by any external agency. To say that they sinned *per liberum arbitrium* (through free choice), as Anselm does twice, is simply to say that they sinned by an exercise of that power. But when he denies that they sinned "through that in virtue of which [their choice] was free," he is emphasizing the teleological nature of freedom; full-fledged freedom of choice is the power for self-initiated action *for some good end,* and the angels did not sin through *that.* Finally, the *potestas peccandi* (power for sinning) through which the angels did fall is simply *liberum arbitrium* unsupplemented by freedom from sin.

Thus Anselm can consistently maintain that the primal sins were committed *per liberum arbitrium* and yet deny that the power to sin is a part of *liberum arbitrium.* If *liberum arbitrium* is simply the power for self-initiated action not compelled by any external agency, then *liberum arbitrium* neither entails nor includes a power to sin. For *liberum arbitrium* can be perfected by something else, as yet unspecified, that renders it incapable of sinning. So the power for self-initiated action as such does not entail or include the power to sin, even though that same power, if unsupplemented by freedom from sin, is itself the power to sin.

Anselm's Definition and Its Immediate Implications

Anselm's arguments in the first two chapters of *De libertate arbitrii* pull in two different directions. As we saw in the last section, chapter 1 hints at a normative definition: free choice is the power to hold on to what is fitting and expedient. Chapter 2, however, suggests a purely descriptive definition: free choice is a power for self-initiated action not compelled by any external agency. In chapter 3 Anselm opts unmistakably for a normative definition: "free choice is the power to preserve rectitude of will for its own sake." Anything that satisfies the normative definition will also satisfy the descriptive definition, since (as Anselm made clear in *De veritate*) the power to preserve rectitude of will for its own sake requires that an agent be able to initiate his own action on the basis of what he believes to be right, and act for the sake of that rightness, without being either compelled or bribed.[18] In keeping with this line of thought, Anselm goes so far as to say that freedom of choice *consists in* having the rational ability to know what is right in conjunction with the will by which one can choose it.[19]

But the entailment does not work the other way around: a power could satisfy the descriptive definition without satisfying the normative definition. Suppose there were a capacity for self-initiated action that is at least sometimes free from external compulsion but was not bestowed upon its possessor for any particular purpose or designed with any particular end in mind. (The free will described by many contemporary libertarians is just such a capacity.) That capacity satisfies the descriptive definition but not the normative definition, and Anselm would not call that capacity *liberum arbitrium*. He would, in fact, find the very idea of such a capacity bizarre. For to suppose that such a capacity exists is to suppose that God created a power for which he had no particular purpose in mind—hardly the act of a rational creator. Accordingly, Anselm shows no interest in what we might call "garden-variety" freedom: freedom with respect to whether one has pasta or pizza for dinner, say. It is, indeed, difficult to imagine Anselm's God granting us a power for self-initiated menu choices, at least under that description. If we in fact have garden-variety freedom, it will be only as a by-product of the morally significant freedom that interests Anselm. Accordingly, in *De concordia* 1.6 Anselm explicitly acknowledges that his discussion in *De veritate* and *De libertate arbitrii* concerns only the freedom necessary for salvation.[20]

Even so, we should not overestimate the importance of Anselm's opting for the normative definition. Although Anselm proceeds, in the remainder of the work, to derive a number of important conclusions using the normative definition, most of the arguments would work equally well if he used the descriptive definition. For example, he argues in chapter 5 that no temptation forces anyone to sin unwillingly:

> S: But how is the choice of the human will free in virtue of this power [i.e., free choice], given that quite often a person whose will is right abandons that rectitude unwillingly because he is compelled by temptation?
>
> T: No one abandons rectitude otherwise than by willing to do so. Therefore, if by 'unwilling' you mean someone who does not will, no one abandons rectitude unwillingly. For a man can be tied up unwillingly, since he does not will to be tied up; he can be tortured unwillingly, since he does not will to be tortured; but he cannot will unwillingly, since he cannot will if he does not will to will. For everyone who wills, wills his own act of willing.[21]

This argument assumes only that actions performed through free choice are uncompelled and self-initiated; Anselm need not appeal to the purpose for which human beings were given free choice. Even the argument that nothing is freer than an upright will (chapter 9) depends explicitly only on the descriptive definition, although the influence of the normative definition is evident in Anselm's specifying the *upright* will.

Freedom and Alternative Possibilities
in *De Casu Diaboli*

The account of freedom that is in place by the end of *De libertate arbitrii* seems to entail the falsity of what contemporary philosophers call the Principle of Alternative Possibilities (PAP), which states (roughly) that an agent performs an action freely only if it was causally possible for that agent to act otherwise than he did. Suppose, for example, that God commands the angel Gabriel to announce the Incarnation to Mary. Because this command is given after the good angels have been confirmed in goodness, it is not possible for Gabriel to do otherwise than obey God.[22] And yet Gabriel announces the Incarnation freely, because in doing so he is preserving rectitude for its own sake: he knows that it is right for him to obey God, he wills that obedience for the sake of its rightness, and he initiates his own act of obedience. It follows that PAP is false; Gabriel acts freely even though he cannot do otherwise.

When we turn to *De casu diaboli,* however, hints of some version of PAP are everywhere. We hope to show that these new arguments extend the account of freedom in *De veritate* and *De libertate arbitrii* but are fundamentally consistent with it. For although free action does not always involve alternative possibilities, it often does; and the reasons why it does arise straightforwardly out of the account of freedom we have already sketched.

The first argument suggesting PAP comes in chapter 5:

T: Do you think the good angels were likewise able to sin before the evil angels fell?

S: I think so, but I would like to understand this through reason.

T: You know for certain that if they were not able to sin, they preserved justice out of necessity and not in virtue of their power. Therefore, they did not merit grace from God for remaining steadfast when others fell any more than they did for preserving their rationality, which they could not lose. Nor, if you consider the matter rightly, could they properly be called just.[23]

It is tempting to see in this argument a straightforward endorsement of PAP. After all, Anselm seems to argue that if the angels who refrained from sinning had not been able to do otherwise—in other words, had not been able to sin—they would not have been free. They could no more have abandoned rectitude than they could have abandoned rationality, and it would be as incongruous to praise them for remaining upright as to praise them for remaining rational.

Despite the initial appearances, however, there is no appeal to PAP in this argument. Rather, the appeal is to the requirement that a free action have its origin in the agent rather than in some external cause. Consider the situation Anselm is envisioning. The good and bad angels were in exactly the same position before the fall: they were equal in nature, in knowledge, and in power. We know that the bad angels fell by exercising their power for self-initiated action: "It was through the power of sinning, and spontaneously, and through free choice, and not out of necessity that... the angelic nature first sinned."[24] If it was not likewise possible for the good angels to fall, that could only have been because some external agency was preventing it; for there was, *ex hypothesi,* nothing internal to their own power of agency to account for that impossibility. And in that case, the good angels did not preserve justice through their own power, but out of necessity.

So Anselm is not assuming PAP. Alternative possibilities come into the picture as a kind of by-product. They are not constitutive of freedom; they just happen to be available, given the requirement that free action have its origin within the agent, in conjunction with the relevant circumstances of the particular case. No doubt alternative possibilities will often be available to agents exercising free choice, but nothing in Anselm's account requires that they always be.

A second passage that seems to involve reliance on PAP is the extended argument of chapters 12 through 14, an argument we summarized at the beginning of this chapter. Anselm argues that an angel must have both a will for justice and a will for happiness if he is to be morally responsible. If he had only one of these wills, he would be able to will nothing but rectitude or nothing but happiness, as the case might be. He would therefore will rectitude or happiness necessarily. Necessity, as we have already seen, is incompatible with freedom. Therefore, an angel without the alternative possibilities provided by the two wills would not be free.

What we shall now show, however, is that this quick summary misrepresents Anselm's argument. Once again, it is not PAP but the requirement of self-initiated action that generates the two-will theory—as we can show by offering a more careful recapitulation of Anselm's argument in chapters 12 through 14. In chapter 12 Anselm argues that in order for an angel to will anything at all, God must give the angel its initial will. For if some agent moves himself to will, he first wills to move himself. Hence, whatever does not yet will anything at all cannot move itself to will. "So it must be the case," Anselm concludes, "that the angel who has already been made apt to have a will but nonetheless does not will anything cannot have his first will from himself."[25] His first will must therefore come from God.

Anselm's use of 'will' (*voluntas*) in this argument and those that are to follow can cause confusion. He explains in *De concordia* that *voluntas* can mean three different things.[26] *Voluntas* can mean the "tool" that the soul uses in order to will (i.e., the faculty or power of will), the disposition of that tool to respond to certain features of what is proposed to it for willing (i.e., desire or motivation or dispositional volition), and the act in which that tool is employed (i.e., occurrent volition). Let us call these respectively "faculty," "disposition," and "volition." When God gives the angel its initial will, is he giving the faculty, the disposition, or the volition? Anselm does of course hold that God gives the faculty of willing, just as he gives every other creaturely power, but the faculty is clearly not what is at issue in the argument just stated. That argument seems to require that we interpret *voluntas* as volition: if there is no volition at all, there cannot be the volition by which the soul wills to employ its faculty of will in a particular way. But the argument would then be obviously mistaken. Surely if the angel has a disposition to will in a certain way, then so long as he has the faculty of willing (and there are no impediments to the use of that faculty), there is no reason why the angel cannot generate his first volition for himself. So what Anselm must mean is that unless God gives the initial *disposition*, the angel cannot have any *volition*. He thinks this because he understands volition as goal-directed: "we do not will anything at all unless there is a reason why we will it." The faculty of will does not engage in pseudo-Sartrean reasonless choice. So if the faculty of will is to be operative at all, God must give the angel at least one motivational disposition in response to which it can engage in actual volition.[27]

In chapter 13 Anselm asks us to suppose that God first gives this angel the will (i.e., the disposition) for happiness, and no other will. Can he move himself to will (i.e., have a volition for) something besides happiness? The teacher and student agree that he cannot:

> S: I can't see how someone who wills nothing besides happiness would move himself to will anything other than happiness. After all, if he wills to move himself to will something else, he wills something else.

> T: Therefore, just as he could not will anything at all on his own when no will had yet been given, so also he cannot have any other willing from himself if he has received only the will for happiness.[28]

For similar reasons, the angel will also be unable to refrain from willing happiness. So unless God gives him some other will, he will will happiness; and the higher his estimation of happiness, the more intensely he will will it. If he cannot have the best things, he will will lesser things—even "the base and impure things that please irrational animals."[29] But no matter what he wills, his will is "the work and gift of God, just as his life and his power of sensation are, and there is neither justice nor injustice in it."[30]

In chapter 14 we are assured that the same conclusions follow if the angel is given only the will for rectitude: he will not be able to help willing rectitude, and his will will be neither just nor unjust. Now he cannot be happy unless he wills to be happy, and he cannot deserve happiness unless he also wills to be just. So if he is to be deservedly happy, he must have both the will for happiness and the will for justice.

At each stage of this argument, Anselm appeals not to anything like PAP, but to the requirement that the agent be able to initiate his own action. The angel can have no volition at all until God gives him a disposition to will in a certain way. If God gives him only the will for happiness, every volition of happiness will have its ultimate origin in God and not in the angel himself; his will is "the work and gift of God."[31] He will not have the power to originate any willing that he did not receive from God; by the descriptive definition of free choice, then, the angel is not free. Similarly, if God gives him only the will for rectitude, every willing of rectitude will have its ultimate origin in God; the angel will again lack the power to initiate any willing that is genuinely his own, and so he will lack free choice. Only if God gives him both wills does he have that power.[32] For then he has the power to will happiness as tempered by justice, and to will happiness without regard for justice. Neither of those volitions is received from God; both have their ultimate origin in the angel himself.

Even though, as we have argued, the arguments of *De casu diaboli* 5 and 12–14 are not driven by PAP, they do show an important connection between freedom as Anselm understands it and the possession of alternative possibilities. Freedom requires that an agent be able to initiate an action that is genuinely his own. Now creatures receive their wills—that is, both their faculty of will and their characteristic dispositions—from God. So if God makes a creature's will in such a way that alternative possibilities are never open to him, every volition of that creature will be "the work and gift of God." The creature will not be able to initiate any action that is genuinely his own, and so he will not be free. It is, therefore, not freedom as such, but *creaturely* freedom, that requires alternative possibilities.[33] And even then, alternative possibilities are required only once, as the case of the good angels makes clear. The good angels had alternative possibilities with respect to their primal choice. Afterward God made them unable to sin; in this way he closed off any alternative possibilities, but he did not destroy their freedom.

Thus, Anselm's arguments up to this point in *De casu diaboli* merely elaborate on the account of freedom that has been in place since the early chapters of *De libertate arbitrii*. But his discussion of the primeval angelic freedom takes an unexpected turn in chapter 23 of *De casu diaboli* when he argues that the angels would not have been free if they had known for sure that they would be punished if they fell. He seems to say that their fear of punishment would have been so great that they would inevitably have willed to retain rectitude, not for the sake of rectitude, but for the sake of avoiding punishment. The just action—willing rectitude for its own sake—would not have been open to them, and by the normative definition of free choice, they would not have been free.

The problem is that the good angels do have this knowledge now, thanks to the example of their fallen brethren. Anselm seems to have a dilemma on his hands. If the good angels are now just, they are preserving rectitude for its own sake, and not merely for the sake of evading punishment. But then there is no reason to think they could not have preserved rectitude for its own sake even if they had known then what they know now. On the other hand, if they are indeed merely trying to evade punishment, they are not just, not praiseworthy, and indeed not free, because their new knowledge is such as to preclude their preserving rectitude for its own sake.

The dilemma owes some of its force to a misreading. It seems natural to read chapter 25 as arguing that the only reason the good angels can no longer sin is that they are aware of the consequences of sin. But in fact the argument is more subtle. Anselm is interested in maintaining that *even if* their knowledge of the consequences of sin is the sole reason the good angels can no longer sin, their not sinning is still to their credit. At the end of the chapter Anselm clearly denies that their inability to sin derives from this knowledge. The teacher remarks, "But in fact you know—because it became evident earlier—that the reason [the good angel] cannot sin is that by the merit of his perseverance he has attained such happiness that he no longer sees what more he could will."[34]

The back-reference is to chapter 6. Chapters 4 and 5 had shown that the fallen angels sinned by willing some additional good that God had not yet given them, and that the good angels could have willed "that something extra" (*illud plus*) but chose instead to retain the just will that God had given them.[35] Anselm then argued in chapter 6 that as a reward for their perseverance in justice, God gave the good angels whatever it was they had passed up in the interests of justice. Thanks to this divine gift, there is nothing for them to will that they do not already enjoy.[36] Now, at the end of chapter 25, Anselm makes sure we do not think he has abandoned this explanation of the sinlessness of the angels.

So Anselm does not after all argue that their knowledge of the consequences of sin renders the good angels unable to sin. But some version of the dilemma we posed above still threatens his account. If the good angels after the fall can have this knowledge and yet retain free choice and choose rectitude for its own sake, why would this knowledge subvert the free choice of angels before the fall? In particular, Anselm thinks that if an angel had this knowledge before the fall, it would necessitate his action.[37] And yet after the fall, it does not necessitate his action. Why would the very same knowledge undermine freedom before the fall but be consistent with freedom afterward?

Remember that the angels have only two wills: the will for justice and the will for happiness. Now imagine two angels, Gabriel and Michael, who are preserving the will for justice. Both know all the consequences of sin, but Gabriel knows this before the fall, whereas Michael first learns this after the fall, by noting the fate of the rebel angels. It follows straightforwardly from the account of freedom given thus far that neither angel can abandon his will for rectitude, but that Gabriel is necessitated, whereas Michael is free. Consider Gabriel first. He can only will happiness and rectitude—and that is God's doing, not his. He cannot sin by willing happiness, because he knows full well he will not get happiness by sinning. He cannot sin by willing rectitude, obviously. So his not sinning is entirely God's doing, not his own. He is necessitated by God's creative acts not to sin.

Michael's case is different. He, too, cannot sin by willing happiness, but that is because he already has all the happiness he can imagine as a reward for his decision to preserve rectitude. His retaining the will to rectitude, though, is his own doing, not God's. As we saw earlier, God gave him the will for rectitude and the will for happiness, but the decision to subject his will for happiness to the demands of rectitude was the angel's own doing. Moreover, he retained rectitude for its own sake. So as long as he sustains that will, he is acting on his own, not out of any necessity. True, he has no temptation to abandon rectitude, but he retains rectitude on his own steam, so to speak, and not because of God's action.

Of course, according to our contemporary way of using modal terms, it seems obviously false to say that Michael is not acting out of necessity. Surely if it is not possible in those circumstances for Michael to sin, it is necessary in those circumstances that he not sin; Michael, it seems, is as much necessitated as Gabriel. Obviously Anselm has something different in mind when he speaks of "necessity," and since he has been regularly opposing necessity to freedom since the first chapter of De libertate arbitrii, we need to be clear about what exactly Anselm takes this freedom-threatening necessity to be. As we noted in the previous chapter, the sort of compulsion that involves antecedent necessity is incompatible with freedom. Thus, when Anselm sets out in De concordia to reconcile free choice with divine foreknowledge, he explains that the kind of necessity that attaches to what God foreknows is not the freedom-threatening kind that "brings it about that a thing exists" (facit rem esse) or that "compels" (cogit) something to come about.[38] Even what God predestines does not happen "by that necessity which precedes a thing and brings it about" (ea necessitate quae praecedit rem et facit),[39] for such causal necessity would destroy freedom.

But the examples of Gabriel and Michael show that Anselm's most fundamental notion is this: an action is necessary just in case its ultimate explanation is external to the agent. Causal determination makes actions necessary because it prevents an agent from initiating any action that is genuinely her own; Gabriel's knowledge of the consequences of sin makes his action necessary for exactly the same reason. No self-initiated action can ever properly be described as necessary, even if it is not possible for the agent to act otherwise in the relevant circumstances.

Anselm's most striking affirmation of this understanding of necessity in action comes in a discussion of God's action in *Cur Deus Homo*. After Anselm has argued that in some sense God *had* to provide a remedy for sin, Boso objects: "If this is so, it seems that God is, as it were, compelled to secure human salvation by the necessity of avoiding impropriety (*indecentia*)... And how will we ascribe our salvation to God's grace if he saves us by necessity?" Anselm replies, "God does nothing by necessity, since he is in no way compelled to do or prevented from doing anything; and when we say that God does something as if from the necessity of avoiding dishonorableness—which he certainly does not fear—it is rather to be understood that he does this out of the necessity of preserving his honorableness. And this necessity is nothing other than the immutability of his honorableness, which he has from himself and not from another and which is therefore improperly called necessity."[40] Because God's immutable uprightness is "from himself and not from another," every upright divine action will be self-initiated; and for that very reason Anselm insists that no such action should be called "necessary." Divine aseity in fact guarantees that *every* action God performs is self-initiated. So all of God's actions are free, even if he never has alternative possibilities available to him.

Reconciling the Two Definitions

It is instructive to see how Anselm's two definitions can be combined into a single general definition without doing violence to Anselm's theory. Recall that Anselm offers a normative and a purely descriptive definition of free choice. According to the descriptive definition, free choice is a power for self-initiated action. According to the normative definition, free choice is the power to preserve rectitude of the will for its own sake; the normative definition entails that a free agent (1) is able to initiate his own action on the basis of what he believes to be right, and (2) is able to act for the sake of that rightness. How can a normative and nonnormative definition be reconciled?

The answer lies in Anselm's motivation for discussing free choice in the first place. Anselm's primary interest in free choice is how it bears on human responsibility for sin and the need for grace. Any other exercise of free choice is ancillary. Thus, his normative definition (his preferred one) explicitly builds in features central to his moral and theological concerns. Anselm believes that some goals are better than others. Specifically, he believes that while justice and happiness are our two most important goals, justice is incomparably more important than happiness. So, if God gave us free will for a purpose, and that purpose is to achieve the best goal through our own free action, then we are acting most freely when we seek to achieve that goal. Further, Anselm seems to think that following this goal is the most rational thing to do as well.

As we shall now show, however, one can abandon Anselm's own story about our ultimate goal without doing much damage to his account of free will. That is, one can accept a teleological account of free choice and reject the notion that the best goal is justice or that one acts most freely when one acts for the sake of justice. If there is no objective hierarchy of goals, an agent will not be more or less free depending on which goals he has chosen, but he will be more or less free depending on how well he satisfies Anselm's descriptive definition of free will.

For if we look at exactly how his descriptive definition (the one Anselm uses when he is not concerned with ultimate goals) would function in actual examples, we will see where we build back in those teleological concerns—properly modified—without realizing it. The normative aspects of Anselm's second definition concern justice. As Anselm says in *De veritate* 12, "Every will not only wills something but also wills for the sake of something. Just as we must examine what it wills, so also we need to understand why it wills."[41] (Notice that this is presented as a general claim, without any reference to rectitude.) And again, "Every will has a what and a why. For we do not will anything at all unless there is a reason why we will it."[42] So we do no violence to Anselm's descriptive definition if we reformulate it as follows: free choice is the power to attain one's goals for the sake of those goals. This definition, which we shall call the enriched descriptive definition,[43] requires that an agent (1) be able to initiate his own action on the basis of what he believes will achieve his goal, and (2) be able to act for the sake of that goal.

The relationship between the enriched descriptive definition and Anselm's preferred normative definition becomes clear in one of Anselm's own illustrative examples in *De concordia:*

> Let us now offer an example involving an upright (that is, a just) will, freedom of choice, and choice itself; and let us consider how the upright will is tempted to abandon rectitude and how it maintains that rectitude by its free choice. Suppose someone is resolved to hold fast to the truth because he understands that it is right to love truth. This person surely already has an upright will and rectitude of will. Another person approaches and threatens to kill the first person unless he tells a lie. We see that it is his decision (*in eius arbitrio*) whether to abandon life in favor of rectitude of will, or rectitude of will in favor of life. This decision ... is free, because the reason by which he understands rectitude teaches that this rectitude ought always to be preserved out of love for rectitude itself, and that whatever is offered to him as a pretext for abandoning rectitude is to be held in contempt, and that it is up to the will to reject or choose as the understanding of reason dictates ... Hence, a decision of the will to abandon this same rectitude is also free and not forced by any necessity, even though it is assailed by the dreadfulness of death.
>
> For although it is necessary that he give up either life or rectitude, nevertheless no necessity determines which he preserves or abandons. Surely in this case the will alone determines which of the two he retains; nor does the force of necessity cause anything, where only the will's choice is operative. And if there is no necessity for someone to abandon the rectitude of will that he has, it is clear that the power to preserve it— i.e., freedom—is not absent. ... In virtue of this freedom both the choice (*arbitrium*) and the will of a rational nature are said to be free.[44]

Anselm's arguments in connection with this example obliterate any distinction between the descriptive and the normative definitions of freedom. Anselm begins by appealing to the key elements of the enriched descriptive definition: the person in the example is free because he knows what goal he ought to aim at and has the power to choose accordingly, and no external force is operating so as to necessitate his choice. But since the goal that he ought to aim at is precisely the preservation of rectitude for its own sake, he satisfies the normative definition. What it is for him to satisfy the enriched descriptive definition is precisely the same as what it is for him to satisfy the normative definition; the two definitions, in other words, are equivalent.

The Usefulness of Anselm's Account
of Freedom

So in the end, the enriched descriptive definition of free choice turns out to be equivalent to the normative definition that Anselm prefers, given the assumption that reason shows us that rectitude of will is the paramount goal to be respected in all action. If we decline to join Anselm in that assumption, the two definitions will not be equivalent; but for that very reason, the reformulated descriptive definition becomes a useful and interesting option for contemporary debates about freedom. We can accept it without committing ourselves to any substantive moral claims, and we disentangle the discussion of freedom from the specifically theological concerns that motivated Anselm.[45]

The greatest advantage of the enriched descriptive definition of free choice is that it satisfies both incompatibilist and compatibilist intuitions about free will. Certainly Anselm takes very seriously the incompatibilist intuition that a free action cannot be causally determined. The reasons that a person has for performing a free action do not determine that he take that action. But while it is true that many free choices are entirely unpredictable, not all of them are. So although Anselm's account satisfies the intuitions of incompatibilists, there are other conditions in which it also satisfies some of the intuitions of compatibilists. What is central to Anselm's definition is that the action be self-initiated and consciously chosen, not that it be one of at least two possibilities. This aspect of Anselm's theory partially satisfies the intuition that as long as a person knows what he is doing and why he is doing it, his action is free, regardless of whether the agent had some other option available to him. Of course, while the compatibilist does not care whether the action is self-initiated, but only that the agent is doing what he wants, the Anselmian insists that the action be self-initiated. But the Anselmian can explain why there is a pull to say that a person who has chosen a particular course of action and is happy with it has sometimes chosen freely, despite a lack of alternatives.

Moreover, in light of arguments purporting to show that which goals and desires one finds oneself with are largely (or even fully) beyond one's control, the enriched descriptive definition helps explain how it is fair (or just) to hold a person responsible for acting on whatever goals he finds himself with. According to Anselm, how one comes by one's goals is irrelevant. He in fact *presupposes* that the motivations of rational creatures derive entirely from outside themselves, although he of course thinks the external source is God rather than heredity, upbringing, or what have you. What is relevant to freedom is not the source of the motivations, but whether, when there is a decision to be made among competing goals, it is the agent himself who is doing the deciding. If the agent initiates the choice and is not determined by circumstances outside his control, then his choice is free and it is permissible to hold him responsible for his action. In the unfortunate, and indeed unlikely, instance in which a person has absolutely no good motives from which to choose, he is still responsible for the action that results from the motive he chose to follow.

What one might see as the greatest strength of Anselm's account—its ability to capture both incompatibilist and compatibilist intuitions—might also be its greatest weakness. We can imagine that a compatibilist would find it incredible that although one's decision to act on a desire might determine one's action, nothing determines which desire one opts to follow. It is true that the Anselmian can give an explanation of her free choice; the explanation will always be in terms of which desire she placed above the others, and she might have reasons for preferring that desire to another. But ultimately, when asked whether that preference determined her action, the Anselmian will say no. In fact, given the same situation, she might conceivably do something else—if there were more than one motive at work in her decision. And that, a compatibilist might well say, is hardly an appealing picture of the relation between free choice and reasons for action.

In reply, an Anselmian should note that the key point behind some brands of compatibilism (especially the freedom-entails-determinism varieties) is that unless my character determines or at least explains my actions, they are not really actions at all, but merely spasms. But the only plausible motivation for that view is the belief that free actions are those that the agent herself originates, those for which the agent is somehow responsible. And Anselm's theory secures that belief. The compatibilist simply refuses to face the problem that worries Anselm in chapters 12 to 14 of *De casu diaboli*. If both the good and the bad angels are to have been free and responsible for their primal choice, it cannot be the case that anything about their desires, powers, or knowledge determined their choice either to preserve or to abandon rectitude. For their desires, powers, and knowledge were all owed to God. Therefore, if their desires, powers, and knowledge had determined their choice, that choice, too, would have been owed to God. God, not the angels, would have been responsible for it; the bad angels would not have been blameworthy, nor the good angels praiseworthy. Indeed, there would have been no distinction between good and bad, because they all had the same desires, powers, and knowledge, and would therefore have made the same "choice." The angels would not have been agents at all, but inert conduits for divine agency.

In contemporary terms, Anselm's arguments amount to this claim: there is no responsible agency unless there is an element of radical voluntarism somewhere. If a certain set of cognitive and affective states, all of which have their origin outside the agent, guarantees a certain choice, the agent is not really an agent at all, but an inert conduit for external causes. An exercise of agency, therefore, is possible only where what the agent has "received" from outside does not guarantee one choice over another. We use the expression "received" in order to bring out the fact that Anselm is replying to the question from 1 Corinthians 4:7 that is quoted at the beginning of *De casu diaboli:* "What do you have that you have not received?" Though Saint Paul's question expects the answer "Nothing," Anselm in effect argues that there is something creatures have that is not received from God: namely, the content of their free choices.[46] For if creatures received from God every exercise of their wills, their actions would be necessary, not spontaneous. Anselm, perhaps unlike such later thinkers as Thomas Aquinas, is not at all zealous about guarding the prerogatives of God as First Cause. On the contrary, Anselm insists that a creature's exercise of free choice is in no way determined by God.

On the other hand, an incompatibilist might flatly refuse to be convinced that anyone in a situation in which he cannot do otherwise is free. It might not move him at all to hear that one is self-consciously, and without compulsion, acting on a choice that one initiated oneself. It might not move the incompatibilist to know that there is nothing else the person is inclined to do and that a million alternatives would not change his action at all. Some people are just resistant to Frankfurt-style stories.

Once again, however, the Anselmian has a promising line of response. The whole motivation behind incompatibilism, after all, is the intuition that if external causal factors are responsible for our actions, then they are not really *our* actions in the sense that matters, and we are not (either causally or morally) responsible for them. The idea of alternative possibilities comes in only because people wrongly conclude that if there is no causal determination there is nothing to narrow down the options to one.

Anselm's theory saves the real motivation for incompatibilism by pre-serving the agent's own causal and moral responsibility for his actions, but without making the unwarranted leap to alternative possibilities, since it shows that there can be cases in which it is the agent's own action-initiating power (will and reason, operating together) and not any external causal power that narrows the options down to one.

MORALITY

It is significant that Anselm's first venture into moral theory is occasioned by a problem in natural theology. Anselm never comes to ethics as an independent area of inquiry, but always in the context of some larger philosophical or theological problem. As a result, it is easy to take his pronouncements on moral matters as mere scattered remarks without much theoretical significance, as *obiter dicta* casually tossed off in the course of answering the questions in metaphysics or theology that really interested him. Yet although it is true that Anselm does not elaborate a detailed ethical theory or focus on morality in any sustained way, there is nonetheless a clearly discernible theoretical framework for his views on morality. This framework remains consistent throughout his career, from the *Monologion* through *Cur Deus Homo* to his last letters.

There is a second reason that it was especially fitting for Anselm to begin his reflections on moral theory in the context of natural theology. For Anselm, what we ought to do is a function of our place in the world, a place established for us by God, who created us for his own purposes and assigned us our role in the order of the universe. In order to be just, human beings must discern their place in the divine ordering and choose to maintain it. Our intellects can fail in that discernment and our wills in that choice, although such failure is generally occasioned by practical impediments rather than theoretical error (one reason, perhaps, that Anselm sees little need to spend time on ethical theory for its own sake). When we do fail, we introduce disorder into God's universe, and some recompense must be made in order to reestablish the perfect beauty of justice. The ultimate recompense, of course, is made on our behalf by a being both divine and human. So theology leads to ethics and ethics brings us back to theology.

Our Purpose

As he comes to the close of his Trinitarian speculations in the *Monologion*, Anselm observes that "the mystery of so sublime a thing seems to me to transcend every power of human understanding."[1] Yet the very incomprehensibility of God threatens to undo all his arguments:

> For if [our conclusion about the Trinity] has been explained by a sound argument, in what way is he ineffable? Or, if he is ineffable, how can our conclusions be correct? ... [And] how could one reply to the point that was made earlier in this very discussion: that the supreme essence is so much above and beyond every other nature that even if sometimes words are applied to him that are common to other natures, their meanings are in no way common? For what meaning did I understand in all the words I thought, if not the common and familiar one? So if the familiar meaning of words is foreign to him, none of my reasoning applies to him. How then is it true that something has been discovered about the supreme essence if what has been discovered is vastly different from him?[2]

As we saw in chapter 7, Anselm resolves the paradox by distinguishing two kinds of knowledge of a thing and, correspondingly, two ways of talking about a thing. We can know something "properly, as the thing itself actually is"; and when we have such knowledge, we express the thing as it is. But there are other things that we cannot know properly, but only "through some likeness or image, as when we see someone's face in a mirror."[3] In such a case, our language, like our knowledge, will be indirect: "we signify through some other thing what we are...unable to express properly, as when we speak enigmatically (*per aenigmata*)." God is a thing of this second sort. Even though we can reach true conclusions about him, we never gain a proper grasp of his essence; we must understand him and speak of him through the conceptions and language we use for created things. So God is indeed ineffable, "because words can in no way express him as he is," and yet knowledge of God remains possible; for "if reason can teach us to form any judgment about him through some other thing, as in enigmatic language (*in aenigmate*), that judgment is not false."[4]

So we always come to know God by knowing other things. The closer a thing is to God, the more satisfactory and informative an image of God it will be. For, Anselm says, "whatever among created things is shown to be more like him must be more excellent by nature. Hence, because of its greater likeness such a thing gives more help to the investigating mind in coming closer to the supreme truth, and because of its more excellent created essence it more fully teaches what that mind ought to believe about the Creator."[5] The most excellent created essence, the one that is most like God, is the rational mind. For the mind is the only creature that can remember, understand, and love itself—or better still, remember, understand, and love God—and is thus "a true image of that essence who through his memory and understanding and love of himself constitutes an ineffable Trinity."[6] The mind can therefore serve as "a mirror for itself"; it cannot look upon God "face to face," but by looking upon itself it sees an image of God.

This image of God is impressed upon the mind through its natural power; it is expressed by the mind through voluntary action. That is, the rational mind fulfills its God-given function to serve as a mirror or image for the contemplation of God when it wills to remember, understand, and love God. This is its preeminent activity and therefore ought to be what it preeminently wills, "for who would deny that whatever better things are in our power should be more in our will?"[7] In fact, we can see that the very purpose for which the rational mind exists is to remember, understand, and love the supreme good. Anselm claims that being rational is the very same thing as having the power "to discern the just from what is not just, the true from what is not true, the good from what is not good, and the greater good from the lesser good."[8] But even when the rational nature exercises that power correctly and makes true judgments, its rationality is pointless unless the rational nature acts in accordance with those judgments. So, Anselm concludes, "it is quite obvious that every rational thing exists in order that it might love something more or less, or reject it altogether, according as its rational discernment judges that the thing is more or less good, or not good at all. So nothing is more evident than that the rational creature was made in order that it might love the supreme essence above all other goods, since he is the supreme good—indeed, that it might love nothing but him or [what it loves] for his sake, since he is good through himself, and nothing else is good except through him."[9]

Knowing the purpose for which rational natures were created is central to Anselm's moral theory, because his central moral notions—rectitude, justice, and order—are understood in teleological terms. As we noted in chapter 3, a thing is right or possesses rectitude when it achieves its intended purpose. Since the purpose of the rational nature is to love God above all else and for his own sake, and to love other things for God's sake, a rational nature possesses rectitude when it does just that. But Anselm prefers to talk not about the rectitude of a rational nature but about rectitude of will, since it is the will that loves (or fails to love) God in the right way. Obviously, as Anselm sees, rectitude of will depends on rectitude of intellect; we are to "love something more or less, or reject it altogether, according as [our] rational discernment judges that the thing is more or less good, or not good at all."[10] But rectitude of intellect is for the sake of rectitude of will, and not the other way around.

Our Place

We have reached Anselm's understanding of rectitude of will by one route that proceeds from his natural theology through considerations about our purpose. But we cannot fully understand Anselm's notion of justice until we follow him along another route that again proceeds from his natural theology—although from quite different aspects of his notion of God—through considerations about our place in the world God has created. Reflecting on our purpose suggests that rectitude of will consists in loving God for his own sake; reflecting on our place suggests that rectitude of will consists in maintaining, so far as it lies within our power, the fitting order that God has established in the universe as a whole. After we examine this second strand in Anselm's thinking about rectitude, we will show how the two coalesce into a single, unified theory.

For Anselm, it is evident to reason that the work of a perfectly rational and perfectly good Creator will be beautiful, since reason discerns that beauty is a great good. But in what does beauty consist? Anselm doesn't directly address the aesthetic question in general, but he certainly makes clear that part of what beauty consists in is order: "If divine wisdom did not add [spontaneous recompense and infliction of punishment] wherever perversity tries to disturb correct order, a certain ugliness would arise from the violation of the beauty of order in the very universe that God ought to make orderly, and God would seem to fall short in his governance."[11] Thus we see that God's good governance consists in part in his establishing and maintaining a beautiful order in the world he creates.

The importance of the notion of order in Anselm's thought cannot be overemphasized. Many of the crucial arguments of *Cur Deus Homo* depend on the idea that there are certain things God cannot do because his doing them would introduce disorder or ugliness; they would ruin the beauty of his creation. Incarnation and Atonement are necessary because they are the only ways to restore or maintain a suitable ordering of the universe, and God is such that he cannot fail to do what is fitting and orderly.[12] For this reason, when Boso frets that unbelievers regard Christian teaching on the Atonement as nothing more than "beautiful pictures," without rational cogency, Anselm in effect replies that the beauty of those pictures *is* their cogency.[13]

This line of thinking also gives Anselm his argument against a form of divine command theory according to which whatever God wills is right, and there are no limits on what God wills. Not surprisingly, Anselm's argument against divine command theory arises in the course of a discussion of what God can or cannot do in forgiving sins. In *Cur Deus Homo* 1.12 Anselm argues that it is not fitting for God to forgive sin unless recompense is made. If God did so, he would leave sin unordered (*inordinatum*), and "it is not fitting for God to leave anything unordered in his kingdom." Boso finds Anselm's reasoning compelling, but he wonders how such a limitation on God's activity can be squared with what we know about God's nature:

> B: God is so free that he is subject to no law and to no judgment; he is so kind that nothing kinder can be conceived. Moreover, nothing is right or fitting except what he wills. Given all that, it seems surprising for us to say that he in no way wills to forgive harm done to himself, or that it is not fitting for him to do so, considering that we often ask his mercy even for harm we have done to *others*.

Anselm replies:

A: What you say about God's freedom and will and kindness is true. But we need to understand these things reasonably, so that we do not appear to contradict God's dignity. Freedom, after all, is only for what is expedient or fitting; and what acts in a way that is unfitting for God should not be called kindness. Now as for the claim that what God wills is just and what he does not will is not just, we should not take this to mean that if God wills something unsuitable, it is just, simply because God wills it. If God wills to lie, it does not follow that it is just to lie. What follows is that he isn't God... And so "If God wills this, it is just" is true only of things that it is not unsuitable for God to will. After all, if God wills that it rain, it is just for it to rain; and if God wills that a certain person be killed, it is just for that person to be killed. Hence, given that it is not fitting for God to do anything unjustly or inordinately, it does not pertain to his freedom, kindness, or will that he should leave unpunished a sinner who does not repay God what he took from him.[14]

Proponents of divine command theory put it forward as a compliment to God's omnipotence. Anselm, however, sees it as an affront to God's dignity to suggest that he would establish arbitrary moral laws or bestow his approval on actions that irrationally contradict his own perfection. For example, God, who is truth himself, cannot condone lying, which in its very essence involves a corruption of truth.

The notion of order is central not only in Anselm's theoretical reflections but in the practical moral advice that he gives. From his earliest letters through his latest, we find one constant refrain: we must maintain the beauty of divine order by submitting our wills to God's. Moreover, nearly everyone is under the authority of earthly masters as well, and Anselm sees these human authorities as extensions of God's regulating arm. As he says in *Cur Deus Homo* 1.12, "the right to exact vengeance belongs only to the one who is Lord of all things. When earthly powers act correctly in doing this, it is really God himself, by whom they were ordained for this very purpose, who does it."[15] So maintaining the beauty of order will require not only that we conform our will to God's will but also that we obey our human superiors. Anselm sets out his conception of obedience in a letter to Eulalia, Abbess of Shaftesbury, in which he explains that "there is true obedience when the will of the subordinate obeys the will of the superior in such a way that no matter where the subordinate is, she wills what she knows her superior wills, provided that it is not contrary to the will of God."[16] We will return to Anselm's important qualification—that we are to obey our superiors provided that what they want us to do is not contrary to the will of God—when we discuss his views about discerning God's will. For now, what is important is to recognize that order and obedience play an astonishingly large role in Anselm's practical advice.

Just as the primary task of those under authority is to maintain order by due submission to their superiors, the primary task of those in authority is to correct disobedience and rectify disorder. When Anselm heard about the insubordination and factionalism that was rampant among the monks of Christ Church, Canterbury, he rebuked them sternly and insisted that everyone "be subject in humble generosity and generous meekness" to the prior, noting that "it was never my will, and with God's protection it never will be my will, that such great and reprehensible disorder should arise in the church commended to my rule, or, should it ever arise, that it be encouraged or permitted."[17] He encouraged Muirchertach, King of Ireland, to exercise this authority unstintingly:

> I beseech the constancy of your good will, insofar as you find things in your kingdom in need of correction, to strive earnestly with God's help to set them right, for the sake of the eternal reward and so that God's grace may increase in you more and more. Nothing that can be corrected is beneath your attention. God holds all people accountable not only for what they do wrong but also for the wrongs that they can correct but fail to correct. And the more power they have for correcting them, the more stringently God holds them accountable for willing and acting well, in accordance with the power that was mercifully bestowed upon them. This seems to apply above all to kings, since they are recognized among human beings as having greater power and facing less opposition. Now if you cannot correct all wrongs at once, that is no reason for you not to strive to progress from better things to even better things. For God in his kindness usually brings good intentions and good efforts to fulfillment, and he repays them with blessed abundance.[18]

There is an unmistakable elegance and beauty in Anselm's theory of a perfectly harmonious universe, set in order by God and his earthly agents and preserved by the due submission of those under authority. It is a thoroughly Benedictine picture, with God as the infinitely wise and kindly abbot of a vast but perfectly regulated network of monasteries. But it is not clear that the theory offers much practical guidance for regulating "the unruly wills and affections of sinners,"[19] even in the relative tranquility that prevails inside the walls of the monastery, let alone in the far more tempestuous affairs of secular life. The shortcomings of Anselm's morality of obedience are evident throughout his letters. One noticeable deficiency is that Anselm tends to encourage a kind of passivity. He is quick to absolve someone of moral responsibility so long as that person is obeying a superior. We see this in an early letter to Hugh the Prior. Hugh was at odds with his superior, who refused to listen to his advice. Anselm advises him that if he cannot get consent to step down from his position, he should keep quiet, obey his superior, and trust that his superior and not he will be held responsible for any mismanagement: "for since the chief position in this endeavor was entrusted to him, not to you, you will not be held responsible if the flock is ill-governed because the shepherd failed to heed your advice."[20] Although Anselm does encourage Hugh to do what he can to mitigate his superior's mismanagement, he offers no advice about how this is to be done, and indeed he seems to regard the whole thing as hopeless. So Hugh needs to find a way consistent with his vows to get out from under his superior's authority; if he cannot do that, then he must keep silent and do as he is told. More than twenty years later, Anselm found himself in a somewhat similar position, entrusted with an administrative responsibility that he found both unpleasant and fraught with moral ambiguities. Much as he had advised Hugh to do, Anselm addressed his superior, Pope Urban II, in a letter that can easily be read as an attempt to induce Urban to relieve him of his bishopric.[21] Anselm could not take it upon himself to abandon his position of responsibility—that would constitute an act of disobedience—but if he could persuade the pope to fire him, he would be morally in the clear.

If Anselm's morality of obedience encourages a kind of passivity on the part of subordinates, it also licenses a kind of inflexibility on the part of authorities. Anselm himself was exceptionally vigorous in enforcing the prerogatives of the See of Canterbury, even when pastoral sensitivity or political savvy would have counseled a more temperate approach. (Anselm had great pastoral sensitivity when questions of due submission were not at issue. He had no political savvy at all.) A particularly striking case arose near the end of Anselm's life. In May of 1108 Thomas, the king's chaplain, was named Archbishop of York. When the archbishop-elect delayed his profession of obedience to Anselm as Archbishop of Canterbury, Anselm wrote several letters to Thomas (worded "extremely severely," as the chapter of York complained)[22] and enlisted the help of Pope Paschal II and King Henry. He also wrote to his friend Samson, the Bishop of Worcester (who happened to be Thomas's father), asking him to help in suppressing this "disorderly (*inordinata*) presumption."[23] Samson acknowledged the justice of Anselm's demands. Nevertheless, he suggested gently, "it is unworthy of you to be so angry over this affair."[24] Samson's plea for calm was unavailing, however. Not long afterward Anselm wrote to Thomas, suspending him from the exercise of his priestly office and threatening with "perpetual anathema" any English bishop who would dare consecrate him bishop.[25]

Rectitude of Will, Justice, and Moral Evaluation

We have been exploring two different ways in which Anselm thinks about rectitude of will. On one way of thinking, we have rectitude of will when we fulfill our purpose by loving God for his own sake; on the other, we have rectitude of will when we maintain the place we have been assigned in God's perfectly ordered universe. But the place assigned to rational nature in the order of the whole *just is* that of knowing God and loving him for his own sake, so the two approaches to rectitude of will lead us to exactly the same doctrine.

We can see more clearly how the two approaches come together by looking first at rectitude in general and then at what is distinctive about the rectitude of rational creatures. Throughout *De veritate* Anselm emphasizes that in ascribing rectitude to created things, we are saying that they do what they ought to do.[26] And what things ought to do is what God created them to do. We can express this equally well by saying that they fulfill God's purpose for them or by saying that they are subject to God's will. What distinguishes rational creatures from the rest of creation is that all other creatures fulfill God's purposes or are subject to God's will naturally (that is, according to the necessity imposed on them by their God-given nature), whereas rational creatures can do so by freely willing to do so:

> A: When a creature preserves the ordering that belongs to it and has been, as it were, commanded for it—whether the creature

> preserves that ordering naturally or rationally—it is said to obey
> God and honor him. This is especially true of a rational nature,
> which has been given the power to understand what it owes.
> When a rational nature wills what it owes, it...preserves both
> its own ordering within the whole universe and, so far as it can,
> the beauty of the universe itself. But when it does not will what it
> owes, it...disrupts the order and beauty of the universe as much
> as it can.[27]

In other words, angels and human beings do what they ought to do, what
they were created to do, when they freely will to love God above all else
and other things for God's sake. To fulfill God's purpose for us just is to
preserve our proper place in the order of the universe. Since we do this
through our will's freedom of choice, rational natures have rectitude when,
and only when, they have rectitude of will: "no one else is understood to be
upright (*rectus*) but those who have an upright will."[28]

As we saw in chapter 11, Anselm connects the notion of rectitude of
will with both justice and moral evaluation. Justice in its most general
sense is equivalent to rectitude in its most general sense. Anything that
fulfills its God-given purpose by acting in accordance with its nature is
doing what it ought to do; it therefore has both rectitude and justice. But
the justice that is the proper subject of moral evaluation can exist only in
rational natures, because only a rational nature can know what is right and
will to do it. And not even everyone who knows rectitude and wills to
preserve it is just. Justice is a matter not only of what we will, but also
of why we will it. A will is just when it preserves rectitude for the sake of
rectitude. Anselm therefore defines justice as "rectitude of will preserved
for its own sake."[29]

This seemingly simple account of justice raises some difficult
philosophical questions. First, in order to be just we must be "aware of
rectitude"[30]—that is, we must know what we ought to do. But how do we
know that? And in what does "awareness of rectitude" consist? The broad
theoretical framework established in the *Monologion* might be taken to
suggest that knowing we ought to do something is tantamount to knowing
that we are achieving our God-given purpose by doing it. Yet if Anselm
requires explicit beliefs about teleology in order for anyone to be just, he
seems to be in the grips of what Rosalind Hursthouse has called "the
Platonic fantasy": "the notion that it is only through the study of philosophy that someone can become virtuous (or really virtuous)."[31]

These are questions about moral knowledge: how we acquire it, and what it consists in. There is a second and related set of questions about moral motivation. For in order to be just, we must not merely do what we ought to do, but do it *because* we ought to do it. Does this mean that justice, and hence praiseworthiness, depend on one's explicitly having some thought along the lines of "This is my duty and for that reason I will do it"? Such a requirement seems overly strong, in that it demands an almost obsessive level of conscientiousness. And if taken strictly, it seems to deny justice and praiseworthiness to actions that one would expect Anselm to commend. Suppose Sandra goes to church because she sees it is her duty to do so, whereas Thomas goes to church because he loves God above all else and wants to praise and thank him. Are we to say that Sandra is just and praiseworthy but Thomas is not? Given the connection between rectitude and teleology, it would surely be an embarrassment to Anselm if in this case it was Thomas alone who fulfilled his God-given purpose by loving God above all else, but Sandra alone who preserved rectitude by doing what she ought because she ought.

Being Aware of Rectitude

We will look first at Anselm's account of moral knowledge. It is central to his account that rationality simply consists in the ability to distinguish right from wrong. In *Monologion* 68 he says that "for a rational nature, its being rational is nothing other than its being able to distinguish the just from the not-just, the true from the not-true, the good from the not-good, and the greater good from the lesser good";[32] he repeats this point in *Cur Deus Homo* 2.1. In both places he immediately goes on to make it clear that the purpose of rationality is not simply to provide us with true beliefs about right and wrong, but to enable us to govern our conduct in accordance with those beliefs. The rational nature, he says, "received this power of discernment so that it might hate and avoid evil, so that it might love and choose good, and so that it might love and choose the greater good to a greater degree."[33] Notice that reason's power for moral discrimination is the power to make immediate, practical, action-guiding judgments, not the power to discern our *telos* or to develop a theoretical understanding of our place in the universe. No doubt reason enables us to achieve this more abstract and global understanding as well, but Anselm is quite clear that

God gave us reason so that we could act rightly, not so that we could be good at metaethics. We see in the letters that when Anselm gives moral advice or instruction, he offers only the bare minimum of theory. He never suggests that his correspondents need to investigate deeper theological or philosophical questions than have already occurred to them.

So Anselm is not a victim of the Platonic fantasy. Only the philosopher (or theologian) will be able to give a satisfactory account of the nature of right action, but any rational being can tell right from wrong. Moreover, Anselm never suggests that in order to "be aware of rectitude," an agent needs to believe of a given action that it has the property of *being right*. An agent may have such a belief, of course, but the awareness of rectitude could well involve a belief that an action conforms to God's will, that it is enjoined upon one by a lawful superior, that it honors God, or simply that it is what one ought to do. In the example proposed above, both Sandra and Thomas count as being aware of rectitude in the required sense.

It will come as no surprise at this point that as a general rule, Anselm thinks that we know what we ought to do by knowing what our earthly superiors require of us. In one of the first letters he wrote as Prior of Bec, Anselm exhorted the monk Henry to preserve the order imposed by divine governance: "Since 'whether we live or die, we are' not our own but 'the Lord's,' we ought to be more concerned with what the Lord, to whom we belong, is making of us than with what we, who are not our own, want. Let us therefore preserve the desire of brotherly charity in such a way that we serve the command of the heavenly will. And let us so exhibit the obedience of subjection that almighty governance demands that we may retain the feeling of the love that divine generosity bestows. For there is no more beneficial way for us to conform to God's ordering than by choosing to obey his will in our governance of our own affairs."[34]

Anselm admonishes Henry to "exhibit the obedience of subjection," by which he means simply, "obey your superior." But as we have already seen, obedience to earthly authorities is always subject to the proviso that we are not to obey if they command something contrary to the will of God. When knowing God's will is not simply a matter of knowing what our earthly superiors command, how do we know God's will? By and large, Anselm seems confident that we just know—or, at least, that someone who is in general seeking to submit to God will have no trouble discerning what God wants. Writing to Robert and his small community of nuns drawn from the Anglo-Saxon nobility, Anselm seems to envision no difficulties in the matter: "Now if you wish to know whether an intention of yours is right, one that is subject to the will of God is unquestionably right. So when you are planning or thinking about doing anything, great or small, ask yourself in your hearts, 'Does God will that I will this, or does he not?' If your conscience replies, 'God truly does will that I will this, and this will of mine is pleasing to him,' then cherish that will, whether or not you are able to carry it out. But if your conscience bears witness to you that God does not will for you to have that will, then turn your heart away from it with all your energy."[35]

Anselm's confidence in this letter that a rightly disposed person will have no difficulty recognizing God's will is typical of his generally sunny view about the capacities of human reason in matters of morality. He regularly bemoans our ignorance and sinfulness in matters pertaining to our ability to understand God, but he is oddly silent about our ignorance in moral matters. In *Cur Deus Homo* 2.13 Anselm argues that the God-man does not take on our ignorance because such ignorance would prevent him from distinguishing perfectly between good and bad. This argument seems to imply that human beings other than the God-man do lack the ability to make consistently reliable judgments about good and bad. Yet he never refers to that inability when he discusses how we are to make moral decisions or why we sin. So it would seem that Anselm does not find this ignorance to be relevant to everyday moral living. Most likely Anselm simply holds that although there is a great deal we do not know, there is plenty we do know. We can easily fill our time acting on what we do know is right, so that we rarely, if ever, need to worry about what we do not know or wring our hands about not knowing what to do.[36]

When we do find ourselves not knowing what to do, it is probably because we are weighing our own desires too heavily. A subsequent letter to the same monk Henry makes this point. Henry was planning to leave the monks of Christ Church, Canterbury, in order to go to Italy to help his sister, who had fallen into the hands of an unscrupulous rich man. Anselm's advice—which boils down to "Stay where you are; this is no big deal and no concern of yours"—might well seem heartless, but it manifests his usual concern with order, and in particular with keeping one's vows and maintaining obedience to one's lawful superiors. Anselm goes further, however, by explaining to Henry why his deliberations have gone astray: "If we join the weight of our love to the weight of the thing loved, we will undoubtedly be deceived in our judgment about the matters on which we have to make a decision." If Henry weighed the "very little good" to be obtained by going to Italy against the numerous and serious evils that he would incur, the evils would clearly outweigh the good; but Henry has tipped the scales by weighing his desire along with the intrinsic merit of the plan.[37]

There is a single but noteworthy exception to Anselm's usual confidence in our ability to discern what we ought to do. Anselm himself agonized over whether God meant for him to accept the Archbishopric of Canterbury and, later, over whether he would be disobeying God if he resigned that office. In August or September of 1095, less than two years into his reign as archbishop, he wrote in frustration to Pope Urban II: "I long to escape from the unbearable anxiety, to lay down the burden; yet on the other hand I fear offending God. Fear of God compelled me to take up this burden and that same fear compels me to keep bearing it. If I discerned God's will in these matters, I would undoubtedly devote my will and my actions to it to the best of my ability. But since God's will is now hidden from me and I do not know what I am to do, I sigh, wandering aimlessly."[38]

Why did Anselm have such difficulty in seeing the will of God, given that in general our consciences give prompt and unambiguous testimony to God's will when we simply "ask ourselves in our hearts" what God wills? The most obvious answer is that Anselm was making the same mistake as Henry: he was weighing his own desires too heavily. It is clear from his letters and other writings by his contemporaries that Anselm hated administrative responsibility. His great passion was for developing his philosophical and theological ideas and shaping the minds of young monks. Administrative duties took him away from his great love, and besides, Anselm recognized that he was not an especially competent administrator. He even offered other people advice for avoiding office, telling one abbot-elect, "with a simple mind and humble effort, resist taking up this burden in every way you can, except by sinning. But if you cannot decline it without sin, take it up obediently and bear it conscientiously."[39] When urged to accept the Archbishopric of Canterbury, he acted in precisely this way. He tells Gilbert, Bishop of Evreux, "I did whatever I could, without sin, to thwart the plans of those who elected me, and I did nothing that I could have avoided doing, without sin, that would make it happen."[40] By the time he wrote his letter to Urban, his service as archbishop had turned out to be even more unpleasant than he had imagined it would be. His misery and his aversion to office loomed so large in his thoughts that he was not able to think properly about God's will.

Or rather, on Anselm's own theory, it seems more accurate to say that he *would not* think properly about God's will. As we have seen, Anselm holds that to be rational *just is* to have the power to discern what one ought to do. If we assume that Anselm was not literally out of his mind with grief, he retained his rationality and therefore his power to discern what he ought to do. What he lost was not the power of discernment but the correct exercise of that power. And since the exercise of that power is always under the control of the will, what we have here is a failure of will and not of intellect.[41]

These considerations illustrate a pervasive feature of Anselm's moral theory, namely, that the deficiencies of what Aristotelians would think of as practical reasoning play almost no role. Unlike Augustine, who gave equal billing to ignorance and difficulty as obstacles to right action, Anselm barely acknowledges the possibility of moral ignorance. We almost always know what we need to know, morally speaking; if we do not, it is our own fault. No less than the voluntarists of two centuries later, Anselm always pins the ultimate responsibility for sin on the will, never on the intellect.[42]

Moral Motivation, Virtue, and Charity

"Awareness of rectitude," then, is a fairly minimal requirement. We need no theoretically sophisticated views about divine governance or human teleology; we need only exercise the power that is definitive of us as rational beings. If we exercise that power properly, we will have no difficulty in knowing what we ought to do. But as we have seen, there is a further requirement for justice. In order to be just, we must not only know what we ought to do; we must also do it *because* we ought to do it—or, in Anselm's preferred formulation, we must "preserve rectitude of will for the sake of that rectitude itself." It is noteworthy that Anselm never offers a positive account of what it is to preserve rectitude of will for its own sake. Rather, he tells us what it is *not*. One does not preserve rectitude of will for its own sake when one does the right thing in ignorance, because one is forced to do it, or for the sake of some "extraneous reward." Presumably, then, as long as one is "aware of rectitude" and does the right thing freely, and not for the sake of something other than rectitude, one counts as preserving rectitude of will for its own sake, and therefore as possessing justice.

As Jeffrey Brower notes, justice for Anselm does not consist "in any particular volition, or series of volitions"; rather, it is a "disposition or habit for choosing what is right for the right reason."[43] But it is important to be clear about exactly what sort of disposition justice is in Anselm's theory. It is not a disposition in the sense of an Aristotelian *hexis:* that is, a stable character trait, firmly rooted as a result of habituation and therefore not easily or quickly lost. As Brower rightly points out, justice for Anselm is not acquired by habituation, or by any human effort; it is bestowed by God.[44] Correlatively, justice is also not strengthened or made stable by habituation; if we make progress in the moral life, this will not be a natural consequence of habituation but a divine gift. Moreover, in this life our possession of justice is always precarious. We cannot either acquire or develop justice by our own efforts, but we can at any point lose it by our own negligence. So Anselm warns the monks of Saint Werburgh at Chester: "Although we can neither have nor preserve anything except through God, it is only as a result of our own negligence that we lose it or fall away from it. Quite often this starts with the slightest matters. Our crafty Enemy often deceives us by persuading us that not much hangs on such things. But what follows is the grave harm of which we read in Scripture: 'One who does not heed small things falls little by little.' "[45] Since justice can be so easily lost, the moral life requires exceptional vigilance:

> This present life is a journey, and as long as we are alive, we do nothing but travel. We are always going either upward or downward: either upward toward heaven or downward toward hell. When we do some good work, we take one step upward; but when we sin in any way, we take one step downward...Now it is important to recognize that one goes downward far more quickly and easily than upward. For this reason, in every will and in every act Christian men and women ought to pay attention to whether they are on the upward or the downward path. Let them wholeheartedly embrace those in which they see themselves ascending. But as for those in which they recognize the downward path, let them flee and renounce them as though they were hell itself.[46]

For this reason, any disobedience, however apparently trivial, is a grave evil: "Do not suppose that any sin is small (though granted, some sins are greater than others). For no act of disobedience ought to be called small: disobedience alone expelled human beings from paradise."[47] Anselm is gentle but firm with a young monk who refuses to do what he is told and copy manuscripts: "Dom Abbot told me many good things about your youthful behavior, but he added one thing that could not please me: you consider it better to do what your own judgment chooses than what obedience requires. For although you have expertise in copying manuscripts, you would rather do anything else that seems better to you than to copy them obediently. You should know for certain that one prayer from an obedient monk is better than ten thousand prayers from one who disdains obedience."[48]

Although obedience is sometimes burdensome and the circumstances unpropitious, there is never any excuse for disobedience and disorderly behavior: "Neither place nor time exempts anyone from being able to live well, since no one anywhere can ever banish a good will from the hearts of human beings against their will, and a system of conduct ordered according to the harmony of things can stand firm in any disorder. For God never demands deeds beyond our ability when he perceives the integrity of our good will and good conduct."[49] One notes here the straightforward practical application of a conclusion Anselm would defend at length in *De libertate arbitrii*: rectitude of will is never taken away, whether by God or by circumstances; it is only thrown away.

Anselmian justice therefore lacks many of the salient features of an Aristotelian moral virtue: it is neither acquired nor strengthened by habituation, it does not guarantee virtuous action in the person who possesses it, and it is easily lost. This would seem to be reason enough to deny that Anselm is a virtue theorist in any meaningful sense. But there are further indications that the role of virtue in Anselm's theory is minimal at best. The traditional vocabulary of the cardinal virtues other than justice, so common in Augustine and Boethius, is almost wholly absent in Anselm.[50] And if a virtue is a disposition that prompts us to perform virtuous acts reliably, readily, and with pleasure, there simply are no virtues (in this life, anyway). We have already seen that there is no guarantee of reliability in acting well; we must watch our every step, lest we find ourselves on a steep downward path. Whether we act readily and with pleasure will depend largely on the state of our desires and emotions, and Anselm does not seem to envision any possibility of training or cultivating the emotions so that they will accord with reason's discernment of the proper course of action.

Besides, justice is a matter of rectitude of will, not rectitude of feeling. And rectitude of will can always be preserved, no matter how unappealing obedience may be. The emotions therefore have no theoretical role to play in Anselm's moral theory, and so there is no place for virtues that would regulate the emotions, even if such regulation were possible.

The theoretical unimportance of the emotions may help explain the surprisingly small role that charity plays in Anselm's writings. For in his letters Anselm seems to treat charity or love as a kind of emotional epiphenomenon. It can motivate someone to act rightly, but we can act rightly without it, and an act does not seem to be any more praiseworthy for having been done out of love. Anselm thanks people for their love or for things they have done out of love, and in his prayers he frequently prays for his own charity to be increased. But even in the letters he seldom speaks of the role of love in behavior without interpreting it in terms of obedience and submission. "To do what renews and enkindles charity," he says, "is not to resist God's governance but to obey it."[51] And loving one's neighbor comes down to wanting him to obey God's will.[52]

We have already noted that Anselm's moral thought is arguably deficient insofar as it fails to give adequate practical guidance. The strikingly small role of charity in Anselm's thought suggests another deficiency, this time at the level of theory rather than practice. One can imagine that Augustine in particular would wonder how Anselm's theory could be adequate as a piece of *Christian* ethics. We have stressed Anselm's reliance on the idea of obeying one's superiors. Anselm has good biblical reasons for stressing obedience: "Let every soul be subject to higher authorities, for there is no authority except from God, and those that exist have been instituted by God. So one who resists an authority is resisting God's governance, and those who resist incur damnation for themselves... Therefore, it is imperative that you be in subjection, not only for the sake of [avoiding God's] wrath, but also for the sake of conscience."[53]

But to a Christian mind, Anselm's emphasis on obedience, biblical though it is, is strangely one-dimensional. For the equally biblical injunctions to "Love your neighbor as yourself" and "Do unto others as you would have them do unto you" are entirely absent from Anselm's theoretical reflections on morality and only barely discernible in his practical advice. Governing one's conduct by these prescriptions requires a subtlety and flexibility of thought that is not apparent elsewhere in Anselm's theory, and they do not permit the unquestioning obedience to authority that Anselm is most comfortable recommending to (or enforcing upon) his many correspondents.

Why are these other biblical injunctions largely absent from Anselm's moral thought? We can only speculate. Acting well out of love for one's neighbor requires a sympathetic understanding of the desires and wishes of others and a discernment of their real needs, and perhaps Anselm thought that such insight was out of the reach of most people. Perhaps a moral theory that made such demands did not fit well with his conviction that to serve God well, one need only think about God. Or perhaps he saw how hard it would be to secure the will's ultimate responsibility for all wrongdoing if reason's discernment of the good were itself a matter of such difficulty.

Whatever the explanation, one cannot avoid the conclusion that Anselm left his moral theory in a somewhat underdeveloped state. He had a clear theoretical framework for thinking about moral issues, but the central place of God's sovereign creative will within that framework led Anselm to focus on vertical relationships of subordination and submission, rather than the horizontal relationships in which love of neighbor would have to play the central role. In fact, Anselm is almost entirely silent about matters of personal conduct in which obedience is not at issue.[54] Anselm himself was by all accounts a loving and generous friend, but as a philosopher he sees little theoretical significance in friendship, or indeed in any other relationship in which there is no clear pattern of authoritative command and willing submission. Yet even for those who share Anselm's strong view of God's sovereign will, submission and obedience are only a part of the moral life; and Anselm has little to say about what remains.

INCARNATION AND ATONEMENT

Christian theologians often distinguish two aspects of the doctrine of Christ: the doctrine of the *person* of Christ, or Christology; and the doctrine of the *work* of Christ, or soteriology. For Anselm, soteriology comes first; only when we understand what Christ must *do* can we understand what Christ must *be*. The work of Christ is to repair the breach that human sin introduced into the relationship between God and humanity. Anselm argues in *Cur Deus Homo* that this work can be accomplished only by a God-man: one person in two natures, fully divine and fully human. This "two-natures" doctrine of Christ is commonly called "Chalcedonian Christology" because it was given its classic formulation by the Council of Chalcedon in 451:

> Therefore, following the holy fathers, we all with one accord teach men to acknowledge one and the same Son, our Lord Jesus Christ, at once complete in Godhead and complete in manhood, truly God and truly man, consisting also of a reasonable soul and body; of one substance (*homoousios*) with the Father as regards his Godhead, and at the same time of one substance with us as regards his manhood . . . recognized in two natures, without confusion, without change, without division, without separation; the distinction of natures being in no way annulled by the union, but rather the characteristics of each nature being preserved and coming together to form one person and subsistence.[1]

Anselm argues that Christian soteriology leads ineluctably to a Chalcedonian Christology.

In the first section of this chapter we show how Anselm sets up his argument by posing, on behalf of the unbeliever, the objection that the Christian account of redemption portrays God as acting in an irrational or unjustified way. Relying on the formulation of this objection given by Brian Leftow, we argue that there are two ways in which Anselm can meet it: he can argue for the fittingness or rational beauty of the Christian account of redemption, or he can argue for its necessity. Although we agree with Leftow that Anselm accepts the argument for the rational beauty of the Incarnation, we show that Anselm thought it was not a feasible strategy for responding to the initial objection because it would not seem convincing to the unbeliever who raised the objection. In the second section we offer an account of the role of such considerations of "fitness" in *Cur Deus Homo*. In the third section we turn to the argument that Anselm did regard as a suitable answer to the unbeliever's objection: the argument that the death of a God-man is necessary to effect a reconciliation between God and human beings. Finally, in the fourth section we consider Anselm's discussion of the metaphysical issues raised by Chalcedonian Christology.

The Fittingness of the Incarnation

By the beginning of chapter 8 of the first book of *Cur Deus Homo*, Boso has shown to his own satisfaction (and clearly to Anselm's satisfaction as well) that one cannot explain the Incarnation by appeal to any supposed obligation on God's part to respect the devil's rights over humanity. The devil had no such rights, and so it appears that God would not have been acting unjustly if he had delivered human beings from the power of the devil by fiat. This conclusion leaves Boso wondering what reason God *did* have to redeem human beings in the way he did, given that he was not under any obligation to do so. Anselm suggests that since we know God's will is never irrational, we can be confident that God had *some* reason for doing what he did, even if we do not see what the reason is. But Boso astutely objects that Anselm's answer will be satisfactory only to those who are already convinced that God in fact did the things Christians say he did. To those who are not already convinced, the Christian account of human redemption appears to describe God as acting irrationally, and "many people will not in any way concede that God wills something if it seems contrary to reason." Anselm then asks Boso to say specifically what he, or the unbeliever on whose behalf he is speaking, finds irrational in the Christian account of human redemption. Boso replies, "To put it in a few words: that the Most High should stoop to such lowly things, and that the Almighty should expend such effort to do something."[2]

Brian Leftow states Boso's reservations in the form of an argument, which he calls the "Divine Cost Argument," or DCA. Let "P" stand for "God saves humanity without becoming incarnate and dying for our sins, and his saving us in this way does not result in an unacceptable balance of good and evil in the world." Then the argument goes like this:[3]

(1) God is perfectly wise.   (premise)
(2) If God is perfectly wise, he pays no unjustified, avoidable costs to
    save humanity.   (premise)
∴ (3) God pays no unjustified, avoidable costs to save humanity.
                                                                    (1, 2, MP)
(4) God is omnipotent.   (premise)
(5) If God is omnipotent, then ($\lozenge$ P $\supset$ God can bring it about that P).
                                                                    (premise)
∴ (6) $\lozenge$ P $\supset$ God can bring it about that P.   (4, 5, MP)
(7) $\lozenge$ P   (premise)
∴ (8) God can bring it about that P.   (6, 7, MP)
(9) If God can bring it about that P, then (if God becomes incarnate or
    atones, he pays an unjustified, avoidable cost to save humanity).
                                                                    (premise)
∴ (10) If God becomes incarnate or atones, he pays an unjustified,
    avoidable cost to save humanity.   (8, 9, MP)
∴ (11) God does not become incarnate or atone.   (3, 10, MT)

According to Leftow, the most promising way to block the conclusion is to argue against either (7) or (9). Anselm, he says, has no case against (7), so his response to DCA is to question (9). He counters (9) by appealing to Chalcedonian Christology. But Leftow objects that Anselm's appeal to Chalcedonian Christology "blocks DCA as an objection to the Incarnation, but not as an objection to the Atonement." He then offers two ways to save the doctrine of the Atonement from DCA, "one of which is Anselm's."[4]

Leftow acknowledges that *Cur Deus Homo* can seem to argue against (7).[5] He instances the argument of Book 2, chapters 4 and 6: "it is necessary

that the goodness of God . . . complete what it has begun in human beings . . .
But this can be accomplished only if there is someone who in payment
for human sin gives God something greater than everything other than
God . . . No one other than God can make this recompense . . . But no one
other than a human being ought to make it . . . [so] it is necessary that a God-
man make it." Though this certainly looks like an argument against (7),
Leftow contends that Anselm's arguments actually support (7). For in order
to show that (7) is false, Anselm would have to show that the following two
claims are *necessarily false:*

(LC) If God offers humanity salvation, he does so via some lesser
compensation for sin.

(NC) If God offers humanity salvation, he does so without any
compensation for sin.

If either (LC) or (NC) is even *possibly* true, then P is possibly true—which
is what (7) says. And Leftow argues that according to Anselm (LC) is
possibly true. The only reason God can't offer humanity salvation by means
of some lesser compensation is that it would not fulfill God's original plan
for humanity: namely, his plan to make human beings equal to angels in
being subject only to himself. Since that plan is *contingent,* it is only
contingent that (LC) is false. In other words, (LC) is possibly true, so P is
possibly true—or, in other words, (7) is true.[6]

Therefore, Leftow concludes, Anselm's response to DCA is to argue
against (9), not against (7). That is, what Anselm is arguing is that even
though God *could have* brought about salvation in some less messy way, his
bringing about salvation by way of Incarnation and Atonement involved
no unjustified or avoidable cost. Indeed, it appears that Leftow reads
Anselm as arguing that God's bringing about salvation in this way involved *no* cost. Leftow notes that (9) rests on the supposition that "pain,
death, and humiliation or 'lowering' are costs God pays. But Chalcedonian
Christians do not hold that 'God the Son dies in his human nature' or 'God
the Son dies *qua* human' entail[s] 'God the Son dies.' . . . Further, if 'God
the Son dies *qua* human' does not entail 'God the Son dies,' it is not clear
why 'God the Son feels pain *qua* human' would entail 'God the Son feels
pain': the inferences are the same formally."[7] By appealing to Chalcedonian Christology, Leftow says, Anselm is arguing that *God* doesn't bear
the cost of salvation, because it was Christ's human nature rather than his
divine nature that suffered and died. As Anselm says,

we claim that the divine nature is undoubtedly impassible, that it cannot in any way be brought down from its lofty heights, and that it expends no effort in anything it wills to do. But we say that the Lord Jesus Christ is true God and true man, one person in two natures and two natures in one person. So when we say that God was subject to lowliness or weakness, we do not understand this according to the sublimity of his impassible nature but according to the weakness of the human substance that he bore. In this way it is evident that no reason opposes our faith, since we are not indicating any lowliness in the divine substance but instead pointing out that there is one person of both God and man. So we do not mean that there was any degradation of God in his Incarnation; rather, we believe that human nature was exalted.[8]

Leftow thinks the appeal to Chalcedonian Christology fails to meet the challenge posed by the DCA. He distinguishes two aspects of that challenge. First, the objection holds that the Christian account of redemption involves a humiliation or degradation of the divine nature; second, it holds that God needlessly and irrationally undergoes pain and death. As a response to the degradation objection, Leftow says, Anselm's appeal to Chalcedon succeeds.[9] As a response to the pain-and-death objection, however, it fails: "While it is true that, on Chalcedonian Christology, God the Son suffers pain and death *qua* human, not *qua* God, the pain and death belong to the Person, not the nature. If God the Son dies *qua* human, then God the Son undergoes human death, even if God the Son does not die *simpliciter* ... To undergo human death *is* to pay a cost. This is clearest if human death is the end of one's existence. But even if it is not—as for God the Son and (as Christians think) the rest of us—it is still the loss of *ante-mortem* life in a human body. This is the loss of a good thing, even if a better replaces it." And similar things can be said about pain. So even though the appeal to Chalcedon meets the objection that God's association with a human nature by itself constitutes a degradation or humiliation of God, it leaves unanswered the unbeliever's complaint that the suffering and death to which that human nature was supposedly subjected were an unnecessary and avoidable price to pay for human redemption. As Leftow puts the point, Anselm's Chalcedonian move undermines (9) "as an objection to the Incarnation, but not as an objection to the Atonement."[10]

Consequently, Leftow thinks Anselm has to acknowledge that God bears the costs of pain and death and needs a way to argue that those costs are not "unjustified [and] avoidable." He offers two ways Anselm can make this argument. The first appeals to notions of rationality, the second to the concept of what is "fitting." It is the second way that Leftow ascribes to Anselm. On this argument the costs of the Atonement are avoidable, but they are *not* unjustified. They are justified because of their fitness, their poetic justice, their beauty. Leftow quotes from *Cur Deus Homo* 2.11, where Anselm writes: "Since humanity sinned through pleasure, is it not fitting for humanity to make recompense through pain? And since humanity was overcome by the devil so easily that it could not have been any easier, and thereby dishonored God by sinning, is it not just for the human being who makes recompense for sin to overcome the devil with such great difficulty that it could not be any greater, and thereby honor God? And is it not appropriate that humanity, which in sinning took itself away from God as much as possible, should in making recompense give itself to God as much as possible?"[11] Leftow describes these considerations as "a set of poetic parallels" that count as reasons for God to redeem humanity in the way that Christians describe. Their "fittingness" is "an aesthetic or quasi-aesthetic value"[12] realized by God's plan of redemption. As a result of such poetic parallels, Anselm says there is "an indescribable beauty that belongs to our redemption, accomplished in this way."[13] And for Anselm, Leftow argues, the beauty of a state of affairs is in itself a reason to bring it about.[14]

Simply by raising the "Beauty Response" (as Leftow calls it), Anselm can block DCA by arguing "that a perfectly rational God might rationally prefer paying the costs [of death and pain] to sacrificing a particular sort of beauty. By making this claim, Anselm could concede that these costs are avoidable and that avoiding them could leave the world with an acceptable balance of moral good and evil, and yet let God's choice be justifiable by appeal to the rationality of loving beauty, or one particular kind of beauty."[15] Leftow argues, then, that these considerations show that premise (9) of the original DCA is false. Even if salvation is possible by some means other than the death of a God-man, the death of the God-man is not an unjustified price for God to pay in order to secure salvation.

The Beauty Response and the Appeal to What Is Fitting

Leftow is right to draw attention to the "aesthetic or quasi-aesthetic" considerations to which Anselm appeals so frequently in *Cur Deus Homo*, but the role of those considerations in Anselm's response to Boso's challenge is more indirect than Leftow's analysis suggests. The progression of the argument in fact shows that appeals to what is fitting are superfluous from a strictly philosophical point of view; Anselm does not use them to establish the truth of the Christian account of redemption, but to show the attractiveness of that truth once it has been established. Indeed, Boso insists from early on in *Cur Deus Homo* that Anselm *not* appeal to considerations of fittingness as though they could serve as independent philosophical considerations in favor of the Christian account of redemption. Anselm tries to use such considerations in response to Boso's initial statement of unbelievers' objections to the Christian account, but Boso immediately rejects them as unpersuasive:

> All these things are beautiful, and they have to be treated like pictures. But if there is nothing sturdy underneath them, unbelievers do not think they provide a sufficient explanation for why we ought to believe that God willed to undergo the things we say he underwent. When someone wants to produce a picture, he chooses something sturdy on which to paint, so that his painting will last. No one paints on water or in the air, since no traces of the picture would remain there. So when we offer unbelievers these instances of what you say is fitting as pictures of an actual fact, they think it is as though we are painting on a cloud, since they hold that what we believe is not an actual fact at all, but a fiction. Therefore, one must first demonstrate the rational solidity of the truth: that is, the necessity that proves that God should or could have humbled himself to the things that we proclaim about him. Only then should one expound on considerations of fittingness as pictures of this truth, so that the body of truth, so to speak, might shine all the more brightly.[16]

In deference to Boso's complaints, Anselm does not raise the "poetic parallels" that Leftow cites from *Cur Deus Homo* 2.11 until *after* he has established that it is necessary for God to become incarnate and lay down his life as recompense for human sin. In other words, Leftow is correct in attributing to Anselm the view that the great aesthetic appeal of redemption as Christians describe it is in itself a reason for God to bring about redemption in that way; but he is wrong in thinking that Anselm uses such considerations of fitness as a way to respond to the DCA.

Nevertheless, we have to acknowledge that Anselm's appeal to considerations of fitness in *Cur Deus Homo* is not exclusively decorative.

Though one cannot use such considerations to convince unbelievers, that is merely a matter of apologetic strategy. Anselm still seems to embrace the idea that if we can discern that some state of affairs is more fitting than any of the alternatives, we can infer on that basis alone that that state of affairs obtains. It is most fitting for God to become incarnate in the person of the Word, so we know that that is what he does. It is most fitting that "there was never a time without someone who belonged to the reconciliation without which every human being would have been made in vain,"[17] so we know that Adam and Eve belonged to it (since they were, for a time, the only human beings around). And we could give many more examples of passages in *Cur Deus Homo,* and indeed elsewhere, in which Anselm appears to accept inferences of the form "*x* is most fitting; therefore, *x*."

Yet that rule of inference has consequences that we might well find troubling.[18] Let MF*x* stand for "*x* is most fitting." Anselm seems committed to the following principle:

(1) MF*x* $\Rightarrow$ *x*.

From (1) we can infer

(2) MF*x* $\Rightarrow$ (MF*x* $\Rightarrow$ *x*)

by the valid rule of inference (A $\Rightarrow$ B) $\Rightarrow$ (A $\Rightarrow$ (A $\Rightarrow$ B)). Now it seems reasonable to suppose that the criteria for fittingness, whatever they might be, are necessary. Something's being the most fitting of all possible alternatives is surely not a contingent matter, but one that is (in contemporary language) invariant across all possible worlds.[19] If that is right, then

(3) MF*x* $\Rightarrow$ $\square$ MF*x*.

From (2) and (3) it follows that

(4) MF*x* $\Rightarrow$ [(MF*x* $\Rightarrow$ *x*) & $\square$ MF*x*].

Now look more closely at the consequent of (4). If every world in which *x* is most fitting is a world in which *x* is true, and every world is a world in which *x* is most fitting, it follows that every world is a world in which *x* is true. Thus,

(5) [(MF*x* $\Rightarrow$ *x*) & $\square$MF*x*] $\Rightarrow$$\square$*x*.

And it follows from (4) and (5), by transitivity, that

(6) MF*x* $\Rightarrow$ $\square$*x*.

So anything that is most fitting is necessary. Now what about those things that are not most fitting? It would seem that they are impossible, since some alternative state of affairs that *is* most fitting will be necessary instead. Hence,

(7) $\sim$MF$x \Rightarrow \sim\Diamond x$.

From (7), by transposition, we infer

(8) $\Diamond x \Rightarrow$ MFx.

And it follows from (6) and (8), by transitivity, that

(9) $\Diamond x \Rightarrow \Box x$.

The result is what contemporary philosophers call "modal collapse": possibility and necessity are equivalent; there is only one possible world.

How should Anselm address this argument? One is tempted to reply that an argument like this, relying as it does on contemporary modal logic, is too alien to Anselm's way of thinking about modality to have any bearing on his thought. But this would be a mistake. When it comes to subsequent or logical necessity, Anselm (as we have seen) accepts the same basic modal inferences and equivalences that we accept nowadays. Nor would it be an adequate response to note that Anselm explicitly denies (6) in one passage. In *De conceptu virginali* Anselm explicitly says that although it was most fitting for Christ to be "conceived from a most pure virgin, this did not happen by necessity, as if a just offspring could not reasonably be generated from a sinful parent through this sort of propagation."[20] Since (6) follows from other principles Anselm seems to accept, this passage from *De conceptu virginali* would at best show that Anselm is inconsistent or fails to grasp the full implications of his own views.[21]

A more promising line of argument would be that perhaps there are, at least in some cases, multiple alternatives tied for "most fitting." The correct inference, then, would not be "x is most fitting; therefore, x," but "x is *uniquely* most fitting; therefore, x." If we interpret MFx in the argument above as "x is uniquely most fitting," the argument will still work as far as (6), but no further. (7) will be false, because some things that are not uniquely most fitting will presumably be possible—those, namely, that are tied for most fitting. And if (7) is false, modal collapse is averted.

As a matter of logic, this response seems perfectly adequate. Whether it correctly represents Anselm's views is another question. Though Anselm never explicitly denies that there can be ties for "most fitting," he never explicitly affirms it either. This is one of the reasons that the texts under-determine the answer to the question, "Was it possible for God not to create?" If creating was uniquely the most fitting thing for God to do, then God had to create; and if creating this particular world was uniquely the most fitting thing for God to do, then God had to create this particular world. But there is simply no way to determine the truth or falsity of those antecedents from anything Anselm explicitly says.

Many contemporary philosophers of religion are concerned about whether God has alternatives because they take the answer to bear on whether God is free and morally praiseworthy.[22] Anselm, as we have seen, does not share this concern. On his view of freedom, God is free whether he has alternative possibilities or not, because (given divine aseity) every action God performs is spontaneous and self-initiated. Our freedom, though, is another matter. And we can use what Anselm holds about crea-turely freedom to show that, whatever he thinks about alternative possi-bilities for God, Anselm has the resources to avoid modal collapse. Let's assume the worst (so to speak) for God. Suppose that in every case there is a uniquely most fitting thing for God to do, so that God has no alternative possibilities. Since there are in fact free creatures, we can conclude that it was most fitting for God to create free creatures. But creaturely freedom, as we have argued, requires genuine alternative possibilities.[23] And if there are genuine alternative possibilities, possibility is not equivalent to ne-cessity, and modal collapse is averted.

The upshot is that, despite appearances, Anselm rejects (1)—and that is the case whether we read MFx as "x is most fitting" or "x is uniquely most fitting." The strongest principle that Anselm can accept is that in cases of what he calls God's efficient will[24]—cases in which God himself is acting, rather than merely permitting some other agent's action—God will always bring about the uniquely most fitting state of affairs, if there is one. This principle is strong enough to allow Anselm to make the inferences he wants to make in *Cur Deus Homo,* since in every such case he is inferring what *God* does from what is most fitting for God to do. Yet the principle is not so strong that it entails there is only one possible world.

It is a consequence of Anselm's view that statements of the form "It is fitting that p" will have different truth values depending on the context of assessment, just as we found with 'ought' and 'can' statements. In any case in which p involves a sinful action, such a statement will be true if we consider God's permissive will—for God cannot permit anything unfitting in the world that he orders perfectly—but false if we consider the moral character of the action—for sin can never be fitting.

The Necessity of the Incarnation

As Leftow's presentation of the Divine Cost Argument makes clear, there are only two ways in which Anselm can meet the objections that Boso voices on behalf of unbelievers. One is to argue that even though God could have reconciled humanity to himself in some other way, he did not act irrationally or unwisely in bringing about redemption in the way Christians say he did. As we have seen, however, Anselm does not think he can make any such argument that would be persuasive to an unbeliever who finds the DCA compelling. Only after the unbeliever has been convinced by some other means does it make sense to elaborate on the fitness of the Incarnation, "so that the body of truth ... might shine all the more brightly."[25]

Consequently, Anselm must take the second approach: he must argue that it is not possible for God to save humanity without becoming incarnate and dying for our sins. But he must argue for a further point on which the DCA is silent. The DCA in effect assumes that if human beings are in need of saving, God has to save them; it simply raises the objection that on the Christian account of human redemption, God secures human salvation in an irrational and unseemly manner. Suppose, however, that Anselm can prove that God cannot save humanity without becoming incarnate and dying. It is still open to the unbeliever to say that in that case, it would have been seemlier and more reasonable for God to have left human beings unsaved, rather than subjecting himself to pain and human death in order to secure their salvation. Anselm must therefore argue not only that God can secure human salvation only through the death of a God-man, but also that if human beings fall into sin, God cannot simply leave them unsaved. We may state the required argument in the following form:

(1) Necessarily, if human beings sin, God offers them reconciliation.
(2) Necessarily, if God does not become incarnate and die, God does not offer reconciliation to human beings. Therefore,
(3) Necessarily, if human beings sin, God becomes incarnate and dies.

Our proposal is that this, and only this, is Anselm's defense of the Incarnation against the objections raised by Boso at the beginning of the work; this, and only this, is his answer to the question posed in the title of the work: Why did God become a human being? Thus, for example, Anselm's speculation that God's original plan for humanity required human beings to be equal to angels is not an essential part of his defense of the Incarnation, because that speculation is not deployed in order to support either of the premises in the fundamental argument of *Cur Deus Homo*. Similarly, whatever may be the interest of Anselm's speculations about the perfect number of rational natures in the heavenly city and the consequent deployment of human beings to fill the places deserted by the fallen angels, those speculations are logically otiose.[26] There is, to be sure, a further question, more literary than philosophical, about why Anselm clutters up *Cur Deus Homo* in the way he does.[27] But it is important to be clear that those speculations really are clutter, not simply from the point of view of contemporary philosophical or theological readers with their own axes to grind, but from the point of view of Anselm's own stated aim in *Cur Deus Homo*.

Now both of the premises in the key argument of *Cur Deus Homo* require defense, and Anselm makes his case for each of them piecemeal. We will follow Anselm's order of presentation in order to show how Anselm's defense of the Christian account of redemption emerges over the course of the work.

Anselm devotes much of Book 1 to a defense of premise (2), the claim that, necessarily, sinful human beings are reconciled to God only through the death of a God-man. The first strand of the argument is found in chapters 11–15, where Anselm argues that reconciliation requires recompense. That is, God does not—he cannot, as a matter of justice—simply cancel the debt of sin. Rather, the debt must be paid, either by way of punishment or by way of recompense.

Although it is customary and perfectly proper to translate Anselm's *debitum* as "debt," it is also important not to press the commercial analogy so far that Anselm's picture of the relationship of human beings to God appears needlessly crude. What human beings owe God is simply what they ought to do. The verb *debere* may equally well be translated "owe" and "ought," and a *debitum* can be either a debt in the commercial sense or an obligation in a broader legal or moral sense. It is true that the breadth of meaning of these words allows Anselm to switch back and forth between the language of commercial transactions and the language of justice and obligation, but we should not be tempted to think that Anselm regards justice as a kind of commercial exchange in which God acts as a rather obsessive auditor who insists that the books be balanced down to the last farthing. Rather, if we must press a differentiation to which Anselm's language does not really lend itself, it is better to say that for Anselm, debt is a species of obligation and can therefore serve as an illuminating analogy for our relationship to God. Something similar can be said about the much-maligned feudal character of the notion of "honor," which Anselm also uses in this section.[28] Accordingly, one cannot immediately dismiss Anselm's doctrine simply because one regards as crude or antiquated the metaphors he uses in developing it.[29]

In fact, for Anselm the notions of *dishonoring God* and of *failing to pay what one owes God* are interdefinable not only with each other, but also with the notion of *sinning,* which is hardly a dispensable notion for the Christian theologian.[30] In chapter 11 he makes the connections among these three notions quite clear: "Every will of a rational creature ought to be subject to God's will . . . This is the debt that human beings and angels owe to God. No one who discharges this debt sins, and everyone who fails to discharge it sins. This is the justice or rectitude of will that makes people just or upright in heart, that is, in will. This is the only and the complete honor that we owe God or that God requires of us . . . Someone who does not pay back to God the honor that is owed him takes from God what is rightly his and dishonors God; and this is what sinning is."[31] Consequently, Anselm can offer two independent arguments for the claim that God cannot simply forgive sins "by mercy alone." The argument of chapter 12 relies primarily (though only obliquely) on the metaphor of debt, that of chapter 13 primarily (and quite explicitly) on the metaphor of honor, but they come to the same thing in the end. God would act unjustly if he made no distinction between the sinful and the just, requiring neither recompense nor punishment for sin, leaving uncorrected the disorder that sin introduces, and acquiescing in the intolerable refusal of rational creatures to subject themselves to God's will as they ought to do. Since God cannot act unjustly, sin must be followed by either punishment or recompense.

Now if sin is simply punished, the demands of justice are satisfied; but human beings are not reconciled with God. So the argument to this point establishes that reconciliation requires recompense. In order to defend (2), Anselm must argue further that only the death of a God-man can serve as recompense. In Book 1 he takes only the first step toward this conclusion by arguing in chapters 20–23 that if human beings sin, they owe God an infinite debt. For even if human beings do not sin, they owe God their very selves and everything they can do, as Boso puts it. Anselm explains: "In this mortal life your love and (this is where prayer comes in) your desire to reach the state for which you were created, and your sorrow that you are not yet there, and your fear of not reaching it, ought to be so great that you should not experience any happiness except in things that give you help or hope in reaching that state. For if you do not love and desire it in accordance with its nature, and feel sorrow that you do not yet have it and that there remains such great uncertainty whether you will ever have it, then you do not deserve to have it."[32] Since such complete obedience is the minimum standard—to fall short of it in any way is to sin—it cannot avail to heal the breach that sin makes between God and humanity.

There is, as Boso notes, enough already in these considerations to make it seem impossible for human beings to be saved. But Anselm goes further, arguing that even the most apparently trivial sin is of infinite gravity and therefore requires an infinite recompense. He asks Boso to imagine that he finds himself under God's watchful eye (*in conspectu Dei*). Someone tells Boso, "Look over there," but God says he doesn't want Boso to look. Anselm asks Boso whether he would take that glance, contrary to the expressed will of God. Boso says he would not do so for any consideration: not to save his own life, not to keep the entire world from destruction, not even to preserve an infinite number of worlds "as full of creatures as this one is." Anselm draws the disheartening conclusion: "That is how seriously we sin every time we knowingly do something, however small, contrary to the will of God; for we are always under his watchful eye, and he always commands us not to sin."[33] Every sin, in short, is infinitely serious and therefore requires a recompense of infinite value.[34]

In chapter 24 Anselm argues further that if human beings do not make recompense, they cannot attain the happiness for which God created them. True, human beings are unable to repay their infinite debt to God; but since this inability is their own fault, a necessary consequence of their free choice to sin, it does not excuse them. It would be contrary to God's justice, and therefore to God's nature, if he were to forgive human beings precisely because they cannot make recompense: "if, on account of their inability to repay what they ought to repay of their own accord, God forgives what he was going to take away against their will, he is lightening the punishment of human beings and making them happy on account of sin, because they have what they ought not to have ... But mercy of this sort is altogether contrary to God's justice, which does not permit anything other than punishment to be repayment for sin. Hence, it is impossible for God to be merciful in this way, just as it is impossible for God to be contrary to himself."[35] So human beings cannot pay their infinite debt, and God cannot justly forgive it. Moreover, no one in a state of sin can justly be given happiness. So, Boso concludes despairingly, "If God follows the rational demands of justice, wretched mortals cannot escape it, and God's mercy seems to perish."[36]

Notice that by the end of Book 1, Anselm has not yet established (2), the claim that, necessarily, if God does not become incarnate and die, God does not offer reconciliation to human beings. He has shown that if human beings are to be happy, their infinite debt must be paid, but he has not yet proposed a God-man as the only available means to pay it. So in the last chapter of Book 1 he makes a more provisional argument. Anselm claims that everyone agrees that happiness is possible for human beings. Yet, he argues, if we leave out any assumptions about Christ we find no way for human beings to be made happy. Clearly, then, we have to believe that human beings can be saved through Christ.

Boso quite sensibly responds that the unbeliever is still entitled to say "I don't see how Christ helps here, so I don't see how human beings can be saved at all." In his reply, Anselm adds one important claim: it is necessary that some human beings will attain happiness: "For if it is unfitting for God to bring human beings who are in any way blemished to that state for which he created them unblemished, lest he seem to regret the good he had undertaken or to be unable to achieve his purpose, much more so is it impossible, on account of that same unfittingness, that no human being is advanced to the state for which he was created."[37] This claim is the first strand in Anselm's argument for (1), the claim that, necessarily, if human beings sin, God offers them reconciliation. So at the close of Book 1, neither of the premises of Anselm's central argument has been fully defended. When Boso summarizes what has been accomplished in Book 1, he says only that Anselm has proved that "sinful human beings owe God, on account of their sin, something that they cannot repay but that they must repay if they are to be saved."[38]

In the first five chapters of Book 2, Anselm takes up the argument for (1). It is evident, Anselm says, that "God made rational nature just, in order that it might be happy in enjoying him."[39] As we have already seen, rationality is simply the power to "to discern the just from what is not just, the true from what is not true, the good from what is not good, and the greater good from the lesser good."[40] Rational nature receives this power of discernment in order to choose according to its dictates:

> Otherwise God would have given it this power of discernment in vain, since its discernment would be in vain if it did not love and avoid things in accordance with its discernment; and it is not fitting that God should bestow so great a power in vain. And so it is certain that rational nature was made for the purpose of loving and choosing the supreme good above all other things, not for the sake of something else, but for its own sake. After all, if rational nature loves the supreme good for the sake of something else, it loves something else and not the supreme good. Now it cannot love the supreme good for its own sake unless it is just. Therefore, it was made rational and just at the same time so that it would not be rational in vain.[41]

Given that rational nature was made rational and just, in order to love the supreme good above all other things and for its own sake, we can conclude further that God intended rational nature to be happy. Otherwise, we would have to say that a rational nature that loved the supreme good above all else but was perpetually estranged from that very good was achieving its God-given purpose. But it is absurd, Anselm says, to think that God's gift of rationality and justice will be, by God's own design, permanently deprived of its proper fulfillment. We can conclude, then, that human beings, as rational creatures, were "made just in order that [they] might be happy in enjoying the supreme good, that is, God."[42]

God's purpose for rational nature does not change simply because human beings have thrown away the justice with which they were created. So if God were to leave human beings in a state of injustice and unhappiness, he would fail in his purpose; he would have created human beings in vain: "it is utterly foreign to [God] that he should allow any rational nature to perish entirely . . . It is therefore necessary that he complete what he began in human nature. And as we have said, this can take place only through a perfect recompense for sin, which no sinner can make."[43]

At this point Anselm has completed his argument for (1). Since God cannot fail in his purpose for rational nature, "which he created so that it might rejoice in him,"[44] a perfect recompense for sin must somehow be made available. But how? In chapters 6, 7, and 9 Anselm argues that only a

God-man, as defined by the Council of Chalcedon, can make recompense for human sin.[45] The one who makes the recompense must be a human being, since only a human being can pay what human beings owe.[46] Yet only God can make this recompense, since the recompense must be proportionate to the sin, which is infinitely serious; and only God can give something of his own that is of infinite value.[47] Therefore, the one who makes the recompense—a recompense that God cannot fail to make available—must be both God and man. And the divine and human natures must come together into a single being:

> If...these two intact natures are said to be conjoined in such a way that the human being is distinct from God, and it is not one and the same being that is both God and human, it is impossible for the two of them to do what needs to be done. God will not do it, because he will not owe the debt; the human being will not do it, because he will not be able to. Therefore, in order for the God-man to do this, it is necessary that the one who is going to make this recompense be both perfect God and perfect man, since only one who is truly God can make it, but only one who is truly human owes it. Therefore, since it is necessary that a God-man be found, one who preserves both natures intact, it is no less necessary that these intact natures come together into one person, just as a body and a rational soul come together into one human being. There is no other way for one and the same being to be perfect God and perfect man.[48]

In short, only a God-man as defined by the Council of Chalcedon can make the recompense that God cannot fail to offer.

So now Anselm has established the necessity of a God-man, but he has not quite finished the argument for (2), because he has not yet shown that the God-man makes recompense *by dying*. We have already seen that the God-man must make recompense by giving God something "greater than everything that is less than God."[49] In chapter 11 Anselm argues that this recompense must be either the God-man himself or something belonging to him, since nothing below him or outside him is great enough to serve as a recompense. Moreover, the recompense must be something that God cannot demand of the God-man as an obligation: "he will lay down himself or something of his own for the honor of God in a way that he is not obligated to do."[50] Now because the God-man will be sinless, he will not be obligated to die, though he will have the power to lay down his life if he chooses. So he can make recompense by laying down his life for the honor of God.

Yet one final question remains. Because Anselm has insisted so strongly that even the most apparently trivial sin is infinitely serious, Boso asks whether the death of the God-man will be a sufficient recompense for the sins of the whole world. Anselm replies, "Suppose that man were present and you knew who he was. And suppose someone said to you, 'Unless you kill this man, this whole world and everything that is not God will perish.' Would you do it in order to save every other creature?" Boso replies that he would not do it even to save an infinite number of worlds from destruction—not even to avoid assuming the burden of "all other sins—not only all the sins of this world that have been or will be, but also, in addition to these, every sin that can even be conceived."[51] Killing the God-man is incomparably more serious than other sins, because it is a sin directly against the person of God.[52] Since the destruction of his life is an evil incomparably greater than any other evil, his life is a good incomparably greater than any other good. It follows, then, that "so great and so lovable a good [is] sufficient to discharge the debt that is owed for the sins of the whole world."[53]

So now Anselm has established (2), and the core argument is complete. God must offer reconciliation to human beings, and such reconciliation is possible only if a God-man gives up his infinitely precious life for the honor of God. But (2) deals only with a necessary condition for reconciliation. It states that God and human beings are reconciled only if a God-man dies, but it does not say that the death of the God-man in fact succeeds in bringing about reconciliation. Indeed, when Boso agrees that the life of the God-man is sufficient to discharge the debt of sin, he means only that it is of sufficient *magnitude* to outweigh sin, not that the offering of the God-man's life automatically reconciles human beings to God. For Boso can still imagine conditions under which the life of the God-man, though intrinsically of sufficient magnitude to discharge the debt of sin, would fail to discharge that debt. First, suppose the God-man is under an obligation to give up his life. In that case, in giving up his life he would merely be giving what he already owed. The infinite value of his life would be needed to discharge his own debt, and so it would not be available to serve as a remedy for sin. Second, even if the infinite value of his life is available to discharge the debt of sin, it might not actually be applied for that purpose. God, to whom the debt of sin is owed, must accept the God-man's self-offering as a recompense for sin. Otherwise, the life of the God-man will not in fact discharge the debt of sin.

Boso goes so far as to argue that the first condition in fact holds: the God-man is under an obligation to give up his life. After all, Boso reasons, Christ understood that laying down his life would be better and more pleasing to God than preserving his life, and "no one will say that he did not owe what he understood to be better and more pleasing to God. How, then, will we claim that he did not owe God what he did ... especially given that a creature owes God everything it is and everything that it knows [is good] and has the power to do?"[54]

Anselm simply denies that creatures owe God the best they are able to do, at least "if you mean the creature owes it as a matter of obligation, and you do not add the qualification, 'If God commands it.'"[55] In certain matters God leaves creatures free to do as they prefer. For example, neither virginity nor marriage is determinately required of human beings. Those who wish to marry are free to do so. Yet virginity is a better state than marriage, so those who choose to remain virgins for God's sake are willingly giving God something that cannot be demanded of them as an obligation; consequently, they can look forward to a reward from God. In the same way, it was Christ's prerogative either to undergo death or not; he was under no obligation to accept death. By offering his life for the honor of God, he gave God something of infinite value that could not be demanded from him as an obligation; consequently, he is entitled to a reward from God.

That reward is the mechanism by which the infinite value of Christ's life is applied to discharge the debt of sin. According to Anselm, justice requires that God reward Christ for his great gift. But since Christ is fully divine, he lacks nothing, and so there is nothing God can give him as a reward that he does not already possess. God must therefore give the reward to someone else, and it is "just and necessary" that he give it to the recipients whom Christ himself chooses: his own fellow human beings. For, as Anselm asks, "To whom will he more fittingly give the fruit and reward of his death than to those for whose salvation he made himself a human being? ... And whom will he more justly make heirs of the reward he does not need, and of the abundance of his own riches, than his own kindred and brothers, whom he sees languishing in poverty and deep misery, bound by their many and great debts, so that what they owe for their sins is forgiven and they are given what they lack on account of their sins?"[56] In this way the value of Christ's self-offering does not merely outweigh in principle the debt of sin; it is actually applied, by the justice and mercy of God, to discharge the debt that human beings cannot otherwise pay.

Christology

Anselm's account of the Atonement is an innovative construction. His Christology proper—that is, his account of the metaphysics of the Word made flesh—is much more conventional and traditional. This difference no doubt reflects the much more settled character of the fundamental doctrines of Christology in Anselm's day. Anselm's aim is simply to give an account in terms of his own metaphysics that is consistent with the Chalcedonian definition and with his own understanding of the demands of the work of Christ.

In *Cur Deus Homo* Anselm determines that only a God-man can carry out the work of reconciliation that God cannot fail to offer. But how can there be a God-man? Divine nature cannot be transformed into human nature, or human nature into divine nature. Nor can some third nature, neither human nor divine, emerge from a mixture of the two. And even if such a hybrid were possible, it would be unavailing for the work of reconciliation, since such a thing would be neither divine nor human. Similarly, a mere conjunction of divine nature with human nature, "in such a way that the human being is distinct from God,"[57] would be of no use, since God would not owe the debt and the human being would lack the power to pay it. Consequently, the God-man must be one being, not two, in whom both the divine nature and human nature maintain their completeness and integrity: "Therefore, in order for the God-man to [effect reconciliation], it is necessary that the one who is going to make this recompense be both perfect God and perfect man, since only one who is truly God can make it, but only one who is truly human owes it. Therefore, since it is necessary that a God-man be found, one who preserves both natures intact, it is no less necessary that these intact natures come together into one person, just as a body and a rational soul come together into one human being. There is no other way for one and the same [being] (*idem ipse*) to be perfect God and perfect man."[58] So the God-man has to be one person with two natures.

It follows, Anselm says, that only one divine person was incarnate. The incarnation does not result in one and the same *nature* that is both divine and human—that is impossible—but in one and the same *person* who is both divine and human. And "this can only be the case in one divine person, since it is unintelligible for distinct divine persons to be one and the same person as one and the same human being. For if one human being is one person with each of a plurality of persons, it is necessary that a plurality of persons that are distinct from one another are one and the same person, which is impossible."[59] But which divine person was incarnate? Anselm argues that many absurd consequences would follow if any person other than the Son were incarnate; and "since it is impossible for there to be any absurdity, however trivial, in God, it was not appropriate for any divine person to be incarnate other than the Son."[60] He also offers positive reasons that it is especially fitting for the Son to be incarnate.[61]

So God the Son is incarnate in such a way that the divine nature and human nature come together in one person, just as the Council of Chalcedon declared. Yet there is a standard objection to Chalcedonian Christology that Anselm needs to meet: "the principle that there is no nature without a concrete hypostasis [i.e., person] or concrete individual."[62] From this principle it follows that if there are two natures in the Incarnate Word, there must also be two persons. In *De incarnatione Verbi* Anselm ascribes such reasoning to unnamed "heretics of dialectic,"[63] clearly treating the argument as one that has actually ensnared some people and not merely as a mistake someone might conceivably make. He writes, "Some people say, 'How do we say that in Christ there are not two persons as there are two natures? After all, before assuming human being, God was a person; and he did not cease to be a person after he had assumed human being. And the assumed human being is a person, since we know that every individual human being is a person. So the divine person who existed before the Incarnation is distinct from the human person who was assumed. Therefore, since Christ is both God and a human being, there seem to be two persons in him.' "[64]

Anselm replies to this argument by suggesting that "human being" is ambiguous between human *nature* and a human *person*.[65] A person "has a collection of distinguishing characteristics along with the nature; it is by those characteristics that human being in general is made an individual and is distinguished from other individuals."[66] If the Word had assumed a *person*, the result would have been two distinct individuals conjoined in some way, and Anselm has already argued that such a pairing of a divine individual with a human individual would have been unavailing for salvation. So the Word did not assume another person but another *nature*.

One and the same collection of distinguishing characteristics belongs to both the Word and the assumed human nature. (We will call this collection "the R-set": the set of characteristics that belong to the Redeemer.) One collection of distinguishing characteristics means one person, even though there are two natures.

This line of response to the heretics of dialectic is clear enough, as far as it goes. Yet as *De incarnatione Verbi* progresses, there are definite signs that Anselm has not adequately worked out the metaphysics of the Incarnate Word. Consider the following statements, all of which Anselm makes in *De incarnatione Verbi* 11:

(1) When we say "Jesus" we designate a person.
(2) Jesus is the human being assumed by the Word.
(3) The Word did not assume a person.[67]

The conjunction of any two of these entails the negation of the third. And consider the implications of these three statements, which we find in the same chapter:

(4) A single collection of distinguishing characteristics belongs to the assumed human being and the Word.
(5) A person is a nature plus a collection of distinguishing characteristics.
(6) By the name "Jesus" we mean, in addition to human nature, the R-set.[68]

From (5) and (6) we can infer

(7) The name "Jesus" signifies a person,

which, as we have seen, Anselm explicitly affirms in *De incarnatione Verbi* 11. But if that inference is legitimate, as Anselm has to admit, it seems we are also entitled to infer from (4) and (5) that

(8) The divine nature, plus the R-set, is a person.

But (2), (7), and (8) together entail

(9) The Incarnate Word is two persons,

which runs afoul of both Anselm's soteriology and the Chalcedonian definition. Furthermore, the conjunction of (9) with (4) entails

(10) One and the same collection of distinguishing characteristics belongs to two distinct persons.

As we have seen, Anselm's denial that (10) is even possible, let alone actual, is the cornerstone of his reply to the "heretics of dialectic."

Can we salvage a consistent and defensible view from what Anselm says in *De incarnatione Verbi*? The most promising approach is to reject (6), the claim that there is an identifiable individual, "Jesus," who consists of the assumed human nature plus the single set of distinguishing characteristics, as well as (8), the parallel claim that there is an identifiable individual (presumably the Word) who consists of the divine nature plus that same set of distinguishing characteristics. Instead, if 'Jesus' signifies a person, it can only signify the one dual-natured person who possesses the R-set; and similarly, if 'the Word' signifies a person, it can only signify that same dual-natured person. We may be led astray—Anselm himself seems to have been led astray—by the fact that when we talk about "Jesus" we have in mind the human features and when we talk about "the Word" we have in mind the divine features. But there is only one identifiable individual, only one person, who has that full set of features, both human and divine. Both 'the Word' and 'Jesus' refer, and can only refer, to that person. At his most clearheaded, Anselm realizes this: "the Son of God cannot be designated or named personally apart from the Son of Man, nor can the Son of Man be designated or named personally apart from the Son of God, since he who is the Son of God is the very same as the one who is the Son of Man, and the same collection of distinguishing characteristics belongs both to the Word and to the assumed human being."[69] Thus, there is no identifiable, nameable individual consisting of just the human nature, or just the divine nature, plus the R-set. (6) and (8) must be rejected; and with those claims out of the way, the rest of Anselm's Christology in *De incarnatione Verbi* is consistent, not only internally, but with the demands of *Cur Deus Homo* and the Chalcedonian definition.

But, one might object, what about the metaphysical principle that a nature plus a set of distinguishing characteristics constitutes a person? Anselm clearly accepts that principle, which also seems quite plausible on independent grounds. (What else would a person be, if not a nature plus a collection of individuating characteristics?) So he ought to accept the implications of that principle. And that principle clearly seems to imply that the human nature plus the R-set constitutes a person, and the divine nature plus the R-set constitutes a person. So once again, the objection continues, Anselm's view is internally incoherent. One principle he

accepts—that a nature plus a set of distinguishing characteristics constitutes a person—entails the falsity of another principle he accepts—that one
and the same set of distinguishing characteristics cannot belong to more
than one person.

Yet Anselm need not reject either principle; the objection is spurious.
He cannot reject the principle that a single set of distinguishing characteristics cannot belong to more than one person, since that principle is
tautological. By definition a set of distinguishing characteristics is the
collection of features that distinguishes it from all other persons of the
same nature. The other principle causes difficulties only because the ob-
jector is applying it incorrectly. Not just any nature plus any set of distinguishing characteristics constitutes a person. Human nature plus the set
of distinguishing characteristics belonging to the archangel Michael does
not constitute anything; those characteristics cannot belong to a human
nature. Similarly, the R-set cannot belong to a divine nature alone, since it
includes characteristics like being born of the Virgin Mary and suffering
under Pontius Pilate, which a divine nature by itself cannot possess. Nor
can it belong to a human nature alone, since it includes characteristics like
being eternally begotten from the Father and being the Word, which a
human nature by itself cannot possess. Only a dual-natured being can
possess the R-set. Human nature plus the R-set, or divine nature plus the
R-set, is no more a person than human nature plus the distinguishing
characteristics of the archangel Michael is a person.

Granted, this defense of Anselm depends on the claim that the R-set is
a single, unified set. But that claim is not a mere ad hoc maneuver. Anselm
devotes the bulk of *Cur Deus Homo* to arguing for the claim that God must
offer human beings reconciliation through the self-offering of a God-man:
one person who is fully divine and fully human. Since, by definition, one
person has one set of distinguishing characteristics, the R-set, which belongs to the God-man, must be a unity. One is therefore entitled to reject
the unity of the R-set only if one has reason to reject the central argument
of *Cur Deus Homo*. No doubt such a reason could be found: Our point is
not that Anselm's soteriology is unassailable, merely that his insistence on
the unity of the R-set is motivated by and derives its warrant from that
soteriology.[70]

There are, to be sure, residual worries about Anselm's Christology in
De incarnatione Verbi. Anselm consistently speaks of the *Word* as becoming
incarnate or as assuming human nature. Yet to speak of the Word is to

speak of a person as distinguished from the divine nature, and the set of features by which the Word is distinguished from the divine nature also includes characteristics that can belong only to a person with a human nature. It would seem, then, that the *Word* cannot become incarnate or assume human nature. Instead, Anselm ought to say that *God* becomes incarnate.[71] Yet Anselm needs to be able to say that the Word becomes incarnate, not only for Scriptural reasons ("The Word became flesh and dwelt among us"), but for the purposes of his polemic against Roscelin. The core of his reply to Roscelin is that the distinction of persons within the Godhead is sufficient to allow the Son to be incarnate without the Father's or the Holy Spirit's being incarnate as well. The personal distinctness of the Word therefore has to be metaphysically prior to the Incarnation, and it is hard to see how that can be the case if, as Anselm also insists, the one set of distinguishing characteristics that belongs to the Word contains characteristics that can only be possessed by a person with a human nature. Furthermore, Anselm clearly supposes in the *Monologion* that he can establish the existence of a divine Word without any reference to human characteristics.

Though Anselm never works out the metaphysics of distinguishing characteristics in any detail, there are indications that his view has the resources to meet this challenge. He always treats collections of distinguishing characteristics as *complete*—that is, as encompassing all the features of a thing that do not belong to its nature. Presumably some of these features will be the rock-bottom individuating features, without which that individual could not exist, and others will be features that the individual happens to have but could have been without. Features that are gained and lost over time would obviously belong in that second class. Anselm suggests something along these lines in *De processione Spiritus Sancti:* "If there are two human beings, one of whom has a son and the other of whom does not, it can be *shown* on that basis that they are distinct, but that is not the *reason* they are distinct. For however things may stand with regard to their having or not having a son, they do not lose their distinctness."[72] What Anselm calls "the reason they are distinct"—alternatively, in this same passage, "the basis of their distinctness" and "the cause of their being distinct persons"[73]—would have to be some feature or features without which that particular individual could not have existed. Other members of an individual's collection of distinguishing features may, as a matter of contingent fact, give us a way of telling that individual apart from others;

but the person's identity and his or her distinctness from other persons with the same nature is secured whether those features are present or not.

If this is indeed how Anselm means us to understand collections of distinguishing characteristics, he can easily explain the personal distinctness of the Word, independently of the Incarnation. There will be some subset of the R-set that is necessary and sufficient to account for the Word's personal distinction from the Father and the Holy Spirit. Call that subset "the W-set." The divine nature, plus the W-set, constitutes the Word. Other features of the R-set, along with the assumed nature, are not the *reason* the Word is distinct from the Father and the Holy Spirit, though they do *show* us that the Word is distinct.

This much is plain sailing. But then how are we to understand the metaphysics of the Incarnation itself in Anselm's terms? If the Word by himself is a person (the divine nature plus the W-set), what becomes of that person when the Word assumes a human nature? We have already seen that there is no nameable, identifiable individual consisting of the divine nature plus the R-set; the only person is the dual-natured God-man. So it would appear that the Word ceases to exist when the Incarnation occurs. Strictly speaking, the Word does not "become incarnate"; rather, the Word ceases to exist and is replaced by a dual-natured person who has all the features the Word once had, plus many more. The only way to avoid this conclusion, it seems, is to assert that the dual-natured person has *always* existed. And as surprising as that view might sound, Anselm actually affirms it in *De conceptu virginali* 21: Jesus' "soul—or rather the whole human being—and God, the Word of God, always existed as one person."[74]

We are left wondering, however, about the modal status of this dual-natured person. Does he exist necessarily, as we might expect given his divine nature, or contingently, as we might expect given his human nature? Suppose first that the existence of the God-man is necessary. Though this does not formally contradict anything Anselm says, it sits uneasily with the argument of *Cur Deus Homo*. God was incarnate in order to effect the reconciliation between God and human beings that was necessary on account of human sin, and it is quite clear from Anselm's account of free choice that the fall did not have to happen.

So suppose instead that the existence of the God-man is contingent. We know that Anselm believes God is necessarily triune, so if there had been no incarnation, there would still have been a second person of the Trinity.

Either that single-natured divine person is the same person as the God-man or he is not. If he is not, then there is a possible but nonactual divine person—surely a disquieting conclusion. It would be better, then, to say that the single-natured second person of the Trinity who would have existed had there been no Incarnation is the same person as the actual God-man. Unfortunately, it is hard to see how a single-natured person could be the same person as a double-natured person. Anselm does not say enough about personal identity to make it clear how that is possible, though neither does he say anything that would rule it out.

Although we might wish that Anselm had addressed these questions (which will arise, in some form, for any Chalcedonian Christology), they lie outside his Christological concerns. He elaborates as much of the metaphysics as is necessary for his soteriological speculations and to defend orthodoxy against the heresy of Roscelin, but he is not interested in the metaphysical problems of Christology for their own sake.

14

ORIGINAL SIN, GRACE,
AND SALVATION

In his work on Incarnation and Atonement, Anselm is confident that he can show by reason alone that what the Church teaches about the person and work of Christ is true. In *De conceptu virginali, et de peccato originali,* however, he has no such confidence. He takes the Church's teaching on original sin as a datum and tries to defend it against objections; he tries to elicit intuitions that are favorable to that teaching and challenge intuitions that oppose it. But sometimes he has nothing more to say against a view than that the Church rejects it, and there is a tentativeness about his approach that suggests he was not altogether convinced that some of the more severe aspects of the doctrine of original sin were fully reasonable. In other works Anselm says he is willing to retract his assertions if they can be shown to be irrational or to contradict Scripture. In *De conceptu virginali* he is hardly willing to admit to having asserted anything he could retract: "I have offered this brief account of original sin so far as my own understanding permits, more by way of exploration than assertion, until God reveals a better account to me in some way."[1]

The Nature and Transmission of
Original Sin

Anselm argues that because of the fall of Adam and Eve, all human beings, from the moment they have a rational soul and thus a will, lack the justice that they ought to have. Sin is, by definition, the lack of justice that one ought to have, so this deficiency in all postlapsarian human beings (Jesus alone excepted) is sin. This sin is called "original" sin for two reasons. First, and most important, "it is received in one's origin": that is, such injustice characterizes the will from the time each particular person begins to exist. Second, "individual human beings derive it from those from whom their nature has its origin."[2] From such sin, damnation follows.

This capsule summary of Anselm's account of original sin raises several questions. At what stage of development does the rational soul come into being, and with it, the deficient will? How and why is original sin transmitted to each new human being from our first parents? How can human beings justly be damned on account of a deficiency in their wills for which they are not responsible and which they are powerless to remedy? And how can they avoid the damnation to which they are liable from the very moment of their origin? We will take each of these questions in turn.

Anselm does not actually say when the rational soul comes into being, but he clearly believes it happens *in utero*. At the earliest stages of development, he says, we do not have a human being, but merely what he calls a "seed" (*semen*): "Now no one thinks [an infant] has a rational soul from the very moment of conception. For it would follow that every time a human seed perishes, even from the very moment of its reception, before it attains human form, the human soul in it is damned because it is not reconciled through Christ, which is completely absurd."[3] Yet by the time an infant is born, the rational soul is clearly present. For all unbaptized children are damned, no one is damned except on account of sin, and sin exists only in the will of a rational nature.[4] So the rational soul, which includes the will, comes into being *in utero*. Nonetheless, newborns cannot actually engage in rational thought—an inability that Anselm attributes, not to their souls, but to their bodies: "in infancy and in the mother's womb the body is so weak that one cannot even understand justice."[5]

Since infants cannot understand justice, and "what does not know rectitude cannot will it,"[6] it might seem reasonable to conclude that infants are not in a state of sin even though they lack justice. For sin is not simply the absence of justice; it is the absence of justice where justice ought to be. Since infants cannot understand rectitude and therefore cannot will it, it would seem to follow, by the principle "ought implies can," that infants are not under an obligation to will justice, and therefore that their lacking justice is not sinful. Anselm ordinarily accepts some version of the principle "ought implies can," so he feels the force of this question. In order to understand his answer, however, we must first examine the second issue we raised earlier: How is original sin transmitted to each new human being from our first parents?

When Adam and Eve fell, human nature fell: "because the whole of human nature was in them, and nothing of human nature was outside them, the whole of human nature was weakened and corrupted."[7] This corruption involved not only their bodies, which became subject to ungoverned appetites of the sort that had previously characterized only the lower animals, but even their souls, which "were infected with carnal affections from the corruption of the body and its appetites, as well as from the lack of the goods that it lost."[8] When human nature is transmitted through natural procreation, the corruption that infected the whole of human nature as a consequence of the primal human sin is transmitted along with it. Yet the fall of Adam and Eve could not change the fact that human nature *ought* to possess the justice with which God had originally endowed it. That ought, that "debt," is transmitted as well. As a result, "it appears to be necessary that in infants human nature is born with the debt of making recompense for the first sin, which it had the power to avoid always, and with the debt of having original justice, which it had the power to preserve always.... This condition can be regarded as original sin in infants."[9]

Anselm argues that it is not because we are human beings, or even because we are descended from Adam and Eve, that we inherit original sin; it is because we come from Adam and Eve through the reproductive nature that God originally gave them. God had subjected this reproductive nature to the will of Adam and Eve in such a way that they had the power to preserve justice for all those who would come from them. But

since Adam[10] refused to be subject to God's will, that reproductive nature—though it remained intact—was not subject to his will, as it would have been if he had not sinned. He also lost the grace that he had the power to retain for all those who would be propagated from him, and all who are propagated by the workings of the nature that he had received are bound by his debt. Therefore, because human nature, which existed wholly in Adam in such a way that there was nothing of it outside him, dishonored God by sinning without any necessity, and could not by itself make recompense for its sin, it lost the grace that it had received and could have retained always for those who would be propagated from it; and every time it is propagated by the reproductive nature that it was given, it contracts sin and, with it, the punishment for sin.[11]

The human nature assumed in the Incarnation is exempt from this debt, however, because it was procreated supernaturally, not by means of the reproductive nature originally given to Adam and Eve. They did not have the power to preserve rectitude for the assumed human nature, so neither did they have the power to lose rectitude for the assumed human nature.[12]

This appeal to Adam and Eve's power either to preserve or to abandon rectitude not only for themselves but for all their natural descendants is a sufficient account, Anselm says, of the rational basis for the transmission of original sin to infants—"provided that we pay heed to pure justice itself, leaving aside our own wills, which so often seriously hinder the mind from understanding rectitude."[13] In addition to addressing the *why* of original sin, Anselm also tries to explain the *how:* the mechanism by which original sin is transmitted. Adam's sin was personal sin. That is, it did not come about as a result of his human nature but through the free choice of his own individual or personal will. Yet Adam's personal sin affected human nature as well: "the person made the nature sinful, since when Adam sinned, human being sinned."[14]

In the transmission of original sin, the causal connection between nature and person works in the opposite direction. Human nature makes each human person sinful. Anselm explains:

> what caused them to lack the justice they ought to have was not their personal will, as was the case with Adam, but the natural deficiency that the nature itself has received from Adam. For there was nothing of human nature that was outside Adam; in him human nature was stripped of the justice that it had possessed, and it always lacks justice unless it receives help. It is for this reason—because the nature subsists in persons and persons do not exist without the nature—that the nature makes the persons of infants sinful. In this way, a person deprived the nature of the good of justice that it had possessed in Adam, and the nature, having become deficient, makes all the persons whom it pro-

creates from itself to be sinful and unjust in virtue of that same deficiency. In this way the personal sin of Adam is transmitted to all those
who are propagated naturally from him, and in them it is original or
natural sin.[15]

In other words, just as the first human persons made human nature sinful
(for human nature subsists only in persons, and there were no other
persons in whom human nature then subsisted), human nature makes all
subsequent human persons sinful (for there are no human persons apart
from human nature). Moreover, Anselm claims that the causal influence
from person to nature continues as well: "just as a person is born sinful
because of the nature, so too the nature is made more sinful by a person,
since when any person sins, human being sins."[16]

The metaphysics of this account seems undeniably odd. Since Anselm
normally thinks of a nature as set of kind-defining features, it is difficult to
make sense at first of the claim that by sinning Adam changed his nature.
On Anselm's usual understanding of nature, that would surely mean that
Adam became a different kind of thing. It would also mean that the death
of Christ would have been unavailing for redemption, because Christ,
being free from original sin, would not have belonged to the same species
as sinful human beings and therefore could not have paid their debt.
Furthermore, it is hard to know how to construe the claim that each sin
committed by a person makes human nature more sinful. Does every
instance of human nature (and thus every human person) become more
sinful subsequent to every personal sin, or does a person's sin damage only
the instances of human nature that are propagated from that person?

The answer to the last question is "neither." Anselm argues that
"original sin is equal in all naturally procreated infants"[17] and that people
do not pass their personal sin along to their children.[18] So it would appear
that personal sin affects only the nature of the person who commits it. Just
as Adam's nature became corrupt as a result of his personal sin, each
individual human being's nature becomes more corrupt as a result of
personal sin. The only difference is that Adam had it in his power to lose
justice for all his natural descendants, and thereby to damage every human
nature, whereas subsequent persons are able to damage only their own
nature.

So in order to understand how personal sin damages human nature,
we have to turn back to the first question: in what sense did Adam's sin
change human nature? Clearly Anselm does not hold that Adam lost any

of his kind-defining features when he sinned. He lost rectitude of will, which is (metaphysically speaking) an accident. As we have seen, he also became subject to both physical and spiritual corruptions that would not have afflicted him if he had preserved rectitude of will. These corruptions, too, are accidents. So in a strict metaphysical sense, Adam's nature remained intact when he sinned. But that nature became subject to difficulties and obstacles that had not previously beset it. For example, Adam retained the capacity for rational thought that belongs to human nature, but his exercise of that capacity was thwarted by the blindness that comes from carnal desires, and he was no longer able to attain the ultimate purpose for which he had been given that capacity: preserving rectitude of will for its own sake.[19] It is not that Adam becomes a different kind of thing, but that he becomes a bad specimen of the kind of thing he was all along; his kind-defining features are not lost, but they become deficient and teleologically incomplete. When subsequent human persons sin, they make their natures worse in the same way that Adam made his nature worse. They encourage carnal appetites, cultivate moral blindness, and in a variety of ways make it more difficult for themselves to exercise the capacities that belong to them as rational animals and to attain the ultimate end for which they were given those capacities.

Culpability for Original Sin

Now that we have explored the transmission of original sin, we can return to our earlier question about the sinfulness of infants. The problem was that it is hard to see how infants can be *required* to possess rectitude of will, given that they are incapable of possessing it. How, then, does their inherited injustice count as sinful? The same metaphysics of person and nature to which Anselm appeals in explaining the transmission of original sin is also meant to explain how infants can be under an obligation to will justice. Human nature in the persons of Adam and Eve was given justice and ought to have preserved it. By abandoning justice, human nature made itself powerless to be just; since this powerlessness is culpable, however, it does not excuse human nature from its obligation to be just. Because that same human nature is present in all infants, it follows that the inability of infants to be just does not excuse them. As Anselm puts it, "The powerlessness [of human nature] in those infants does not excuse human nature for not paying back in them what it owes, since it brought that powerlessness upon itself by abandoning justice in its first parents, in whom the whole of human nature existed; and it is always indebted to have the power that it received for the sake of always preserving justice."[20]

Consider the familiar analogy of a drunk driver. Ordinarily, relying on "ought implies can," we would say that someone who was incapable of avoiding a car accident is excused from blame for the accident, precisely because he couldn't avoid it. But if his inability to avoid the accident was a consequence of his voluntarily drinking to excess, we would not excuse him from blame, because he brought that inability on himself. In the same way, human nature brought its present state upon itself by voluntarily throwing away justice in the person of Adam. Consequently, its inability to recover justice does not excuse it; its obligation to possess justice remains. Human nature in infants thus culpably lacks the justice it ought to possess. And since the injustice of the nature passes to the person, infants are culpably unjust. They are not punished as severely for their sin as they would be if they had sinned personally, but they are punished nonetheless. If they die in that state of culpable injustice, they are damned.

Anselm realizes that the damnation of unbaptized infants is not obviously just: "There are some whose minds are unwilling to accept that infants who die unbaptized ought to be damned solely on account of this injustice of which I have spoken, since no human being judges that they deserve to be blamed for some other person's sin, and because infants are not yet just and capable of understanding at that age; and they do not think that God should judge innocent children more strictly than human beings would judge them."[21] His first reply is that in fact God *should* judge children more strictly than we do. We would be wrong to demand from other human beings a justice that we did not confer and that is not owed to us. But God did grant justice to human nature, and that justice is owed to him, so he is right to hold human nature accountable for lacking justice—even when that human nature subsists in infants, who are "not yet just and capable of understanding."

Anselm's second reply is to argue that the strictness of God's judgment is actually not out of line with our own moral judgments. He invites us to consider an analogy: "Suppose a man and his wife who have been promoted to some great dignity and possession, not by their own merit but by grace alone, together commit some serious crime for which there is no excuse, and because of this crime they are justly dispossessed and reduced

to servitude. Who would say that the children they have after their con-
demnation do not deserve to be subjected to servitude as well, but rather
should by grace be restored to those good things that their parents justly
lost?"[22] One can imagine that this analogy would have been more persuasive in Anselm's day than it is in ours, since many of us will have mer-
itocratic and individualistic intuitions that undercut its force. We might
agree that the children should not be restored to the rank and possessions
that their parents justly lost—certainly in practice we would not restore
them—but we would not think it fair to subject the children to servitude
(or imprisonment, or the denial of the franchise, or whatever the analogous punishment in the current day might be). Even if, as would certainly
happen in practice, the children grew up in the poverty resulting from
their parents' deprivation, their poverty would not be permanent—not, at
least, as a matter of law. They would be allowed to work their way back
into prosperity and respectability. And if their parents died in debt, and
without the means to satisfy the creditors, the children would not inherit
that indebtedness.

Anselm would doubtless see this reaction as superficial. We have acknowledged that we would not in practice restore the children to their
parents' former status. Is this not, he would ask, because it is *just* for them
to participate at least to that degree in their parents' degradation? And if
indeed it is just, then they are justly deprived on account of a sin that is not
their own. Of course (he might continue) they would be able in principle to
work their way back into prosperity and respectability, because they have
not been deprived of the capacity to do so—though they have been justly
deprived of the resources that might enable them to do so with ease. But the
unmerited dignity that our first parents threw away was not merely prosperity or respectability; it was justice itself. We, their children, are justly
deprived of that justice, and it is a consequence of that deprivation that we
are powerless to work our way back into the dignity that our first parents
culpably renounced. To say otherwise would be blatant Pelagianism.

Whatever the merits of his analogy, Anselm is convinced that the only
way to make sense of the Church's teaching and practice is to affirm that
infants are in a state of sin. For the Church teaches that unbaptized infants
are damned, and only the sinful are damned. What, then, of those who
have been baptized? Given his understanding of rectitude of will, Anselm
cannot think that baptized infants possess rectitude of will, since they are
not able to understand rectitude. So baptized infants, just like unbaptized

infants, lack justice and are powerless to acquire it by their own efforts. But once they have been baptized, their powerlessness is no longer culpable, and God no longer demands justice from them as something required. Since injustice or sin is the absence of *required* justice, baptized infants are not unjust or in a state of sin. If they die in that state, they are admitted to heaven "through the justice of Christ, who gave himself on their behalf, and through the justice of the faith of their mother the Church, which believes on their behalf."[23]

Notice that baptism brings about no intrinsic change in its subject. Baptism does not erase the corruption that has been inherited from Adam. It does not confer virtues or change the will. Anselm does not speak of it as inaugurating a new life: it is a washing, and nothing more.[24] The only change brought about by baptism is relational. God ceases to demand what he had previously demanded; he accepts as innocent the powerlessness that he had previously treated as culpable.

Grace and Salvation

For infants, who cannot will rectitude, this merely relational change is sufficient for salvation. More, however, is required of those who are able to exercise their rational capacities well enough to understand what rectitude demands, and thus to choose rectitude or reject it. They must actually will rightly, and they must do so for the sake of rectitude itself. Anselm insists that one wills rightly because one possesses rectitude, and not the other way around: "Now there is no doubt that a will wills rightly only because it is upright. Vision is not acute because it sees acutely; rather, it sees acutely because it is acute. And in the same way, a will is not upright because it wills rightly; rather, it wills rightly because it is upright. And when it wills this rectitude, it undoubtedly is willing rightly. Therefore, it wills rectitude only because it is upright. But a will's being upright is the same thing as its having rectitude. So it is clear that it wills rectitude only because it has rectitude."[25] This rectitude is not present at birth, and it is not conferred by baptism, so we must ask how someone comes to possess it.

The initial gift of rectitude is from God; it is an unmerited gift of grace. Since free choice is the power to preserve this rectitude of will for its own sake, Anselm's resolution of the problem of grace and free choice is altogether straightforward: we obtain rectitude of will by grace, and we preserve it (or abandon it) by free choice. Even so, Anselm also emphasizes the ways in which grace assists free choice in preserving rectitude of will. When temptation assails the will, grace "helps by mitigating or altogether removing the power of the temptation that assails free choice, or by increasing the felt strength of rectitude itself."[26] Indeed, everything that disposes someone to receive or preserve rectitude of will—the reading of Scripture, hearing a sermon, or anything else that serves as a "seed of right willing"[27]—is a matter of grace.

We must not think of the initial gift of rectitude as complete righteousness. It will be limited in both breadth and intensity. One might be given rectitude of will in one particular area; for example, "someone receives the rectitude of willing sobriety."[28] Anselm's model is clearly the Benedictine notion of continuous conversion, which involves not a dramatic once-for-all change but instead a steady and ever-deepening turning to God in obedience and love. The initial gift of rectitude enables those who possess it to seek greater rectitude: "those who say, 'Turn us, O God,' have already turned to some extent, since they have an upright will when they will to be turned. They pray in virtue of what they have already received, in order that their turning might be increased, like those who were already believers and said, 'Increase our faith.' It is as if both were saying, 'Increase in us what you have already given us; bring to completion what you have already begun.'"[29]

Only those in whom this turning (conversio) is brought to completion will be granted eternal life. As Anselm puts it,

> I do not hold that eternal life is promised to all the just; it is promised only to those who are just without any injustice. For they are the ones who are properly and without qualification called "just" and "upright in heart." Some people, after all, are just in one respect and unjust in another: for example, someone who is chaste but envious. The blessedness of the just is not promised to such people, for just as true blessedness is without any shortcoming, so too it is granted only to those who are just without any injustice. For since the blessedness that is promised to the just will be a likeness to the angels of God, it follows that just as there is no injustice in the good angels, so too no one with any injustice will have fellowship with them.[30]

Anselm declines to offer any account of how anyone attains such perfect justice in this present life; he simply says that we know it is possible, "through holy efforts and through God's grace."[31]

The eternal life that is promised only to the perfectly just is so great a good that all other goods are worthless in comparison. For the sake of that good we ought to flee all earthly pleasures; we should find our only happiness in this life "in things that give [us] help or hope in reaching this state."[32] Now in keeping with Anselm's understanding of the relationship between rectitude and happiness, he cannot mean that we are to pursue rectitude of will in order to attain the joys of heaven. That would truly be a case of preserving rectitude of will for the sake of an extraneous reward, rather than for its own sake. Instead, Anselm means that we would dishonor God by loving any temporal happiness without reference to him; we would be failing to give God his due.

In light of these considerations, we can understand even better the urgency, the sense of precariousness, that we saw in the moral admonitions in Anselm's letters. Since any love for temporal things without reference to God is sin, it is perilously easy to sin. And since any sin, any injustice, is sufficient to disqualify us from eternal happiness and fit us for eternal misery, we are in this life perpetually on the brink of hell. Small wonder, then, that Anselm so often writes as though no one outside a monastery has any hope of salvation.[33] We can understand as well why Anselm says things to his correspondents that would otherwise appear heartless. He goes so far as to congratulate his sister and brother-in-law on having lost all but one of their children in infancy: "If you are wise and give the matter your wise consideration, you will understand that God has done you a great mercy, because he took away from you an incitement to love this present age and to long for things that pass away, by taking from you your heirs in this life and making your children his own heirs, his own children, in eternal life. Now give thanks to God because you have been relieved of your burden and set free to hasten toward God with all your heart, all your effort, and all your strength; and be anxious for nothing but the salvation of your souls."[34] We see here yet another reason for Anselm's overwhelming concern for vertical relationships of subordination and submission—chiefly of submission to God, and derivatively of submission to our earthly superiors—at the expense of horizontal relationships in which love of neighbor would have to play a central role. Even the love of our own children is "an incitement to love this present age," a temptation to stray from the uncompromising love of that perfect good that can tolerate no rival for the affections of an upright will.

EPILOGUE

Anselm is deceptively simple. Our own collaboration on Anselm began because he is the sort of figure on whom a medievalist and an analytic metaphysician can profitably work together. Anselm's work (unlike, say, Augustine's) is thoroughly argumentative in a way that is hospitable to an analytically trained philosopher, yet it is not burdened by the elaborate technical machinery that makes a figure like John Duns Scotus so difficult for the nonspecialist. And Anselm seemed a safe bet, frankly, because his work looks relatively easy and he did not write a great deal.

Yet this easy work has turned into a book, and the book could easily have been twice as long as it is. Somewhat to our own surprise, we have been concerned almost exclusively with exposition. One cannot assess the philosophical merits of Anselm's arguments and views without first getting clear on what they are, and that by itself can be a formidable task. For what can, on first acquaintance, seem careless or underdeveloped almost invariably proves, on further analysis, to be thoughtful and subtle. One frequently finds that Anselm has anticipated all sorts of objections and quietly supplied the wherewithal to meet them. He does not always have the apparatus he needs in order to offer solutions that will satisfy a contemporary philosopher, but his wrestling with the issues is always honest.

Another reason that Anselm's work is more difficult, and indeed more satisfying, than it appears is connected with the fact that (as we pointed out in the introduction) Anselm's work is highly reactive. Much of his writing is done in response to a request or as a reaction against some emergent heresy. As a result, he only writes about what he's interested in at the time; but in doing so, he assumes all of his philosophy. Consequently, it is difficult to take up one of his works and interpret it by itself. Anselm is the kind of thinker whom contemporary tenure-and-promotion committees love, for he has a research program, an overarching project, and it is a lifelong one. For that reason, Anselm's views in any given work can be fully appreciated and understood only in light of his work as a whole.

That overarching project is aptly described, in Anselm's own familiar phrase, as faith seeking understanding. It is the "seeking understanding" part that people generally emphasize, but the "faith" part is every bit as important for understanding Anselm. He is interested in philosophical explorations only insofar as they bear on matters of faith, which means that fundamentally he is interested only in God and in the economy of redemption. He simply does not care about other things, at least not as independent subjects of inquiry. One wants him to have a worked-out view of universals, for example, but he just doesn't. What is important to Anselm is that God creates all things in accordance with the one divine Word that is consubstantial with the One who utters it, and that creatures in some way reflect the perfect goodness that God does not merely have but actually *is*. Anselm simply doesn't care enough about the metaphysical details of the relationship between God's goodness and creaturely goodness, or about the ontological status of creaturely natures and their relation to the one Word, to work out an account of properties.

Yet although Anselm can be disappointingly uncurious—or, perhaps we should say, frustratingly single-minded about his own interests and impatient with what he regards as inessentials—he is a valuable interlocutor for contemporary philosophers and theologians. He is a careful thinker, and an honest one. He is generous; he really tries to understand people's objections. He does much more than simply rehash received wisdom. Indeed, he is a bold thinker, and very creative in his way. Though even his most sympathetic readers (among whom we count ourselves) will not agree with everything he says, Anselm's arguments and views almost always command respect. He may sometimes be wrong, but he is seldom boringly wrong.

NOTES

NOTES TO INTRODUCTION

1. Eadmer, *The Life of St Anselm, Archbishop of Canterbury,* ed. R. W. Southern (Oxford: Clarendon Press, 1962); R. W. Southern, *Anselm: A Portrait in Landscape* (Cambridge: Cambridge University Press, 1991). For two admirable brief accounts of Anselm's life and works, see the first chapter of G. R. Evans, *Anselm,* Outstanding Christian Thinkers Series (Wilton, Conn.: Morehouse-Barlow, 1989), and G. R. Evans, "Anselm's Life, Works, and Immediate Influence," in Davies and Leftow, 5–31.

2. Southern suggests a dating of 1060–63 for *De grammatico,* though he acknowledges that this is a matter of conjecture. Schmitt prefers a later date.

3. Evans, "Anselm's Life," 9.

4. Ibid., 20.

5. M prol. (I:7).

6. M 1 (I:13).

7. P prooem. (I:93).

8. Schmitt dates *On the Fall of the Devil* to 1085–90.

9. For more detail, see the introduction to *Anselm: Three Philosophical Dialogues,* trans. Thomas Williams (Indianapolis: Hackett Publishing Company, 2002), vii–xiv.

10. Southern, *Anselm,* 186–94, lays out the reasons for cynicism, as well as the evidence for taking Anselm's protestations as sincere. Sally Vaughn makes the best case for thinking that Anselm welcomed the archbishopric in *Anselm*

of Bec and Robert of Meulan: The Innocence of the Dove and the Wisdom of the Serpent (Berkeley: University of California Press, 1987), 129–35.

11. Eadmer, *Life of St Anselm,* II.ii.

12. At the synod of Soissons in 1092 or 1093 Roscelin's views were condemned and he was forced to recant.

13. DIV 1 (II:5).

14. CDH praef. (II:42).

NOTES TO CHAPTER I

1. M 16, 34.

2. M 16, 32, 33, 34, 44, 48, 53, 60, 64; CDH 1.15, 2.13.

3. M prol. (I:7).

4. Ibid.

5. Ibid.

6. DIV 6 (II:20).

7. Mann, "Anselm on the Trinity," 257.

8. *De Trinitate* 1.2.4.

9. DIV 6 (II:20–21).

10. DC 3.6 (II:272).

11. DC 3.6 (II:272).

12. M 33 (I:53).

13. M 1 (I:13).

14. P prol. (I:93–94).

15. P 1 (I:100).

16. P prol.

17. Psalm 14:1; 53:1.

18. P 4 (I:104). Or, as Anselm assures Gaunilo, "the meaning of this expression has such great force that the thing it expresses is, from the mere fact that it is understood or thought, necessarily proved both to exist in reality and to be whatever we ought to believe about the divine nature" (AR, I:138–39).

19. P 3 (I:103).

20. P 4 (I:104).

21. DIV 6 (II:20).

22. See page 8.

23. DIV 1 (II:6).

24. Letter 136 to Fulk, Bishop of Beauvais, ca. 1091/92 (III:280–81).

25. DIV 1 (II:8), quoting Acts 15:9, Psalm 19:8 (= 18:9), and Psalm 19:7 (= 18:8).

26. DIV 1 (II:8–9).

27. DIV 1 (II:9).

28. This firsthand acquaintance can come through the senses (M 1, DG 14), by introspection (M 70, P 25, DLA 6, DC 3.1 and 3.10), through intelligent observation (M 8, P 24, DCD 25, CDH 2.11, DC 3.9), and through undergoing something (CDH 1.9).

29. 1 Corinthians 2:15.

30. DIV 1 (II:9).

31. DIV 1 (II:10).

32. DIV 2 (II:11).

33. DIV 11 (II:30).

34. CDH praef. (II:42).

35. DIV 1 (II:9).

36. M 1 (I:14).

37. CDH comm. (II:39–40), quoting Job 14:5.

38. CDH 1.6–7.

39. See in particular CDH 1.10 and 1.18.

40. CDH 1.18 (II:82).

41. CDH 2.17 (II:126).

42. CDH comm. (II:40).

43. CDH comm. (II:40).

44. But see DC 3.6 for reflections on a closely related question: "Now we should understand 'faith is from hearing' to mean that faith is from what the mind conceives as a result of hearing: not that the mind's conception by itself brings about faith, but that faith cannot exist apart from that conception. Faith—one's believing what one hears—comes about when, through grace, rectitude of will is added to the conception" (II:271). Cf. Thomas Williams, "God Who Sows the Seed and Gives the Growth: Anselm's Theology of the Holy Spirit," *Anglican Theological Review* 89 (2007): 611–27.

NOTES TO CHAPTER 2

1. M 10 (I:24–25).

2. M 10 (I:25). Ignore, for the time being, the strangeness of saying that perceptible and imperceptible words were "discovered" (rather than invented). We will return to that issue in chapter 3.

3. M 10 (I:24).

4. As will become very clear over the course of this chapter, Anselm's theory of the relationship between thought and its objects is best expressed if we use the verb 'think' with a simple direct object, rather than with 'of' or 'about'. Such usage will admittedly seem a bit awkward at first, but it is perfectly respectable (if somewhat old-fashioned) English. See *Oxford English Dictionary,* 2nd ed., s.v. "think, *v.*²," B.4.c: "*trans.* with simple obj. To form a

definite conception of (something real) by a conscious mental act . . . cognize," though with no example more recent than William James (1890).

5. M 10 (I:24).

6. M 11 (I:26).

7. See M 3, 7, 18, 32, 67; P 2–5, 9, 11, 14–15, 18, 20, 22: AR (*passim*); DV 1; DCD 4, 15; DIV 4; CDH 1.12, 1.19, 1.23, 2.14, 2.20. The exact relationship between (un)thinkability and (im)possibility is hard to make out, however. Is (un)thinkability identical with (im)possibility, indefeasible evidence for (im)possibility, necessarily coextensive with (im)possibility, or what? We are inclined to believe that for Anselm (1) (un)thinkability and (im)possibility are necessarily coextensive and (2) something's being (un)thinkable is *explained by* its being (im)possible, and not vice versa; but the texts probably underdetermine the interpretation.

8. DIV 12 (II:30).

9. M 10 (I:25). Anselm will later deny that *mortal* properly belongs to the human essence (CDH 2.11, II:109).

10. M 31 (I:48).

11. The Latin uses *per* or the instrumental ablative.

12. King, "Anselm's Philosophy of Language," 87.

13. DIV 1 (II:9).

14. DIV 1 (II:10).

15. *Categories* 1, 1ᵃ12–15. We adapt the translation from that given by Paul Vincent Spade in *Thoughts, Words, and Things: An Introduction to Late Mediaeval Logic and Semantic Theory,* 189–190. Spade's account of Anselm's semantics of denominatives (198–200), on which we draw in this section, differs from ours primarily insofar as he is interested in tracing the development of what will later become connotation theory.

16. DG 14 (I:160).

17. Even if Anselm did not know *De interpretatione,* he knew the Aristotelian-Boethian slogan, as we can tell from his use of variations on the expression *constituere intellectum* in DG 14 (I:160), DCD 11 (I:249–250), and LF (43).

18. *De magistro* 2.

19. Ibid.

20. *De magistro* 3. Anselm probably did not know *De magistro,* but he most likely knew *De doctrina christiana,* in which Augustine sets out the account of signification that gives rise to the puzzles so abortively addressed in *De magistro.* For an account of the books that were probably available to Anselm, see Southern, *Anselm,* 53–59.

21. Of course there are other words that pose a problem for the idea that every sign is the sign of something—such words as 'because', 'for', 'although',

'and', 'if', 'besides', and 'notwithstanding'—but we are following Anselm in focusing on the difficulties that arise for *names*.

22. King, "Anselm's Philosophy of Language," 89. Although our reading of Anselm's account of privative, indefinite, and empty names differs markedly from King's—compare the present section with King, 89–90—our approach to Anselm's theory of language in general is deeply indebted to King.

23. DCD 9 (I:247).

24. DCD 10 (I:247).

25. DCD 11 (I:248).

26. DCD 11 (I:249).

27. DCD 11 (I:250): *Multa quippe dicuntur secundum formam quae non sunt secundum rem.*

28. LF (43).

29. LF (43). Note that Anselm here offers the same account for all three of the problematic kinds of name: privative ('injustice'), indefinite ('not-man'), and empty ('nothing').

30. DIV 11 (II:29).

31. DG 13 (I:157). We say "apparently" because these words are quoted from the student, not the teacher, though the teacher does not disclaim them. The teacher's words are actually rather cryptic: "The name 'human being' signifies *per se* and *ut unum* those things of which the whole human being consists. Among these, substance occupies the foremost position, since it is the cause of the others and possesses the others, not in the sense that it needs them but in the sense that they need it...Hence, although they are all simultaneously and as one called by the one name 'human being,' this name chiefly signifies...the substance" (DG 12, I:156). It is not clear what is meant by 'substance' here.

32. So Anselm insists repeatedly in DIV 11 (I:29). We see no reason for Anselm not to say that 'human being' also signifies individual human beings *qua* instances of a nature (as opposed to *qua* individuals), but he does not in fact say so.

33. For the metaphysical structure of individuals, see chapter 9.

34. DIV 11 (I:29).

35. DG 12 (I:157).

36. See M 21 and 24, DC 1.5 and 2.2, and King, "Anselm's Philosophy of Language," 97.

37. LF (28). The way this is worded suggests (contrary to King, "Anselm's Philosophy of Language," 101) that it is not the verb itself that has a predicative force that "needs a name in order to be discharged," but rather that the act of predicating the verb of something (the act of tokening a verb in the

predicate position in a well-formed statement) is what provides the additional signification—in other words, brings it about that the verb does not merely signify a doing but signifies that the doing is an activity or effect of a particular agent. The distance between these two possibilities, however, is minimal, and perhaps nothing hangs on the distinction.

38. LF (27).

39. LF (27).

40. LF (28).

NOTES TO CHAPTER 3

1. Aristotle, *Metaphysics* 4.7 (1011b 25–8).

2. DV 2 (I:177). We will hyphenate 'what-is' and 'what-is-not' for ease of reading.

3. DV 1 (I:176).

4. G. R. Evans, *Anselm and a New Generation,* 136.

5. DV 2 (I:178).

6. DV 2 (I:178).

7. DV 2 (I:179).

8. Someone to whom the terminology of 'type' and 'token' is unfamiliar can most easily grasp it by considering the following: "The cat sat on the mat. The cat sat on the mat. The cat sat on the mat." Within the quotations marks are three *tokens* of the same *type*.

9. This is not to say that creatures do not act purposively—some of them obviously do—but that in acting purposively they perform actions, make statements, and so forth, whose *genuine* purposes are determined, not by their own wills, but by God's creative activity. For example, *my* purpose in making a statement may be to hurt a colleague's feelings, but it does not follow that that is what the statement is actually *for*.

10. Although Anselm does not state explicitly that natural-language statement-types were made by God, Anselm describes the powers and purposes of statements using exactly the same sort of language he uses to describe the powers and purposes of creatures generally. Thus, statements "received the power to signify" (*accepit significare*) just as an angel created by God "received the power to will" (*accepit velle*). And a statement's signifying what it received the power to signify is "natural"—Anselm's usual word for what follows from the nature God gave a thing—just as, if an angel received only the power to will happiness, its willing happiness would be "natural." In *De veritate* 5, in fact, Anselm expressly notes that the invariable truth of statements is an instance of the rectitude that actions have when a thing acts in accordance with the nature God gave it: "For just as fire, when it heats, does

the truth, since it received the power to heat from the one who gave it being, so also the statement 'It is day' does the truth when it signifies that it is day, whether it is actually day or not, since it received naturally the power to do this."

11. Anselm's usual word, as we have noted, is *oratio. Propositio* occurs a few times in *De veritate,* but it is not distinguished in sense from *oratio.*

12. We take the expression "lush and giddy platonism" from William E. Mann, "Simplicity and Properties: A Reply to Morris," *Religious Studies* 22 (1986): 343–53, at 348.

13. DV 3 (I:180). Note that if Anselm thought of propositions as a kind of mental language, as some later medieval thinkers will, then he would have no need to suppose that God creates natural-language statement-types. For then utterances would express mental language or thought, which is the same in all human beings because it is a function of the powers we were given by God. In this way the truth of statements could be analyzed in terms of the truth of thought or mental language. Unfortunately, Anselm does not think of propositions in this way.

14. For truth in the will, the teacher appeals to John 8:44, which says that the devil "did not abide in the truth." "It was only in his will," the teacher says, "that he was in the truth and then abandoned the truth." For truth in action, the teacher appeals to John 3:21: "He who does the truth comes to the light."

15. DV 4 (I:181).

16. DV 5 (I:182).

17. DV 9 (I:189).

18. The qualification "perceptible by the mind alone" excludes rectitude that can be perceived by the senses, such as the rectitude (that is, the straightness) of a stick.

19. DV 7 (I:185).

20. See DCD 20. The idea of God's permitting things that he does not bring about raises other philosophical issues, which we consider in chapter 11.

21. DV 8 (I:186).

22. Would Anselm then infer that John ought to kill Samantha? The answer is not altogether clear from the text, but we are inclined to say yes. Anselm acknowledges that expressions of the form "S ought to φ" do not always imply that S is under an obligation to φ. So he can consistently affirm both that John is not under an obligation to kill Samantha (indeed, that he is under an obligation not to kill her) and that he ought to kill her.

23. It is important not to confuse this claim with the superficially similar (and relatively uncontroversial) claim that the propositional content, and hence the truth-value, of an utterance can change depending on the circumstances

of the utterance. Anselm holds the much stronger and more counterintuitive view that one and the same utterance, with just one determinate propositional content and in one determinate set of circumstances, can have different truth values according to different ways of assessing the utterance.

24. More literally, "...the supreme Truth is not a rectitude because it owes something. For all things owe [something] to it, but it owes nothing to anything." DV 10 (I:189–190).

25. DV 9 (I:190).

26. M 18 (I:33), quoted verbatim in DV 1 (I:176).

27. DV 10 (I:190).

28. DV 13 (I:196–97).

29. DV 13 (I:197).

30. DV 13 (I:198).

31. DV 10 (I:190).

32. DV 13 (I:199).

NOTES TO CHAPTER 4

1. M 1 (I:13).

2. M 1 (I:13–14).

3. M 1 (I:14).

4. M 1 (I:14).

5. M 1 (I:14).

6. M 1 (I:15).

7. M 1 (I:15).

8. M 2 (I:15).

9. M 4 (I:17).

10. DPSS 14 (II:214).

11. M 4 (I:16–17).

12. M 2 (I:15).

13. M 1 (I:15).

14. Leftow, "Anselm's Perfect-Being Theology," in Davies and Leftow, 132.

15. M 3 (I:15): "Omne...quod est, aut est per aliquid aut per nihil." Although *est* often has a predicative sense in Anselm, either instead of or (more usually) alongside its existential sense, *est* has to be read existentially in this argument.

16. LF 40.1–2.

17. M 3 (I:15–16).

18. Richard Rodgers, "Something Good," from the film version of *The Sound of Music*.

19. See also chapter 2 of this volume, "The Signification of Verbs."

20. M 3 (I:16).

21. M 3 (I:16).

22. M 3 (I:16)

23. M 4 (I:17).

24. An actual quantitative infinity is (roughly) an infinitely numerous collection of items all of which exist at the same time. Medieval thinkers were generally willing to allow the possibility of a quantitative infinity by successive parts, in which the infinitely numerous items exist successively rather than all at once.

25. M 4 (I:17).

26. DIV 2 (II:13).

27. M 27 (I:45).

NOTES TO CHAPTER 5

1. G. R. Evans, "Anselm's Life, Works, and Immediate Influence," 24.

2. Ibid., 27.

3. According to P prooem. (I:94), the original Latin title of the *Monologion* was *Exemplum meditandi de ratione fidei;* the original title of the *Proslogion* was *Fides quaerens intellectum.*

4. P 2 (I:101).

5. In "Why Anselm's Proof in the *Proslogion* Is Not an Ontological Argument," *Thoreau Quarterly* 17 (1985), 32–40; and "Russell or Anselm?" *Philosophical Quarterly* 43 (1993): 500–504, G. E. M. Anscombe argues that the phrase should instead be translated "For if it is only in the mind, what is greater can be thought to exist in reality as well." If one understands what Anselm is saying in this way, he is not suggesting that existence in reality is greater than existence in the mind. Since we will go on to argue that Anselm is not at all comparing the greatness of real existence with that of merely intentional existence, we would be happy to adopt Anscombe's suggestion. Unfortunately, it seems to us to require an impossible construal of Anselm's Latin; moreover, we take it that Anscombe's interpretation has been decisively repudiated in Jasper Hopkins's introduction to *A New, Interpretive Translation of St. Anselm's Monologion and Proslogion* (Minneapolis: The Arthur J. Banning Press, 1986), 26–33.

6. GR 6 (I:128).

7. Nicholas Wolterstorff, "In Defense of Gaunilo's Defense of the Fool," in C. Stephen Evans and Merold Westphal, eds., *Christian Perspectives on Religious Knowledge* (Grand Rapids, Mich.: William B. Eerdmans, 1993), 87–111.

8. Ibid., 90.

9. Ibid., 89.

10. Ibid., 87. "Disingenuously" is our word, not his, but Wolterstorff does note one remark of Anselm's that "reads as though it were the conclusion to a passage in which Anselm points out the disanalogy" when it fact it is no such thing (88).

11. Williams, Thomas, "Saint Anselm," *The Stanford Encyclopedia of Philosophy* (Summer 2006), http://plato.stanford.edu/archives/sum2006/entries/anselm/; "Gaunilo," in Donald Borchert, ed., *The Encyclopedia of Philosophy,* 2nd ed. (Detroit: Macmillan Reference USA, 2006).

12. Eadmer, *Vita Sancti Anselmi,* in Southern, *The Life of St Anselm,* 31.

13. AR 1 (I:130).

14. M 10 (I:25). Anselm will later deny that *mortal* properly belongs to the human essence: see CDH 2.11 (II:109).

15. M 10 (I:24).

16. M 11 (I 26).

17. Paul Vincent Spade, "Ambiguity in Anselm," *International Journal for Philosophy of Religion* 7 (1976): 433–445, at 436 n. 5, and 437.

18. P 3 (I:102).

19. *Id ipsum quod res est. Id ipsum* is not especially emphatic in Anselm's usage, and *id ipsum quod* appears several times where it simply means "that which" (where *id quod* or simply *quod* would have done just as well). So one should not take the expression to require anything like full understanding or a complete grasp of the object in order for an object to be "thought" in the second and proper sense. In fact, we do not have a full understanding or complete grasp of God, but God is still thought in the proper sense.

20. P 4 (I:103–4).

21. P 4 (I:104).

22. GR 4 (I:126–27).

23. AR 8 (I:137).

24. No doubt children and philosophically unsophisticated adults can think God in the sense that they get God before their minds by means of some image or true description of God. Admittedly, that sort of thinking does not require serious and sustained reflection about the necessary conditions for being an unsurpassable good, but it also does not make possible the kind of argument that Anselm wishes to make in the *Proslogion.*

25. There are, if not seven different arguments, at least seven distinct stretches of text in which Anselm makes a case for (A2): (1) section 1, paragraph 2; (2) section 1, paragraph 3; (3) section 1, paragraph 4; (4) section 2, paragraph 3; (5) section 3; (6) section 4, paragraph 1; (7) section 9.

26. The English translation of this sentence, much like the Latin original, leaves the modal operators where they are grammatically at home but philosophically less than perspicuous. To avoid scope ambiguity, we would represent this sentence as follows: □ (it can be thought to exist ⊃ □ [it exists]).

27. AR 1 (I:130–31).

28. The rehash of *Proslogion* 2 is given in the fourth of the seven passages identified above.

29. GR 6 (I:128).

30. AR 3 (I:133).

31. Anselm's only other mention of the Lost Island reinforces the idea that he takes Gaunilo to be objecting to (A2). Anselm writes, "So you see how right you were to compare me to that stupid man who was willing to affirm the existence of the Lost Island *solely because the island would be understood if someone described it*" (AR 5 [I:135–136]).

32. AR 3 (I:133).

33. AR 5 (I:134)

34. AR 5 (I:135)

35. AR 5 (I:135).

36. Or rather, it is not *obvious* that there is any such feature in the notion of "that which is greater than everything else." We need an additional argument, as Anselm says, and he proceeds to tell us what the argument is. That than which nothing greater can be thought is that which is greater than everything else; that than which nothing greater can be thought cannot be thought not to exist; therefore, that which is greater than everything else cannot be thought not to exist (AR 5 [I: 135]).

37. P 2 (I:101).

38. Wolterstorff 108–11.

39. AR 7 (I:137).

40. Anselm had a bit of a thing about painting. The art seems to be his favorite source of analogies, some of them instructive (as at CDH 1.1), some of them noticeably strained (as at CDH 1.4).

41. P 2 (I:101). More literally, "he understands that what he has now painted exists."

42. P 2 (I:101).

43. Anselm does explicitly appeal to necessary existence in chapter 3 of the *Proslogion,* which simply restates the argument of chapter 2 with a specific example of an existence-entailing feature of that than which nothing greater can be thought. The popularity of the notion that chapter 3 offers a different and independent argument from that of chapter 2, rather than an elaboration or gloss on the argument of chapter 2, is an excellent example of the way in

which the secondary literature can put obstacles in the way of our under-standing of Anselm. There is nothing in the *Proslogion* itself to suggest that the chapter 3 argument is a new and distinct argument—the *utique* at the beginning of the chapter is evidence enough for its connection with what comes before—and in light of Anselm's reply to Gaunilo it seems obvious that necessary existence is simply one example, though perhaps the most straightforward and striking example, of an existence-entailing feature of that than which nothing greater can be thought.

NOTES TO CHAPTER 6

1. Two differences between the *Monologion* and the *Proslogion* that do not arise in the body of the discussion are worth noting briefly here. Most strikingly, Anselm explores Trinitarian doctrine at length in the *Monologion* but barely mentions the Trinity in the *Proslogion*. Presumably this is because even Anselm does not think there is any clear argumentative path from the concept *that than which nothing greater can be thought* to the Trinity. Even the brief discussion of the Trinity in P 23 depends on the Augustinian psycho-logical analogies explored in the *Monologion*. In the *Proslogion* Anselm simply identifies the Trinity with that than which nothing greater can be thought and exhibits some of the implications of the concept for the relationships among the three divine persons, but he does not try to derive the three-personal nature of God from the claim that God is that than which nothing greater can be thought. Second, God's justice and mercy, discussed in the next-to-last section of this chapter, are prominent in the *Proslogion* but hardly mentioned in the *Monologion*. Two reasons for this difference suggest them-selves. First, the *Monologion* minimizes God's active engagement with creatures, concentrating instead on the causal dependence of creatures on God. Second, and probably more important, the arguments of the *Proslogion* arise out of the believer's inner struggle, in which mercy and justice are relevant, rather than out of the more dispassionate considerations of the *Monologion*. Even though we see no reason to think that the argument of P 2 (and following) is anything other than an argument, the "rousing of the mind to the contemplation of God" in P 1 is still quite relevant. As we argued in chapter 5, Anselm's "rousing of the mind" focuses on the seeming hiddenness and elusiveness of God, which ac-count for the frustration the believer feels in attempting to approach God, but which also offer the very considerations of greatness on which the *Proslogion* argument rests. The *Proslogion* argument in turn not only reveals God more fully, but reveals him in a way that explains his apparent hiddenness.

2. The argument of M 80 suggests that Anselm thinks that the term 'God' is reserved for a being regarded as worthy of worship: "Surely everyone who

says that God exists (whether one God or more than one) understands him to be nothing other than a substance that he thinks human beings ought to worship because of his preeminent dignity, and to entreat in any pressing need, beyond every nature that is not God" (I:86). This explains why Anselm uses the word 'God' from the very beginning of the *Proslogion*, which opens with worship and prayer.

3. M 7–8.

4. M 13 (I:27).

5. M 14 (I:27).

6. M 15 (I:28). "Nouns or verbs" could equally well be translated "names or words." As the argument progresses, it becomes clear that Anselm is talking about predicates of any kind.

7. M 16 (I:30).

8. M 15 (I:28). Note that Anselm does not actually need the general principle that no relative predications reveal what a thing is in order to support the claim that relatives are not predicated substantially of God, since he immediately derives the latter claim from the doctrine of divine aseity rather than from the general principle. But he will need the general principle later for the purposes of his Trinitarian theology, so he goes ahead and states it here.

9. M 15 (I:28–29).

10. Brian Leftow, in "Anselm's Perfect-Being Theology," 135–39, offers the most analytically rigorous treatment of the argument of M 15. He goes astray, however, in treating a formulation that comes late in chapter 15 as though it were an independent formulation, rather than a shorthand restatement of the earlier (and, as he rightly says, "better") formulation.

11. M 16 (I:30).

12. M 17 (I:31).

13. P 18 (I:114). This argument recurs in DIV 4 and 7.

14. P 18 (I:115). See Leftow, "Anselm's Perfect-Being Theology" (148), for criticisms of this argument.

15. M 21 (I:36).

16. M 22 (I:39).

17. M 22 (I:41).

18. M 23.

19. M 24.

20. Katherin Rogers, "Anselmian Eternalism," *Faith and Philosophy* 24 (2007): 3–27, argues among other things that Anselm's view of divine eternity requires him to be an eternalist (or, in her terminology, a four-dimensionalist). Brian Leftow responds in "Not So Anselmian," *Faith and Philosophy* (forthcoming). We agree with Leftow both that Rogers's argument from

divine eternity to eternalism is unsuccessful and that Anselm is a presentist, but we develop Anselm's view in somewhat different ways.

21. M 28 (I:46).

22. M 28 (I:46).

23. M 22 (I:40). One could, we suppose, give an eternalist reading to *cum praeterito, quod iam non est* by translating it as "with the past, which does not exist now," rather than as "with the past, which no longer exists"—though such a translation would be highly tendentious and artificial, and only someone bent on finding eternalism in Anselm would dream of adopting it. But there is no eternalist reading available for *cum futuro, quod nondum est:* "with the future, which does not yet exist." So this passage is clearly presentist.

24. Note that in laying out the different possibilities concerning God's relation to time in M 21, Anselm takes it for granted that there is nothing in time that is analogous to the way in which a plurality of distinct places are all equally real.

25. Trenton Merricks, "On the Incompatibility of Enduring and Perduring Entities," *Mind* 104 (1995): 523–41, argues that presentism entails endurantism and that eternalism rules out endurantism. Nonetheless, there are philosophers who argue that presentism is compatible with perdurantism as well as philosophers who hold both eternalism and endurantism. Given how contested the relationship is between theories of time and the perdurantism/endurantism debate, we can at best say that Anselm's commitment to presentism is highly suggestive of endurantism, not that it outright entails endurantism.

26. M 21 (I:37).

27. Ibid.

28. DIV 13 (II:31–32). It is not immediately obvious how conceiving of the Nile "as existing for its whole lifetime" is meant to help with the issues of Trinitarian theology that Anselm is considering. We read the analogy as follows. Notice that we have two sets of words in the relevant passage. On the one hand, Anselm speaks of the "spring," the "river," and the "lake," the analogues for the three Persons of the Trinity. On the other hand, he speaks of the one "Nile," "stream," "body of water," and "nature"; these are the analogues for the single divine nature. Anselm needs us to think about the Nile "as existing for its whole lifetime" because if we look at all the water that will make up the spring in its lifetime, that (quantity of) water will be the same as the (quantity, stream, body of) water that will make up the river over its lifetime, and similarly for the lake. If we think of each of them only momentarily (which is how Anselm, as a presentist, usually thinks), we will miss the point that they're all made of exactly the same stuff. After all, when

we think of the spring, the river, and the lake as they all exist at a given time, they are made up of different water. But if we consider the spring, the river, and the lake over the Nile's entire lifetime, we are conceiving one and the same Nile/body of water/nature/stream.

29. Ibid.

30. Merricks, "Incompatibility," makes an argument along these lines.

31. Yet it is noteworthy that if some contemporary philosopher were to press Anselm on the supposed incompatibility of presentism with perduring entities, he would have the resources to meet the challenge. We suspect that in the back of Anselm's mind in this passage is Augustine's frequent appeal to utterances as examples of temporally extended events whose parts come into being and pass away. For Augustine, these parts add up to a whole only because the soul can hold the parts together in its attention; as far as their own extramental existence is concerned, the parts of the utterance must all cease to exist in order for the utterance itself to be completed. (See, for example, *Confessions* 11.27.35.) In a similar spirit, Anselm could argue that the utterance and the four-dimensional Nile are not strictly speaking perduring entities at all, but mental constructs. To ascribe this view to Anselm would, however, go well beyond the textual evidence.

32. DC 1.5 (II:254).

33. M 22 (I:41): *labile praesens.*

34. DC 1.5 (II:254).

35. M 24 (I:42), alluding to the definition of eternity in Boethius, *Consolation of Philosophy,* Book 5, prose 6.

36. M 25 (I:43).

37. M 25 (I:43).

38. M 26 (I:44).

39. M 27 (I:45).

40. M 27 (I:45).

41. M 28 (I:46).

42. M 28 (I:46).

43. M 28 (I:46).

44. P 9 (I:106–7).

45. P 9 (I:108). The argument echoes the words of a widely used collect: *Deus, qui maxime parcendo et miserando potentiam tuam manifestas* (in Cranmer's rendering, "God, which declarest thy almighty power most chiefly in showing mercy and pity").

46. P 10.

47. P 11 (I:109).

48. P 11 (I:109).

49. See, for example, Leftow, "Anselm's Perfect-Being Theology," 152–53.

50. In addition to Leftow, "Anselm's Perfect-Being Theology," see Thomas V. Morris, "Perfect Being Theology," *Noûs* 21 (1987): 19–30, and Katherin A. Rogers, *Perfect Being Theology* (Edinburgh: Edinburgh University Press, 2000).

51. Leftow, "Anselm's Perfect-Being Theology," 135–39.

NOTES TO CHAPTER 7

1. M 26 (I:44).

2. M 65 (I:76).

3. M 15 (I:28).

4. The language in the quoted passage is *convenire substantialiter;* we take this to be equivalent to *dicatur de . . . substantia, est . . . significativum substantiae, designat essentiam,* and *significat essentiam,* all of which appear within the next few lines as ways of posing the same question.

5. The expression "unqualified perfections" *(perfectiones simpliciter)* is associated in particular with John Duns Scotus. See William E. Mann, "Natural and Supernatural Knowledge of God," in Thomas Williams, ed., *The Cambridge Companion to Duns Scotus* (Cambridge: Cambridge University Press, 2003), 238–62, at 247–48.

6. M 15 (I:29).

7. To forestall pettifoggery from the perennially obtuse: this is not "what he is like" in the sense of "what he resembles," but in the usual sense that expression has in colloquial English. When normal speakers of English ask "What is he like?" they are requesting a description, not a simile.

8. M 16 (I:30).

9. For a defense of the doctrine of univocity, see Thomas Williams, "The Doctrine of Univocity Is True and Salutary," *Modern Theology* 21 (2005): 575–85. For an overview of approaches to theological language in the Middle Ages, see Thomas Williams, "Describing God," in Robert C. Pasnau, ed., *The Cambridge History of Medieval Philosophy,* forthcoming.

10. M 26 (I:44).

11. M 22 (I:40).

12. M 22 (I:41).

13. This reading of what Anselm means by 'above' and 'beyond' in this context is confirmed in M 65 (I:76–77): "through his unique loftiness he is far above all things and through his natural distinctive character he is vastly beyond all things."

14. M 26 (I:44).

15. As Peter King notes ("Anselm's Philosophy of Language," 104 n. 4), "Anselm regularly calls the significate of a sign its signification *(significatio).*"

16. M 64 (I:74–75).

17. "Necessary proofs": *probationibus necessariis* and *necessariis rationibus* (M 64 [I:75]); "the solidity of certainty": *certitudinis...soliditas* (ibid.).

18. M 65 (I:75).

19. M 65 (I:76).

20. In fact Anselm rarely talks about the *sensus* of individual terms. Other than here in M 65 he does so only at DG 4, DC 3.6, and possibly RG 7. In each of those cases we could replace *sensus* with *significatio,* but always with the emphasis on informational content rather than the significate. Anselm frequently talks about the *sensus* of phrases or sentences, and in those contexts *sensus* always means "meaning."

21. DG 4 (I:149).

22. For such usage, see M 23 and 25, RG 4, DCD 1, DPSS 13.

23. DG 20, DIV 11, DPSS 16.

24. M 29, 38, 43, 49, DIV 2, DPSS 16.

25. M 65 (I:76): "We often say many things that we do not express properly, as they are."

26. M 65 (I:76).

27. M 65 (I:76).

28. As Peter King, "Anselm's Philosophy of Language" (96), suggests.

29. M 65 (I:76).

30. On this score Anselm would surely have agreed with an argument John Duns Scotus made against Henry of Ghent's doctrine of analogical predication. Scotus argued that all our mental contents derive from our experience of creatures. So if we have any concepts at all that apply to God, they must be the very same concepts that apply to creatures, since those are the only concepts we have. See *Ordinatio* 1, d. 3, pars 1, qq. 1–2, n. 35. Note that in DLA 1 and 14 Anselm takes it as unproblematic that the definition of *liberum arbitrium* is the same for God's *liberum arbitrium* as it is for ours, even though God's *liberum arbitrium* is very different from ours.

NOTES TO CHAPTER 8

1. M 8 (I:24).

2. M 9 (I:24). The Latin of the second sentence is compact in a way that resists translation: "Patet itaque quoniam priusquam fierent universa, erat in ratione summae naturae quid aut qualia aut quomodo futura essent."

3. M 10 (I:24). For Anselm's notion of "utterance" (*locutio*), see chapter 2.

4. M 11 (I:26).

5. M 11 (I:26).

6. *De diversis quaestionibus 83,* q. 46.2: "Sunt namque ideae principales quaedam formae vel rationes rerum stabiles atque incommutabiles, quae ipsae

formatae non sunt ac per hoc aeternae ac semper eodem modo sese habentes, quae divina intellegentia continentur."

7. Whether there really is a "standard doctrine of divine ideas" is not altogether clear. Statements of the textbook version of the doctrine of divine ideas are hard to find in Augustine, and even the term "idea" is infrequent, being confined mainly to the celebrated discussion of the topic in q. 46 of *De diversis quaestionibus 83.* It is probably best to read Anselm as taking his cue from Augustine's occasional remarks on the divine ideas and developing them in ways suggested by Augustine's Trinitarian doctrine in general. Such a reading is consonant with Anselm's own description of his relationship to the fathers, and especially Augustine, in DIV 6.

8. M 29 (I:47), rehearsing an argument already made in M 12.

9. M 29 (I:47).

10. M 30 (I:48). Henceforth we will use a capital letter to distinguish the one divine Word from ordinary words, though no such device was available to Anselm.

11. *De diversis quaestionibus 83,* q. 46.2: "nec eadem ratione homo qua equus; hoc enim absurdum est existimare. Singula igitur propriis sunt creata rationibus."

12. M 31 (I:48). "Patterned after it" translates *ad exemplum illius facta.*

13. M 31 (I:49).

14. M 31 (I:49).

15. Anselm uses the word *singularis* to express several claims: that the supreme nature exists in a unique way (M 26, 28), that it is an individual (M 27), and that it is simple and unitary (M 17 ff.).

16. M 31 (I:49/14–20).

17. He does, however, say so in M 26.

18. M 36 (I:50).

19. The survey of the primary texts and secondary literature found in Katherin Rogers, *The Neoplatonic Metaphysics and Epistemology of Anselm of Canterbury* (Lewiston, NY: Edwin Mellen Press, 1997), 112–24, amply illustrates the difficulties.

20. Try to imagine two portraits talking about what their originals must be like—how they are, somehow, more *real;* how they can move from place to place without being carried—without having any direct knowledge of things like their originals. The imagined dialogue will inevitably take on many of the characteristics of theological discourse.

21. M 32 (I:50).

22. M 32 (I:51).

23. M 33 (I:52).

24. M 34 (I:53).

25. M 34 (I:53).

26. M 34 (I:53).

27. Many, perhaps most, divine ideas theorists balked at the notion of uninstantiated kinds, and the view that there are ideas of individuals was also highly controversial. Our point is simply that there is nothing in the theory of divine ideas as such to exclude those sorts of ideas. The reasons for disallowing certain types of ideas came from considerations extraneous to the theory of divine ideas itself. For example, if one supposes that the principle of individuation is something *per se* unintelligible, there is a strong case to be made that there are no divine ideas of individuals. But if the principle of individuation is something *per se* intelligible, divine ideas of individuals seem unobjectionable.

28. M 36 (I:54–55).

29. M 10 (I:25).

NOTES TO CHAPTER 9

1. M prol.

2. The psychological analogies do not appear at all in DIV or DPSS. DIV offers an analogy for the Trinity drawn from sensible things in order to provide a model for the predications involved in talking about the Trinity, rather than (strictly speaking) as an analogue for the metaphysical relations that constitute the Trinity. DPSS dispenses with analogies altogether, perhaps because in that work Anselm is debating with fellow Christians who already accept the three-personal character of God and therefore do not need them.

3. M 79 (I:86).

4. Anselm's other Trinitarian work, DPSS, differs from M and DIV in using premises drawn from Scripture and the Creed (see note 2). Anselm could not do so in M because he was trying to provide purely rational arguments; he could not do so in DIV because he was trying to confute a heretic who "either does not believe Scripture or else interprets it in some perverse sense" (DIV 2 [II:11]).

5. We first find these words in a letter from the monk John (Letter 128, III:270–71). Anselm quotes them, at least in part, every time he engages with Roscelin's challenge: in his brief reply to John (Letter 129, III:271–72), in his instructions to Bishop Fulk of Beauvais on how to respond on Anselm's behalf at the upcoming Council of Rheims (Letter 136, III:279–81), and in various drafts of DIV (see I:282 ff. and II:4 ff.). Anselm is never sure whether it was Roscelin who stated the comparison to "three angels or three souls" or his correspondent who introduced the comparison as a gloss on Roscelin's challenge.

6. DIV 2 (II:11).

7. Can we call God's nonessential features "accidents," as we did in the case of creatures? Augustine says no (*De trinitate* 5.4.5–5.5.6), on the grounds that accidents imply mutability and God is immutable. Anselm considers this reasoning and is inclined to reject it: "among the things that are called accidents, some do imply a degree of mutability, but others in no way destroy immutability" (M 25 [I:43]). Nonetheless, perhaps out of deference to Augustine, he avoids talking about God as having accidents.

8. It is on this basis that Anselm would reply to a criticism raised by William Mann in "Anselm on the Trinity." Mann criticizes Anselm for holding, inconsistently, both that the Father begets the Son necessarily and that relations do not belong to the essence of anything:

> But recall *No-rel.*, the principle that no relational term ascribed to any being refers to that being's essence. Anselm invoked *No-rel.* to support his thesis that no relational term ascribed to God refers to God's essence. But the terms, "begets" and "spirates," are relational and ascribed to God. Now Anselm faces a dilemma. Take the case of begetting; analogous remarks apply to spiration. Either the Father begets the Son essentially or not. If the former, then *No-rel.* is false. If the latter, that is, if the Father does not beget the Son essentially, then it would seem that the Son's existence is as contingent as the existence of any creature. But that consequence flies in the face of everything that Anselm has said about the Father and the Son, in particular, that the Father's existence is necessary and that the Father and the Son are coeternal, coequal, and consubstantial. (274)

But we have seen how Anselm would reply to this criticism. The relational properties that distinguish the persons are necessary, but they do not belong to the common divine essence.

9. DIV 3 (II:14–15).

10. DIV 3 (II:15).

11. DIV 3 (II:15).

12. We consider the image of the Nile briefly in our discussion of time in chapter 6; see in particular note 28. Gillian Evans examines Anselm's approach to analogies of the Trinity in "St. Anselm's Images of Trinity," *Journal of Theological Studies*, n.s. 27 (1976): 46–57.

13. M 12 (I:26).

14. See chapter 4, "Divine Simplicity, Eternity, and Omnipresence," for the details of these arguments.

15. M 29 (I:47). Nothing hinges on the choice of the word 'subsist' here; substituting 'exist' would make no difference to the argument.

16. Anselm will not argue until M 42 that it is appropriate to call the divine utterer "Father," but we will go ahead and employ the usual Trinitarian vocabulary at this stage in order to avoid awkward circumlocutions.

17. M 29 (I:47–48).

18. Cf. Evans, "St. Anselm's Images of Trinity," 57: "we may take it that Anselm made use of these images [of the Trinity] only in order to explain to others what was already perfectly clear to himself."

19. M 33 (I:52–53). This passage also suggests a second use for the appeal to the human mind's self-understanding: an *a fortiori* argument that reinforces the conclusions already drawn. Given that our own weak minds, when functioning at their best, generate a consubstantial likeness or word, surely the perfect divine mind will generate a consubstantial Word through its perfect self-understanding.

20. See M 33 (I:52): "the one who utters by means of these words has the same substance as they have, and yet he is not a word." Anselm speaks of "words" in the plural because he has not yet identified the supreme spirit's self-utterance with his utterance of creation.

21. M 29 (I:48).

22. The classic example in recent philosophical theology of the use of relative identity to illuminate the doctrine of the Trinity is Peter van Inwagen, "And Yet They Are Not Three Gods, But One God," reprinted in *God, Knowledge, and Mystery: Essays in Philosophical Theology* (Ithaca, NY: Cornell University Press, 1995), 222–59. Anselm's implicit appeal to relative identity has little of the theoretical sophistication of van Inwagen's, but the two accounts are recognizably in the same spirit. The notion of relative identity is highly controversial; indeed, van Inwagen himself has no use for it except in the context of Trinitarian theology.

23. M 38 (I:56). Anselm makes a similar argument at the beginning of M 43 and repeatedly in DPSS 1.

24. M 43 (I:59).

25. M 43.

26. M 43, 44, 45.

27. M 80.

28. M 43 (I:59).

29. M 79 (I:86). Anselm here departs in small but noteworthy ways from the example of Augustine. In *De trinitate* 5.8.10–5.9.10, Augustine complains that the distinction the Greeks make between *ousia* and *hypostasis* is obscure. Moreover, he says, one cannot sensibly say in Latin that God is one essence and three substances, as the Greek usage would suggest. So we must say that God is one substance or essence and three persons—where 'person' is used just because we have to say *something* in answer to the question "Three what?" Anselm shows himself to be more ecumenically minded than Augustine, not merely in forbearing to criticize Greek theological vocabulary but also in defending "one essence, three substances" as appropriate Latin usage, alongside the more usual "one essence, three persons."

30. DIV 2 (II:11). In DPSS 1 (II:178), however, Anselm notes that in Trinitarian contexts 'Spirit' is *construed* as a relative name (*pro relativo nomine ponitur*).

31. M 48 (I:63–64).

32. *De trinitate* 14.11.14.

33. The entire constructive Trinitarian project in the *Monologion* rests on this Augustinian notion of memory, so it is regrettable that Anselm does nothing to clarify his understanding of memory. It is arguably far too inchoate and obscure an idea to bear the weight that Anselm tries to place upon it.

34. Anselm's pneumatology, and especially his teleological understanding of the Holy Spirit, are explored at length in Thomas Williams, "God Who Sows the Seed."

35. M 49 (I:64). The word "affection" (*affectus*) is especially interesting here, since commentators have been inclined to deny any affect in Anselm's God on the strength of P 8, in which Anselm argues that God does not feel the *affectus* of compassion, though we feel the *effectus* of his merciful action. In light of Anselm's willingness to acknowledge affect in God in the *Monologion,* we should perhaps interpret the denial of compassion as a point about divine impassibility rather than a statement about divine emotionlessness in general. That is, compassion has to be excluded from the divine life, not because it is an emotion, but because it is a *reaction* to something external.

36. M 53 (I:66).

37. M 54 (I:66).

38. John Milbank, "The Second Difference: A Trinitarianism without Reserve," *Modern Theology* 2 (1986): 213–34, at 214–15. The expression *a Patre Filioque tamquam ab uno principio* does not appear anywhere in Anselm, but we can take it as a fair representation of Anselm's doctrine in M 54.

39. Augustine makes the triad of power, wisdom, and love a key structural principle in the *Confessions,* as James J. O'Donnell has shown. The use of appropriated names in Trinitarian formulas is nothing new, though it has been on the rise in recent years because of the desire to avoid gendered language in speaking of God. Such formulas are not (as some seem to think) inherently modalist, though we acknowledge that in many cases there are other grounds for suspecting the Trinitarian theology of those who use them.

40. M 59 (I:70).

NOTES TO CHAPTER 10

1. CDH 2.17 (II:122).

2. *Summa contra Gentiles* 3.148.

3. Anselm uses the word *coactio* only three times, and in each place it is contrasted with *prohibitio* (constraint): CDH 2.10 and 2.17, and DC 1.1.

4. It might seem odd for Anselm to say that all necessity is compulsion or constraint and then to speak of a kind of necessity that does not compel anything to be. In fact, however, there *is* compulsion involved in this second kind of necessity: the thing compels or brings about the necessity, rather than the necessity's compelling or bringing about the thing. We will examine the two sorts of necessity in detail below.

5. CDH 2.17 (II:125). "Creation" translates *conditio*. The derivation of *conditio* from *condere*, to create, is a false etymology; but Anselm surely did not know that, and he would have found frequent use of *conditio* to mean "creation" in his readings in Augustine.

6. LF (27–28).

7. CDH 2.17 (II:125).

8. DV 5 (I:181–82).

9. DV 12 (I:192).

10. CDH 1.18 (II:80). That *creatura insensibilis* means "incapable of experiencing God" rather than "incapable of sensation" is made clear earlier in the passage, where Anselm contrasts "the lesser nature that would not experience God" (*minor quae non sentiret deum natura*) with "the greater nature that ought to enjoy God."

11. DCD 21 (I:268).

12. DCD 24 (I:272).

13. DLA 2 (I:209).

14. DLA 2 (I:210).

15. In addition to the texts already cited, spontaneity is contrasted with compulsion at DLA 9, DCD 16, and CDH 1.8–9 and 1.22; with necessity at CDH 1.10 and 2.5 and DC 2.3; and with both compulsion and necessity at CDH 2.16 and 2.18 and DC 1.3.

16. LF (23–24).

17. DCD 12 (I:253). Similar examples are given at DV 8, DLA 5, and CDH 2.17.

18. Compare the similar explanations given at DCD 12 and P 7. Problems similar to those raised in this section are also raised in LF.

19. These are all taken from DC 1.2–3.

20. DC 1.2 (II:249).

21. DC 1.2 (II:249).

22. DC 1.2 (II:250).

23. LF (27–28).

24. DCD 3 (I:236–37).

25. DPSS 1 (II:181).

26. Simo Knuuttila, "Anselm on Modality," in Davies and Leftow, 111–31, at 122.

27. DC 1.1 (II:245).

28. The argument is strongly reminiscent of an argument Augustine offers in *De libero arbitrio* 3.3.

29. DC 1.1 (II:246).

30. DC 2.3 (II:262).

31. DC 1.3 (II:250): "Tomorrow's sunrise...is understood to be future in accordance with *two* necessities: both antecedent necessity, which brings it about that a thing exists (for the fact that its future existence is necessary accounts for why it will exist), and subsequent necessity, which does not compel anything to be (for the fact that it is future is what accounts for its being future by necessity)." Notice that, as Anselm recognizes, every case of antecedent necessity will also involve subsequent necessity, but not vice versa.

32. DC 1.2 (II:248–49).

33. Brian Davies has raised the objection that Anselm, as someone who accepts the doctrine of divine simplicity, cannot consistently say that divine foreknowledge is not part of the causal history of creaturely actions. The objection, we take it, is that according to the doctrine of divine simplicity, God's foreknowledge is identical with God, so to say that divine foreknowledge is not part of the causal history of creaturely actions is tantamount to saying that *God* is not part of the causal history of creaturely actions—surely, Davies suggests, an implication that Anselm cannot accept. We reply that Anselm is perfectly happy to accept the claim that, in at least one crucially important way, God is not part of the causal history of free creaturely actions. For (as we shall argue in detail in the next chapter) Anselm consistently argues for an understanding of creaturely freedom according to which the free actions of creatures originate in the creatures themselves, and not in God (except in the derivative sense that the powers that creatures exercise in their free actions are received from God). Admittedly, this reply sidesteps a closely related question. If indeed Anselm holds that free creaturely actions are in some respect independent of God's causal activity, it follows that the content of God's foreknowledge is in just that respect dependent on what creatures do; and since (for Anselm) creatures have the power to act otherwise than they do, it follows that God's foreknowledge could have been otherwise than it is. Consequently, Davies can argue, Anselm must say that the divine nature could have been otherwise than it is—for according to the doctrine of divine simplicity, God's foreknowledge is identical with the divine nature. This is a problem Anselm simply does not see, so it is less clear how we ought to reply on his behalf. One approach, explored by Katherin Rogers in *Perfect Being Theology,* is to grant that in some sense the divine nature is contingent,

but to argue that this sort of contingency is innocuous. Another approach, which we are inclined to prefer, is to seek a way of qualifying the doctrine of divine simplicity so that one can deny the strict identity of God's nature with God's foreknowledge and yet satisfy the philosophical and theological intuitions that impel Anselm to embrace divine simplicity.

34. Anselm's theory of free will strictly entails only that human beings have power over the past at least once. Nevertheless, given the contingent fact that human beings fell, he thinks that we must frequently have alternatives available to us in order for our actions to be free, and therefore that we frequently have power over the past.

35. DC 2.3 (II:262): "and just as what is foreknown is immutable in eternity even though it is subject to change in time before it exists, this is true of everything included in God's predestination." However, Anselm doesn't fully work out all the implications of this feature of free choice, and someone might well hesitate to accept Anselm's solution without knowing more about what Anselm thought this power over the past consisted in. Contemporary philosophers of religion have discussed such powers at considerable length. See, for example, John Martin Fischer, *God, Foreknowledge, and Freedom* (Palo Alto: Stanford University Press, 1989).

36. CDH 2.17 (II:122).

37. There is considerable debate about whether Descartes actually held this "Cartesian" view. For an overview of the issue, see David Cunning, "Descartes' Modal Metaphysics," *The Stanford Encyclopedia of Philosophy* (Fall 2006), Edward N. Zalta (ed.), http://plato.stanford.edu/archives/fall2006/entries/descartes-modal/.

38. CDH 2.16 (II:122).

39. CDH 2.17 (II:123).

40. CDH 2.17 (II:124).

41. CDH 2.17 (II:123).

42. CDH 1.12 (II:70). We return to this passage in the next chapter in the context of Anselm's rejection of divine command theory.

NOTES TO CHAPTER 11

1. Anselm uses *libertas arbitrii* and *liberum arbitrium* interchangeably. We shall translate as "freedom of choice" and "free choice," respectively, with no distinction in meaning.

2. DLA 3 (I:212). At DLA 13 this definition is endorsed as complete (*perfecta*): that is, as stating a necessary and sufficient condition for freedom of choice.

3. See DLA 1 and 14.

4. DV 1.

5. See our discussion of Anselm's account of truth in chapter 3.

6. DV 4 (I:181).

7. Thus, in the passage cited above, the student says that the devil "voluit quod debuit, ad quod scilicet voluntatem acceperat." The construction admits of two different readings; and although the difference appears slight at first, we think it is important. On one reading, the last 'quod' has the same referent as the preceding 'quod'; on the other, the last 'quod' refers to the whole clause "voluit quod debuit." On the first reading, Anselm's meaning is "he willed that which he ought to will—in other words, he willed that for the sake of which he had received a will." On the second reading, his meaning is "he willed what he ought to will—which is the very reason why he had received a will." (Our translation above is deliberately ambiguous but is perhaps more naturally taken in the first way.) The first reading suggests a material, the second reading a purely formal specification of the will's end. The parallels to the account of truth in statements give some warrant to the first reading. Anselm offers a material specification of the end of statements (statements are for signifying the way things are), not a purely formal one (statements are for signifying what they ought to signify). More important, however, the philosophical barrenness of a purely formal specification tells decisively in favor of the first reading. Anselm cannot sensibly say that God gave us a will so that we could will what God gave us a will to will—we would get either an empty circle or an infinite stutter ("we should will what God gave us a will to will, which is willing what God gave us a will to will, which is willing..."). Fortunately, the first reading makes for better Latin as well as better moral philosophy.

8. DV 12 (I:192).

9. DV 12 (I:193).

10. DV 12 (I:194).

11. DV 12 (I:194).

12. See the preface to DV (I:173–74).

13. DLA 1.

14. Notice that Anselm's assumption here, namely that moral praiseworthiness and blameworthiness require free choice, is commonly made in the contemporary debate as well.

15. DLA 1 (I:208).

16. DLA 2 (I:209).

17. DLA 2 (I:209–10).

18. DV 12; see section 2 above. Anselm makes a similar argument in DLA 13.

19. DLA 4; cf. DLA 12.

20. The same restriction applies to the discussion in DC itself, where Anselm notes more than once that he is relying on the account of freedom developed in the earlier works, applying it to show that freedom is compatible with divine foreknowledge, predestination, and grace.

21. DLA 5 (I:214).

22. We have not yet been told *why* this is not possible—that explanation is delayed until chapter 6 of DCD—merely *that* it is not possible (DLA 1 and 14).

23. DCD 5 (I:242–43).

24. DLA 2 (I:209).

25. DCD 12 (I:254).

26. DC 3.11.

27. In his review of *The Cambridge Companion to Anselm,* in which an earlier version of this chapter appeared, Jasper Hopkins wrote, "the analysis of *freedom* might stress that a 'self-initiated action' is not an unmotivated action and that self-initiation can include the mere fact of one's *consenting* to what temptation prompts" ("The Philosophy of Anselm," *British Journal of the History of Philosophy* 13 (2005): 745–53, at 751, emphasis in original). We take it that the paragraph to which this note is attached amply makes the first of Hopkins's points, and we will allow our quotation of Hopkins in this note to make the second.

28. DCD 13 (I:256).

29. DCD 13 (I:257).

30. DCD 13 (I:257).

31. DCD 13 (I:257).

32. In correspondence, Eleonore Stump raised the following objection: "Why shouldn't we suppose that what God gives an angel is the power to initiate anything the angel takes to be good, where it is up to the intellect to determine what counts as good, in any sense of 'good'? Then the angel could initiate an action for happiness or for justice, and it would really be his own will which did the initiating, even though the angel had only one will and not two." The answer is that God has given the angel a properly functioning intellect, so he will always see justice as better than mere happiness (see DC 1.6). If the angel's only motivational disposition is toward willing what his intellect takes to be good, he will of course will what has greater goodness (justice) in preference to what has lesser goodness (happiness). In that case, the angel's willing justice has its ultimate origin not in the angel but in God, who gave him the motivational disposition and the properly functioning intellect that together guarantee his willing justice.

33. So Anselm's view entails that God, who receives nothing from outside himself, *never* needs alternative possibilities in order to be free. We take up this issue at the end of this section.

34. DCD 25 (I:273).

35. Anselm commendably refrains from indulging in speculative angelic psychology and tells us that he has no idea what the something extra could have been. Scotus, who read *De casu diaboli* attentively, is somewhat less circumspect. See John Duns Scotus, *Ordinatio* 2, d. 6, q. 2.

36. DCD 6 (I:243): "adhærentes iustitiæ nullum bonum velle possint quod non gaudeant."

37. DCD 24.

38. DC 1.3 (II:250).

39. DC 2.3 (II:262).

40. CDH 2.5 (II.99–100). "Honorableness" and "dishonorableness" translate *"honestas"* and *"inhonestas,"* respectively.

41. DV 12 (I:193–94).

42. DV 12 (I:194).

43. We call it "enriched" because it makes explicit certain requirements Anselm takes to be implied by the original descriptive definition, not because it actually adds something new.

44. DC 1.6 (II:257).

45. Because the enriched descriptive definition is silent about what an agent's goals are or should be, and hence says nothing about the content of the agent's "knowledge," it is ultimately merely Anselmian, not Anselm's. Anselm insists that we have only two motivations—one for happiness, the other for justice. The only sorts of choices that are of interest to him are ones that involve a conflict between the two. Any other decisions require a conflict among intermediate goals and their potential to make a person happy. Mistakes in this regard are all due to lack of knowledge or lack of rationality. Anselm wants to be able to say that people are most free when their motivation for action is justice (preserving rectitude for its own sake). Thus, those who act on the belief that a base hedonistic life leads to happiness, not realizing that such a life is incompatible with justice, are less free than those who recognize the incompatibility but choose happiness over justice (not realizing that ignoring justice will preclude ultimate happiness). They in turn are less free than those who once chose justice over happiness, now realize that the choice of justice leads to happiness, and maintain their desire to uphold justice for its own sake. By contrast, if we refrain from building a substantive moral theory into the enriched descriptive definition, there will be no such hierarchy of degrees of freedom. If, say, a person foolishly believes that smoking combats colds, then the smoker can smoke as freely as the nonsmoker refrains.

46. In order to preserve the appearance of answering "Nothing" to the Pauline question, Anselm argues that free choices are received from God in

the sense that creatures received from God the powers that they exercise in making free choices. This way of expressing his view allows Anselm not to run afoul of the letter of Paul's point while arguably violating its spirit.

NOTES TO CHAPTER 12

1. M 64 (I:74).
2. M 65 (I:75–76).
3. M 65 (I:76). Anselm's language in *Monologion* 65–68 repeatedly recalls (without ever quoting) 1 Corinthians 13:12, which in the version Anselm knew reads as follows: "Now we see in a mirror, enigmatically (*in aenigmate*), but then face to face. Now I know in part, but then I shall know as I am known."
4. M 65 (I:77).
5. M 66 (I:77).
6. M 67 (I:78).
7. M 68 (I:78).
8. M 68 (I:78). Cf. CDH 2.1.
9. M 68 (I:78–79). Cf. CDH 2.1.
10. M 68 (I:78–79).
11. CDH 1.15 (II:73).
12. The principle that God always acts in a fitting and orderly way raises interesting modal questions, which we will address in the next chapter.
13. CDH 1.4. This is not to say that Anselm does not seek to offer logically compelling arguments for the claims under dispute. But in doing so, he is making concessions to unbelievers and immature believers who are not yet able to perceive in one synoptic glance the beauty or orderliness that is intellectually satisfying to a more developed understanding. For Anselm himself, the aesthetic insight comes first; the discursive arguments are developed later, in order to "raise up" those of weaker intellect "just a little to gaze upon the reason of the things we believe" (CDH comm. [II:40]).
14. CDH 1.12 (II:70).
15. CDH 1.12 (II:70).
16. Letter 403 to Eulalia, Abbess of Shaftesbury, and her nuns, Autumn 1106 (V:347).
17. Letter 182 to Prior Henry and the other monks at Canterbury, ca. 1095 (IV:67).
18. Letter 427 to Muirchertach, King of Ireland, 1106 or 1107 (V:373–74).
19. Collect for the Fifth Sunday in Lent, *Book of Common Prayer* (1979).
20. Letter 6 to Hugh the Prior, ca. 1071 (III:108).
21. Letter 1093 to Pope Urban II, August or September 1093. There is another way to read this letter, in which it poses a theoretical problem about

moral knowledge rather than a problem for the practical application of Anselm's morality of obedience. We examine the letter in greater detail below in the section on moral knowledge.

22. Letter 454 from the Chapter of the Church of York, October 1108 (V:402).

23. Letter 464 to Sampson, Bishop of Worcester, ca. December 1108 (V:413).

24. Letter 465 from Sampson, Bishop of Worcester, December 1108 or January 1109 (V:415).

25. Letter 472 to Thomas, Archbishop-elect of York, March or April 1109. Anselm did get his way, if only posthumously. The bishops unanimously supported Anselm's demands, and "the King sided with the bishops because he had no wish at all to bring upon himself the excommunication of Father Anselm" (Eadmer, *Historia novorum* 209). Thomas made the required profession before he was consecrated in July 1109, three months after Anselm's death.

26. The qualification "to created things" is crucial. God has rectitude—indeed, God *is* rectitude—even though he is not subject to any "ought" or duty. See DV 10 and chapter 3, "The Supreme Truth."

27. CDH 1.15 (II:72–73).

28. DV 12 (I:196).

29. DV 12 (I:194).

30. *[R]ectitudinem...agnoscit* (DV 12 [I:192]); *rectitudinem...percipit* (DV 12 [I:193]).

31. Rosalind Hursthouse, *On Virtue Ethics* (Oxford: Oxford University Press, 1999), 137.

32. M 68 (I:78).

33. CDH 2.1 (II:97). Cf. M 68 (I:78–79): "every rational thing exists in order that it might love something more or less, or reject it altogether, according as its rational discernment judges that the thing is more or less good, or not good at all."

34. Letter 5 to Henry the monk, ca. 1071 (III:106), quoting Romans 14:8.

35. Letter 414 to Robert and his nuns, 1106–9 (V:360).

36. And in fact the argument of CDH 2.13 depends on the claim that the overwhelming *magnitude* of Christ's earthly work required flawless discrimination between good and bad. Ordinary human beings have a much more limited scope of activity and so presumably do not need perfect evaluative judgment. So long as they can discriminate between good and bad in their limited affairs, they will have all they need.

37. Letter 17 to the monk Henry, before 1074 (III:124). Cf. DCV 23 (II:165): "our own wills, which so often seriously hinder the mind from understanding rectitude."

38. Letter 193 to Pope Urban II (IV:83).

39. Letter 61 to Fulk, abbot-elect, ca. 1078 (III:176). In letter 88 Fulk writes back to Anselm, now abbot-elect at Bec, quoting this advice word for word and telling Anselm, "I see no way you can refuse this burden" (III:214).

40. Letter 159 to Gilbert, Bishop of Evreux, before 4 December 1093 (IV:26). Anselm wrote to Gilbert, who had blessed him as Abbot of Bec, because of rumors that Gilbert suspected him of jockeying for ecclesiastical preferment out of greed and ambition. Other letters attempt similar rebuttals. For the debate over Anselm's true attitude toward the archbishopric, see the introduction.

41. Assuming, that is, that Anselm is reporting his feelings accurately, and not overdramatizing in order to induce Urban to make things easier on him by just telling him what to do—as an alternative reading of this letter, explored above, would suggest.

42. For an excellent discussion of the rise of voluntarism in the thirteenth century, see Bonnie D. Kent, *Virtues of the Will: The Transformation of Ethics in the Late Thirteenth Century* (Washington, DC: The Catholic University of America Press, 1985).

43. Jeffrey E. Brower, "Anselm on ethics," in Davies and Leftow, 222–56, at 248.

44. Ibid., 249.

45. Letter 231 to the monks of the monastery of Saint Werburgh at Chester, ca. 1102 (IV:136–37), quoting Ecclesiasticus 19:1.

46. Letter 420 to Basilia (V:365–66). See also Letters 2, 167, 183, 184, and 403.

47. Letter 403 to Eulalia, Abbess of Shaftesbury (V:348). The imagery here is suggestive, since Anselm thinks of the monastery as a kind of earthly paradise, and one can be expelled from a monastery for disobedience. Note Letter 333, in which Anselm compares the monastery to the Garden of Eden.

48. Letter 232 to the monk Hugh, ca. 1102 (IV:139).

49. Letter 96 to Richard and the other monks of Bec resident in England, ca. 1080–81 (III:222–23).

50. *Fortitudo* for Anselm always means "strength," never "courage." *Prudentia* sometimes has the sense of "practical wisdom" in the letters, but there is no clear doctrine of practical wisdom in Anselm. The word *temperantia* never appears in Anselm.

51. Letter 37 to Lanzo the novice (III:145).

52. Letter 134 to Ermengard. Ermengard's husband wants to become a monk. Anselm counsels her that if she truly loves him, she will want him to do what God has inspired him to do.

53. Romans 13:1–2, 5.

54. The one noteworthy exception occurs in CDH 2.18, where he argues that since neither marriage nor celibacy is commanded by God, people ought to get married if they prefer marriage but remain celibate if they prefer celibacy.

1. *Book of Common Prayer* (1979), 864.

2. CDH 1.8 (II:59).

3. "Anselm on the Cost of Salvation," *Medieval Philosophy and Theology* 6 (1997): 73–92, at 75–76. We have reorganized Leftow's argument in order to make it easier to follow, but we have made no changes in the substance of the argument. Leftow takes up a closely related issue in "Anselm on the Necessity of the Incarnation," *Religious Studies* 31 (1995): 167–85, where he argues that "Anselm's case that God 'must' save humanity by becoming incarnate and atoning for human sin comes down to this: God's nature and prior choices make it the case that God ought to save humanity in this way, and God's nature is such that he will do what He ought" (180). In light of our comments in the preface, it is perhaps important for us to note here that Leftow is most emphatically *not* someone who has obscured Anselm's soteriology by bad exegesis—quite the contrary.

4. Leftow, "Anselm on the Cost of Salvation," 76.

5. We will argue in the following section that CDH in fact *does* argue against (7).

6. Leftow, "Anselm on the Cost of Salvation," acknowledges in a footnote (80 n. 23) that Anselm might have a stronger case that (LC) is necessarily false *given* God's plan to make human beings equal to the angels. But, as we must note, this revision would not be enough to save Anselm's argument from a version of DCA, because an unbeliever could surely complain that it was foolish of God to make such a plan, knowing what it would require of him should human beings fall (and knowing, furthermore, that they would in fact fall: see CDH 2.6). Fortunately, as we will show, Anselm's arguments in fact support the claim that (LC) is necessarily false independently of any considerations about God's plan for human beings. For any sin, however apparently trivial, is of infinite gravity. It therefore requires an infinite recompense. And no being less than God can offer an infinite recompense.

7. Leftow, "Anselm on the Cost of Salvation," 81.

8. CDH 1.8 (II:59).

9. We note here two slight infelicities in Leftow's presentation of his argument: (1) According to Leftow, Anselm "suggests that God is not less perfect for having a life containing a human life." That is correct, but it isn't

quite right to say that Anselm derives this suggestion from the Chalcedonian two-natures theory. Chalcedon allows him to say that Christians are not "indicating any lowliness in the divine substance," but the two-natures theory by itself does not provide the resources to show that there is no degradation involved in the divine nature's union with a human nature that *is* subject to such "lowliness." (2) Moreover, despite his explicit statement that Anselm uses the appeal to Chalcedon to deny that the costs of redemption are really costs at all—or costs paid by *God,* at any rate—Leftow in fact correctly presents Anselm as arguing not that God pays no cost to redeem humanity, but that the costs are justified because they are not really humiliations but glories.

10. Leftow, "Anselm on the Cost of Salvation," 82–83.

11. CDH 2.11 (II:111).

12. Leftow, "Anselm on the Cost of Salvation," 91.

13. CDH 1.3 (II:51).

14. Leftow, "Anselm on the Cost of Salvation," 91. Note, in support of Leftow's point, the large role Anselm gives to the beauty of order in his moral theory. See chapter 12, pages 196–97.

15. Leftow, "Anselm on the Cost of Salvation," 92.

16. CDH 1.4 (II:51–52).

17. CDH 2.16 (II:119).

18. We owe the argument that follows to Tom Flint.

19. Consider: Could the most fitting number of rational natures have been other than what it in fact is? Could things have been such that an Incarnation of the Holy Spirit would have been more fitting than the Incarnation of the Word?

20. DCV 18 (II:159).

21. And indeed there is a strong appearance of inconsistency in this case, since in CDH 2.8 Anselm clearly seems to think that God could not have become incarnate otherwise than in a virgin.

22. See, for example, William L. Rowe, *Can God Be Free?* (Oxford: Clarendon Press, 2004); Michael J. Murray and Michael Rea, *An Introduction to the Philosophy of Religion* (Cambridge: Cambridge University Press, 2008), chapter 1.

23. This is not to say that in every case in which a creature acts freely, there are alternative possibilities. See chapter 11, pages 182–85.

24. See LF for details.

25. CDH 1.4 (II:52, Boso speaking).

26. CDH 1.16–18. Anselm explicitly marks this discussion as a digression both at the beginning and at the end. At the beginning, when Boso asks Anselm to explain the replacement of angels by human beings, Anselm replies, "You have misled me. We set out to discuss nothing but God's Incarnation,

and now you're throwing in extra questions for me." Boso does not dispute that these are indeed "extra questions," but he encourages Anselm to answer them anyway: "Don't be angry: 'God loves a cheerful giver.' And the best way for anyone to show that he is cheerful in giving what he has promised is to give more than he promised" (CDH 1.16 [II:74]). Then, at the end of the discussion, Boso says, "Now return to the point from which we digressed" (CDH 1.18 [II:84]).

27. Perhaps the cluttered character of *Cur Deus Homo* is attributable in part to the haste in which Anselm completed it, but in the preface Anselm blames his haste only for omissions, not for disorganization (unless perhaps the complaint that his work was not fully *exquisitum* is an acknowledgment that CDH is not as carefully structured a work as he generally wrote).

28. The discussion in David Brown, "Anselm on Atonement," in Davies and Leftow, 279–302, at 290–95, is very helpful in this context.

29. Richard Campbell, "The Conceptual Roots of Anselm's Soteriology," in D. E. Luscombe and G. R. Evans, ed. *Anselm: Aosta, Bec and Canterbury* (Sheffield: Sheffield Academic Press, 1996), 256–63, offers a valuable corrective to "sociological and juridical" readings of Anselm's key concepts.

30. Perhaps certain caveats are necessary here, since there are arguably theologians who regard the notion of sinning as crude and antiquated and yet are recognizably Christians. The point is that such theologians are not going to be the kind of people who are looking for an account of the Atonement, because they don't think there's anything to atone for. Anyone who *is* looking for an account of the Atonement will have to think it makes sense to talk about sin. And since everything Anselm says about debt or honor can be restated in terms of sin, one can't dismiss Anselm's account of Atonement just because one thinks talk of debt is crude and talk of honor is antiquated feudalism.

31. CDH 1.11 (II:68).

32. CDH 1.20 (II:87).

33. CDH 1.21 (II:88–89).

34. Here Anselm recurs to a point he first made in CDH 1.11, where he argued that someone who takes from another what the other rightly possesses must not merely restore what he stole but also give more, as compensation for the injury or affront done to the other. Hence, Anselm says in 1.21, "you do not make recompense unless what you pay back is greater than the thing for the sake of which you ought not to have committed the sin" (II:89). But the compensatory damage requirement, as we might call it, does not actually play an essential role in Anselm's argument for the necessity of Incarnation and Atonement. The infinite seriousness of sin is enough to establish the point that a nondivine human being cannot make recompense for sin. The compensatory damage requirement plays more of a rhetorical role: Anselm uses it to drive

home the hopelessness of the human condition apart from Christ and, later, the sufficiency of the death of Christ as recompense for sin (see CDH 2.14).

35. CDH 1.24 (II:93).

36. CDH 1.24 (II:94).

37. CDH 1.25 (II:95).

38. CDH 1.25 (II:96).

39. CDH 2.1 (II:97).

40. M 68 (I:78).

41. CDH 2.1 (II:97).

42. CDH 2.1 (II:98).

43. CDH 2.4 (II:99).

44. CDH 2.4 (II:99).

45. In chapter 8 Anselm argues that Christ's human nature should be assumed from a virgin woman descended from Adam. We do not regard this as part of the core of the argument, although it is quite possible that Anselm did.

46. An overly literal reading of the commercial metaphor will make hash of Anselm's point, since it is not in general true that only the person who owes a debt can discharge it. We all know that if Jim gets into financial trouble, Bob can bail him out. What Anselm is getting at is that sin ruins the proper relationship between God and humanity. Unless there is some change *in humanity,* the breach in that relationship does not get healed.

47. Note that this rules out (LC) without any need to appeal to supposed facts about God's plan for humanity in relation to angels. It is true that Anselm does appeal to such facts in CDH 1.5 in arguing that human beings could not be redeemed by angels. (If they had been, they would be rightly judged to be subservient to the angels, whereas God intends for human beings to be equal to the angels.) But that argument comes before the main problem of the work is stated and the main line of argument is introduced and developed, and Anselm does not return to it. These are not reasons to think Anselm would disavow the argument, but they do indicate that he does not regard it as essential to the central points of CDH. The central claim of CDH is that humanity cannot be redeemed by anyone other than a God-man; the argument of 1.5 simply elucidates an additional reason why humanity cannot be redeemed by an angel in particular.

48. CDH 2.7 (II:102).

49. CDH 2.11 (II:110).

50. CDH 2.11 (II:110).

51. CDH 2.14 (II:114).

52. When Anselm says that other sins are incomparably less serious because they are *extra personam Dei,* "person of God" could mean simply "divine person" (the usual sense in Anselm of *persona Dei*); but it seems more

likely that "person" here has the sense it has in the legal expression "sins against the person."

53. CDH 2.14 (II:114). In chapter 15 Boso asks how the death of the God-man can overcome the sin of those who killed him, since killing him is so incomparably evil. Quoting 1 Corinthians 2:8 ("If they had known, they would never have crucified the Lord of glory"), Anselm argues that those who put Christ to death did so in ignorance and were therefore not guilty of an incomparably great sin. In fact, no one could knowingly kill the God-man.

54. CDH 2.18 (II:128).

55. CDH 2.18 (II:128).

56. CDH 2.19 (II:130–31).

57. CDH 2.7 (II:102).

58. CDH 2.7 (II:102).

59. DIV 9 (II:24–25); cf. CDH 2.9.

60. DIV 10 (II:26). These absurdities include the following: (1) if the Father or the Holy Spirit were incarnate, there would be two sons in God: the Son of God and the son of the Virgin. This would be confusing, and it would also mean that the Son of God would outrank the son of the Virgin in terms of his nativity, since being born of God is greater than being born of a human mother. (2) If the Father were incarnate, there would be two grandsons in God. The Father would be the grandson of the Virgin's parents, and the Son would be the grandson of the Virgin (the Son of the son of the Virgin), even though he would in no way derive from the Virgin.

61. DIV 10 (II:26–27). Most strikingly, Anselm argues that human beings sinned most particularly against the Son, that most perfect likeness of the Father, by arrogating to themselves a false likeness to God in asserting their own autonomous wills in defiance of the divine will. There is therefore a particularly satisfying poetic justice in their redemption by the Son.

62. U. M. Lang, "Anhypostatos-Enhypostatos: Church Fathers, Protestant Orthodoxy and Karl Barth," *Journal of Theological Studies* NS 49 (1998): 630–57, at 647.

63. DIV 1 (II:9).

64. DIV 11 (II:28).

65. In English, to be sure, 'human being' more naturally suggests an individual human person; it is only with some effort that one can school oneself to interpret "Christ assumed human being" as meaning "Christ assumed human nature." The Latin *homo* is genuinely ambiguous in the way Anselm suggests. So is the English 'man', but we have sought to avoid translating *homo* as 'man', except in the expression 'God-man'—and even there only on the grounds that the ugliness of 'God-human-being' is too high a price to pay to avoid "gendered" language.

66. DIV 11 (II:29).

67. DIV 11 (II:29).

68. DIV 11 (II:29).

69. DIV 11 (II:29).

70. It is no objection that DIV was written before CDH. The discussion of the collection of properties belongs to the latest stage of Anselm's revisions of DIV, which he finished in 1094. He began writing CDH in 1095. Since it is clear from CDH 1.1 that Anselm's arguments in CDH had been worked out in discussion before he began to commit them to writing, it is quite reasonable to suppose that by the time he drew up the final version of DIV, he had already worked out the soteriology that he would defend in CDH.

71. And in fact Anselm does say this at DCV 21. But this is not his usual language.

72. DPSS 2 (II:186).

73. "The reason they are distinct": *ob hoc sunt ab invicem alii;* "the basis of their distinctness": *unde alius sit [Spiritus Sanctus] a Patre;* "the cause of their being distinct persons": *causa ut diversae sint personae.*

74. DCV 21 (II:160).

NOTES TO CHAPTER 14

1. DCV 29 (II:173). The difference in tone is obvious when one compares this statement to M prol., DIV 6 ("I think he will find in [the *Monologion* and *Proslogion*] discussions of this matter that he will not be able to refute and will not wish to belittle"), CDH comm. and pref., and the last paragraph of DC.

2. DCV 1 (II:140).

3. DCV 7 (II:148).

4. DCV 3.

5. DCV 2 (II:141).

6. DV 12 (I:192).

7. DCV 2 (II:141). This passage alone is enough to counter any reading of Anselm as an extreme realist or Platonist with respect to universals. Whatever exactly human nature is, for Anselm, it can undergo change; and it does not exist apart from its instances. Platonic forms, by contrast, are immutable, and they have being independently of the things that participate in them.

8. DCV 2 (II:141).

9. DCV 2 (II:141–42).

10. Anselm uses "Adam" here, as he often does throughout DCV, as a shorthand for "Adam and Eve": see DCV 9.

11. DCV 10 (II:152). In DCV 23 Anselm will say that original sin is present in all human beings because we were "in Adam," but he makes it

clear at the beginning of the chapter that this is merely a different way of making the same point that he had argued for in chapter 10: that the pro-creation of all subsequent human beings, except for the supernaturally con-ceived God-man, depends on the reproductive nature that was given to Adam and Eve.

12. DCV 12. According to this reasoning, Anselm notes, the supernatu-rally procreated human nature would have been free from Adam's debt even if it had not been joined in unity of person with a divine nature (DCV 13) and even if it had been procreated through a sinful human parent (DCV 18).

13. DCV 23 (II:165).

14. DCV 23 (II:165).

15. DCV 23 (II:165).

16. DCV 27 (II:170).

17. DCV 24 (II:168), 27 (II:170).

18. DCV 24.

19. M 68, CDH 2.1

20. DCV 2 (II:142).

21. DCV 28 (II:170–71).

22. DCV 28 (II:171).

23. DCV 29 (II:173).

24. With one possible exception in the Prayer to St. Peter (III:31), Anselm always treats baptism purely as a cleansing from sin, rather than as the be-ginning of a new, supernatural life. He also emphasizes the *additional* obli-gation imposed in baptism, that of fidelity to the promises made on one's behalf. As he says in his letter to Bishop Fulk about Roscelin, "It is just to demand from [Christians] that they hold unshaken the pledge made in baptism" (III:281). He treats this obligation as similar to that imposed by ordination vows: see Letters 319 (V:247) and 329 (V:261).

25. DC 3.3 (II:265–66).

26. DC 3.4 (II:268).

27. DC 3.6 (II:270).

28. DC 3.4 (II:268).

29. DC 3.6 (II:272), quoting Psalm 85:4 (84:5) and Luke 17:5.

30. DC 3.4 (II:268).

31. DC 3.4 (II:268).

32. CDH 1.20 (II:87).

33. This sounds like an exaggeration, but if one reads through Anselm's letters, it is not until Letter 189 that one finds the first indication that anyone living "in the world" can be saved.

34. Letter 211 (IV:108). He writes to them in a similar vein in Letter 258.

REFERENCES

ABBREVIATIONS

References in endnotes to the Latin text of Anselm use the following abbreviations:

AR	Anselm's *Reply to Gaunilo*
CDH	*Cur Deus Homo*
DC	*De concordia*
DCD	*De casu diaboli* (*On the Fall of the Devil*)
DCV	*De conceptu virginali et de originali peccato* (*On the Virginal Conception, and On Original Sin*)
DG	*De grammatico*
DIV	*De incarnatione Verbi* (*On the Incarnation of the Word*)
DLA	*De libertate arbitrii* (*On Freedom of Choice*)
DPSS	*De processione Spiritus Sancti* (*On the Procession of the Holy Spirit*)
DV	*De veritate* (*On Truth*)
GR	Gaunilo's *Reply on Behalf of the Fool*
LF	Lambeth Fragments
M	*Monologion*
P	*Proslogion*

Parenthetical citations by volume and page number refer to the critical edition of F. S. Schmitt, *S. Anselmi Cantuariensis Archiepiscopi Opera Omnia* (Stuttgart–Bad Canstatt: Friedrich Fromann Verlag, 1968). Parenthetical citations by page number alone refer to Schmitt's edition of the Lambeth Fragments in "Ein neues unvollendetes Werk des hl. Anselm von Canterbury," *Beiträge zur Geschichte der Philosophie und Theologie des Mittelalters* 33, no. 3 (1936): 22–43.

Adams, Marilyn McCord. "Anselm on Faith and Reason." In Davies and Leftow, 32–60.

———. "Saint Anselm's Theory of Truth." *Documenti e studi sulla tradizione filosofica medievale* 1 (1990): 353–72.

Anscombe, G. E. M. "Russell or Anselm?" *Philosophical Quarterly* 43 (1993): 500–504.

———. "Why Anselm's Proof in the *Proslogion* Is Not an Ontological Argument." *Thoreau Quarterly* 17 (1985): 32–40.

Augustine. *De magistro.* In *Contra academicos. De beata vita. De ordine. De magistro. De libero arbitrio,* ed. W. M. Green and K.-D. Daur. Turnhout, Belgium: Brepols, 1970.

——— . *De trinitate,* ed. W. J. Mountain and F. Glorie. Turnhout, Belgium: Brepols, 1968.

Barnes, Jonathan. *The Ontological Argument.* London: Macmillan, 1972.

Barth, Karl. *Anselm: Fides Quaerens Intellectum.* Richmond, Va.: John Knox Press, 1960.

Book of Common Prayer. New York: Church Publishing, 1979.

Brower, Jeffrey E. "Anselm on Ethics." In Davies and Leftow, 222–56.

Brown, David. "Anselm on Atonement." In Davies and Leftow, 279–302.

———. " 'Necessary and Fitting' Reasons in Christian Theology." In *The Rationality of Religious Belief,* ed. W. Abraham and S. Holtzer. Oxford: Oxford University Press, 1987.

Campbell, Richard. "The Conceptual Roots of Anselm's Soteriology." In *Anselm: Aosta, Bec and Canterbury,* ed. D. E. Luscombe and G. R. Evans, 256–63. Sheffield: Sheffield Academic Press, 1996.

———. *From Belief to Understanding.* Canberra: ANU Press, 1976.

Colish, Marcia L. "St. Anselm's Philosophy of Language Reconsidered." *Anselm Studies* 1 (1983): 125–41.

Cunning, David. "Descartes' Modal Metaphysics." In *The Stanford Encyclopedia of Philosophy,* ed. Edward N. Zalta (Fall 2006). http://plato.stanford.edu/archives/fall2006/entries/descartes-modal/

Davies, Brian, and Brian Leftow, eds. *The Cambridge Companion to Anselm.* Cambridge: Cambridge University Press, 2005.

Deme, Daniel. *The Christology of Anselm of Canterbury.* Burlington, Vt.: Ashgate, 2003.

Eadmer. *Historia novorum in Anglia,* ed. Martin Rule. Wiesbaden: Kraus Reprint, 1965.

Ekenberg, Tomas. *Falling Freely: Anselm of Canterbury on the Will.* Uppsala: Uppsala Universitet, 2005.

Evans, G. R. *Anselm.* Outstanding Christian Thinkers. Wilton, Conn.: Morehouse-Barlow, 1989.

———. *Anselm and a New Generation.* Oxford: Oxford University Press, 1980.

———. "Anselm's Life, Works, and Immediate Influence." In Davies and Leftow, 5–31.

———. "St. Anselm's Images of Trinity," *Journal of Theological Studies* 27 (1976): 46–57.

Fairweather, Eugene R. "Truth, Justice, and Moral Responsibility in the Thought of St. Anselm." In *L'homme et son destin d'après les penseurs du moyen âge. Actes du premier congrès internationale de philosophie médiévale,* 385–91. Louvain: Nauwelaerts, 1960.

Fischer, John Martin. *God, Foreknowledge, and Freedom.* Palo Alto, CA: Stanford University Press, 1989.

Gasper, Giles E. M. *Anselm of Canterbury and His Theological Inheritance.* Burlington, Vt.: Ashgate, 2004.

Gracia, Jorge J. E., and J. J. Sanford. "Ratio quaerens beatitudinem: Anselm on Rationality and Happiness." In *Rationality and Happiness: From the Ancients to the Early Medievals,* ed. J. Yu and Jorge J. E. Gracia. New York: University of Rochester Press, 2003.

Henry, Desmond Paul. *The Logic of Saint Anselm.* Oxford: Oxford University Press, 1967.

Hestevold, H. S. "The Anselmian Single-Divine-Attribute Doctrine." *Religious Studies* 29 (1993): 63–77.

Holopainen, Toivo. *Dialectic and Theology in the Eleventh Century.* Leiden: Brill, 1996.

Hopkins, Jasper. *A Companion to the Study of St. Anselm.* Minneapolis: University of Minnesota Press, 1972.

———. *A New, Interpretive Translation of St. Anselm's Monologion and Proslogion.* Minneapolis: The Arthur J. Banning Press, 1986.

———. "The Philosophy of Anselm." *British Journal of the History of Philosophy* 13 (2005): 745–53.

Hursthouse, Rosalind. *On Virtue Ethics.* Oxford: Oxford University Press, 1999.

Kent, Bonnie D. *Virtues of the Will: The Transformation of Ethics in the Late Thirteenth Century.* Washington, D.C.: The Catholic University of America Press, 1985.

Keshgegian, Flora A. "The Scandal of the Cross: Revisiting Anselm and His Feminist Critics." *Anglican Theological Review* 82 (2000): 475–92.

King, Peter. "Anselm's Intentional Argument." *History of Philosophy Quarterly* 1 (1984): 147–65.

———. "Anselm's Philosophy of Language." In Davies and Leftow, 84–110.

Klima, Gyula. "Saint Anselm's Proof: A Problem of Reference, Intentional Identity and Mutual Understanding." In *Medieval Philosophy and Modern Times,* ed. G. Holmström-Hintikka. Dordrecht: Kluwer, 2000.

———. "Conceptual Closure in Anselm's Proof: Reply to Tony Roark." *History and Philosophy of Logic* 24 (2003): 131–34.

Knuuttila, Simo. "Anselm on Modality." In Davies and Leftow, 111–31.

———. *Modalities in Medieval Philosophy.* London: Routledge, 1993.

Lang, U. M. "Anhypostatos-Enhypostatos: Church Fathers, Protestant Orthodoxy and Karl Barth." *Journal of Theological Studies* NS 49 (1998): 630–57.

Leftow, Brian. "Anselm on the Cost of Salvation." *Medieval Philosophy and Theology* 6 (1997): 73–92.

———. "Anselm on the Necessity of the Incarnation," *Religious Studies* 31 (1995): 167–85.

———. "Anselm's Neglected Argument." *Philosophy* 77 (2002): 331–47.

———. "Anselm's Perfect-Being Theology." In Davies and Leftow, 132–56.

———. "Not So Anselmian." *Faith and Philosophy,* forthcoming.

Lewis, Delmas. "Eternity, Time, and Tenselessness." *Faith and Philosophy* 5 (1988): 72–86.

Luscombe, D. E., and G. R. Evans, eds. *Anselm: Aosta, Bec, and Canterbury.* Sheffield: Sheffield Academic Press, 1996.

Malcolm, Norman. "Anselm's Ontological Arguments." *Philosophical Review* 69 (1960): 41–62.

Mann, William E. "Anselm on the Trinity." In Davies and Leftow, 257–78.

———. "Natural and Supernatural Knowledge of God." In *The Cambridge Companion to Duns Scotus,* ed. Thomas Williams, 238–62. Cambridge: Cambridge University Press, 2003.

———. "The Perfect Island." *Mind* 85 (1976): 417–21.

———. "Simplicity and Properties: A Reply to Morris," *Religious Studies* 22 (1986): 343–53.

Marenbon, John. *Early Medieval Philosophy (480–1150).* London: Routledge & Kegan Paul, 1983.

———. Review of Katherin A. Rogers, *The Anselmian Approach to God and Creation* and *The Neoplatonic Metaphysics and Epistemology of Anselm of Canterbury. Religious Studies* 36 (2000): 498–504.

McIntyre, John. *St. Anselm and His Critics: A Re-interpretation of the Cur Deus Homo.* Edinburgh: Oliver and Boyd, 1954.

Merricks, Trenton. "On the Incompatibility of Enduring and Perduring Entities." *Mind* 104 (1995): 523–41.

Milbank, John. "The Second Difference: A Trinitarianism Without Reserve." *Modern Theology* 2 (1986): 213–34.

Millican, Peter. "The One Fatal Flaw in Anselm's Argument." *Mind* 113 (2004): 437–476.

Morris, Thomas V. "Perfect Being Theology," *Noûs* 21 (1987): 19–30.

Murray, Michael J., and Michael Rea. *An Introduction to the Philosophy of Religion.* Cambridge: Cambridge University Press, 2008.

Priest, Stephen. "Reality and Existence in Anselm." *Heythrop Journal* 41 (2000): 461–62.

Resnick, I. M. *Divine Power and Possibility in St. Peter Damian's* De divina omnipotentia. Leiden: Brill, 1992.

Roark, Tony. "Conceptual Closure in Anselm's Proof." *History and Philosophy of Logic* 24 (2003): 1–14.

Rogers, Katherin A. "Anselm on Eudaemonism and the Hierarchical Structure of Moral Choice." *Religious Studies* 41 (2005): 249–268.

———. "Anselmian Eternalism." *Faith and Philosophy* 24 (2007): 3–27.

———. *The Neoplatonic Metaphysics and Epistemology of Anselm of Canterbury.* Lewiston, NY: Edwin Mellen Press, 1997.

———. *Perfect Being Theology.* Edinburgh: Edinburgh University Press, 2000.

Rowe, William L. *Can God Be Free?* Oxford: Clarendon Press, 2004.

Serene, Eileen F. "Anselm's Modal Conceptions." In *Reforging the Great Chain of Being* (Synthese Historical Library 20), ed. Simo Knuuttila. Dordrecht: Reidel, 1981.

———. "Anselmian Agency in the Lambeth Fragments: A Medieval Perspective on the Theory of Action." *Anselm Studies* 1 (1983): 143–56.

Southern, R. W. *Anselm and His Biographer,* 2nd ed. Cambridge: Cambridge University Press, 1983.

———, ed. *The Life of St Anselm, Archbishop of Canterbury, by Eadmer.* Oxford: Clarendon Press, 1962.

———. *Saint Anselm: A Portrait in Landscape.* Cambridge: Cambridge University Press, 1991.

Spade, Paul Vincent. "Ambiguity in Anselm." *International Journal for Philosophy of Religion* 7 (1976): 433–45.

———. *Thoughts, Words, and Things: An Introduction to Late Mediaeval Logic and Semantic Theory.* http://pvspade.com/Logic/docs/thoughts1_1a.pdf

Thomas Aquinas. *Summa contra gentiles.* Rome: Marietti, 1946.

van Inwagen, Peter. "And Yet They Are Not Three Gods, But One God." Reprinted in *God, Knowledge, and Mystery: Essays in Philosophical Theology,* 222–59. Ithaca, NY: Cornell University Press, 1995.

Vaughn, Sally. *Anselm of Bec and Robert of Meulan: The Innocence of the Dove and the Wisdom of the Serpent.* Berkeley: University of California Press, 1987.

Viger, Christopher. "St. Anselm's Ontological Argument Succumbs to Russell's Paradox." *International Journal for Philosophy of Religion* 52 (2002): 123–28.

Weidemann, Hermann. "Anselm und die Insel: Das ontologische Argument im Spiegel surrealistischer Kunst." *Archiv für Geschichte der Philosophie* 86 (2004): 1–20.

Wierenga, Edward. "Anselm on Omnipotence." *The New Scholasticism* 62 (1988): 30–41.

Williams, Thomas. "Describing God." In *The Cambridge History of Medieval Philosophy,* ed. Robert C. Pasnau, forthcoming.

———. "The Doctrine of Univocity Is True and Salutary." *Modern Theology* 21 (2005): 575–85.

———. "Gaunilo." In *The Encyclopedia of Philosophy,* 2nd ed., ed. Donald Borchert. Detroit: Macmillan Reference USA, 2006.

———. "Saint Anselm." *The Stanford Encyclopedia of Philosophy* (Summer 2006). http://plato.stanford.edu/archives/sum2006/entries/anselm

———. "God Who Sows the Seed and Gives the Growth: Anselm's Theology of the Holy Spirit." *Anglican Theological Review* 89 (2007): 611–27.

———, trans. *Anselm: Three Philosophical Dialogues.* Indianapolis: Hackett, 2002.

———, trans. *Anselm: Basic Writings.* Indianapolis: Hackett, 2007.

Wolterstorff, Nicholas. "In Defense of Gaunilo's Defense of the Fool." In *Christian Perspectives on Religious Knowledge,* ed. C. Stephen Evans and Merold Westphal, 87–111. Grand Rapids: William B. Eerdmans, 1993.

INDEX

DATE DUE
